NEDERBURG

THE FIRST TWO HUNDRED YEARS

TEXT BY PHILLIDA BROOKE SIMONS · PHOTOGRAPHS BY ALAIN PROUST

CHAPTERS 10 AND 11 ARE BASED ON MATERIAL PROVIDED
BY NEDERBURG AND THE STELLENBOSCH FARMERS' WINERY

STRUIK
WINCHESTER

AN IMPRINT OF
STRUIK PUBLISHERS (PTY) LTD
CORNELIS STRUIK HOUSE
80 MCKENZIE STREET
CAPE TOWN 8000

REG. NO. 63/00203/07

FIRST PUBLISHED 1992

MANAGING EDITORS DOUGLAS VAN DER HORST AND VALERIE STREAK
EDITORS HELEN LAURENSON AND VALERIE STREAK
DESIGNER WILLEM JORDAAN
DUSTJACKET DESIGNER WILLEM JORDAAN
PROJECT CONSULTANT JOANNE SIMPSON
PROOF-READERS LENI MARTIN AND HELEN LAURENSON
PICTURE RESEARCHER ALLISON MURPHY
INDEXER LEONIE TWENTYMAN JONES

TYPESETTING AND PAGE MAKE-UP BY DIATYPE SETTING CC, CAPE TOWN
REPRODUCTION BY UNIFOTO (PTY) LTD, CAPE TOWN
PRINTED BY TIEN WAH PRESS (PTE) LTD, SINGAPORE
STANDARD EDITION BOUND BY TIEN WAH PRESS (PTE) LTD, SINGAPORE
SPONSORS' AND COLLECTORS' EDITIONS BOUND BY PETER CARSTENS, JOHANNESBURG

THE SPONSORS' EDITION IS LIMITED TO 26 COPIES LETTERED FROM A TO Z
THE COLLECTORS' EDITION IS LIMITED TO 100 COPIES NUMBERED FROM 1 TO 100
THE STANDARD EDITION COMPRISES 2 500 UNNUMBERED COPIES

ISBN 0-947430-40-7 (SPONSORS' EDITION)
ISBN 0-947430-39-3 (COLLECTORS' EDITION)
ISBN 0-947430-38-5 (STANDARD EDITION)

CONTENTS

ACKNOWLEDGEMENTS

During the preparation and writing of this book, I have benefited from the ready assistance of many people, to all of whom I am extremely grateful.

First, I must thank the management of Stellenbosch Farmers' Winery and specifically of Nederburg for making it possible for the story of a famous Cape wine farm to reach a wide reading public. André Steyn, administrative director of S.F.W., and Tony Starke, company secretary, have been particularly helpful to me. For information regarding the Nederburg Auction I am grateful to both Bennie Howard, group public relations manager, and Arlene Johnston, while details of the Nederburg Opera and Ballet Awards were provided by Marietha Channell.

To the personnel at Nederburg itself, especially managing director Ernst le Roux, and public relations manager Pieter Marais, I am greatly indebted. They, like all the rest of the staff, have readily provided me with information on all the many occasions that I visited Nederburg.

My deep appreciation goes to the publishers, Struik Winchester of Cape Town, for entrusting me with a task that has proved of immense interest and much wider scope than at first envisaged. Peter Borchert and Douglas van der Horst have supported and encouraged me throughout.

Without the expertise and aid of Margaret Cairns I should never have been able to comprehend the complexities of land tenure at the Cape, and the challenging mystery of Nederburg's founding date might well have remained unsolved. Dr Anna Böseken gave me valuable advice and Jean Blanckenberg cheerfully came to my aid in the Registry of Deeds and the Cape Archives.

Rona Currey allowed me to make use of relevant extracts from her personal diaries. To her go my gratitude and affection. I must thank Peter and Eileen Pare, children of Maurice Pare, as well as Helen Plumbly and Derek Power, who provided me with the story of the Pare family.

It is difficult to express adequately my appreciation of the co-operation I have received from John Lyall and his wife, Barbara. They welcomed me, then a stranger, to their home in Cornwall where, during a happy and busy week, I studied all Colonel Robert Lyall's invaluable documents — including the re-discovered and vital Nederburg grant. John has also been extremely helpful in making available photographs of Nederburg and other material in his possession. My thanks are due, too, to Francis and Alethea Lyall, and also to James for his part in the quest for the grant.

With the help of those who remember them, I came to feel that I, too, had personally known the Graue family. My deepest thanks in this respect go to Peter and Dorothea Corder, Gisela and Michael Pardoe, Werner Thielscher, Denis and Dorothy Taylor, Corrie Coetzee and Herthe Pass. Bruno and Bianca Mori gave me details of the association between Monis Wineries of Paarl and Nederburg and lent me photographs formerly belonging to the Graues as well as their personal correspondence.

To Lothar Barth, former chairman and managing director of Stellenbosch Farmers' Winery, go my special thanks. His profound knowledge of the wine industry and of Nederburg in particular was of enormous help. I am extremely grateful to Dr Nino Costa for much vital information and especially for the lucid way in which he explained the development of Johan Georg Graue's philosophy of selection and cold fermentation. It has been a privilege and an inspiration to get to know Günter Brözel whose contribution to Nederburg's story — and to that of the wine industry in South Africa — has been immeasurable. I must thank Ansie Kemp for sharing with me her experiences — often amusing — of 16 years as Nederburg's public relations officer.

Many other people gave me their help in a variety of ways. They include Dorothy Bagnall, Charles Currey, Mary Faure, Nieske Hiemstra-Weitz, Bayman Jacobs, Dr W. G. le Roux, Ralie Malherbe, Andrew Marais, Hannes Marais, Jenny McQueen, Diana and Eric Simons, Helene van der Westhuizen, Karl-Heinz Wilhelm and, from Safmarine, Richard Warnes and Daniella Lengner. I thank them all.

To the staffs of the Cape Archives, the Registry of Deeds, the Master's Office and the South African Library — all in Cape Town — my thanks are due, as they are to Mrs G. Malherbe of the Huguenot Museum in Franschhoek, Mrs W. A. de Klerk of the Drakenstein Heemkring in Paarl, Pat Gordon of *The Argus* library, Commander Mac Bisset of Fort Wynyard Coast and Anti-Aircraft Artillery Museum, and Liz Biggs of the Simon's Town Museum. In London I gratefully received the assistance of the staff of the India Office Library and the personal attention of Graham Nattrass of the British Library.

For help given me during the final stages of the book's preparation I am grateful to Helen Laurenson and Valerie Streak who proved meticulous and sympathetic editors. Allison Murphy searched diligently and successfully for archival illustrative material; Leonie Twentyman Jones painstakingly compiled the index and Leni Martin demonstrated her phenomenal accuracy as a proof-reader.

The text of this book has been immeasurably enhanced by its visual beauty. For this I am indebted to photographer Alain Proust and designer Willem Jordaan; also to project consultant Joanne Simpson.

Finally, I must thank my family, particularly my husband, Richard Simons, for the patience with which they endured my single-minded preoccupation with Nederburg for almost two years.

PHILLIDA BROOKE SIMONS, RONDEBOSCH, CAPE, APRIL 1992

Nederburg's story is more than a narrative of the events that have taken place on a famous and beautiful farm overlooking Paarl's wide valley. It is a tale of the dreams and the disappointments, the sorrows and the successes and the day to day events that, over two centuries, have made up the lives of the many men and women who lived and loved and laboured and — some of them — died there. It is a story of people of vision — rough stable-hand's son or sophisticated entrepreneur — who developed it from a patch of wilderness into one of South Africa's most eminent wine farms; who laid out its vineyards and orchards and harvested its grapes and pressed its wine. More than that: the history of Nederburg is inextricably linked with its background, whether of mighty mountains and brilliant blue skies or of the unfolding saga of the South African wine industry that weaves, thread-like, through the tapestry of the nation's history.

For half a century or more following 1791 when Philippus Bernardus Wolvaart was granted his 57 morgen and a bit, facts and figures concerning Cape farms were officially and regularly recorded. For an idea, albeit a sketchy one, of what life was like in the Boland two centuries ago, turn to the *opgaafrollen*. Annual census returns taken for tax purposes, they provide details, among other things, of the number of vines every farmer planted, the children he fathered, the slaves he kept, the cattle that grazed on his fields and the firearms he took with him when he went hunting. Local churches, too, are an invaluable source of information, for they registered marriages and baptisms and kept meticulous minutes of meetings — some humdrum, others surprisingly gossipy. And for the details of a man's earthly possessions, look up the inventory taken by field-cornet or magistrate's clerk when a householder went insolvent or died.

Yet to trace the personalities and habits of the Cape's early inhabitants, to place flesh on bare bones or a twinkle in the eye, is quite another matter — for these are human details that seldom emerge from the records. We know how much wine the farmers produced and how many barrels their cumbersome wagons brought into Cape Town for export or sale, but there is little chance of finding out whether they were pillars of respectabilty or disreputable blackguards; whether they beat their slaves, gave money to the poor or were unfaithful to their wives. The picture of Nederburg's first century as a farm rises relatively clearly from the tattered pages of official documents, but its owners remain faceless and shadowy.

As the 19th century wore on, bureaucracy at the Cape relaxed — at least as far as statistical records were concerned — and the researcher finds that following the time when Jacobus Petrus Hauptfleisch became master of Nederburg, there is no way of knowing what was sown there or how much was reaped; nor has it been possible to discover anything about the man himself.

Things changed after the turn of the century. A great deal is known about both the lives and personalities of Nederburg's next three owners — Harry Currey, Maurice Pare and Robert Lyall — though only Colonel Lyall's records (and they are copious and detailed) of his life and work at Nederburg have been traced. If Currey and Pare kept them, they have been lost. Yet these two men, as well as Colonel Lyall, led interesting lives before they became farmers and these 'before Nederburg' experiences have been recounted in this book, even though, at first sight, they may appear to have little relevance. In fact, they show what is hardly less important to Nederburg's history than the story of its wines — the *kind* of man who has chosen to make it his home. Each of them has, in his own idiosyncratic way, left a legacy of something neither tangible nor visible but which, over the years, has suffused Nederburg with its own indefinable ambience.

The period since the purchase of Nederburg by Johann Georg Graue in 1937 to the present day would make a story in itself. Fortunately, a wealth of documentary evidence exists in the form of detailed business records — ledgers and day-books, minutes of meetings, reports and so on — as well as privately-owned papers, letters and numerous newspaper articles. Then, there are still alive today many people willing to share their recollections of the dramatic transformation of Nederburg over the past half-century and more. Interviews with them, more than anything, have brought these years to life.

The story of Nederburg, then, is a human one concerning the people associated with it over its first 200 years. Sometimes that association has been lifelong: the younger Willem Petrus Retief, for example, was born at Nederburg and — 68 years later — died under its thatched roof. Other owners, like Harry Currey, it seemed barely to touch. Of them all, Johann Georg Graue, without question, will be best remembered. To him, Nederburg involved an entire way of life, a dream that was realized, the heartbreak of personal tragedy, a torch that was lit, passed on, and continues to burn brightly today.

■

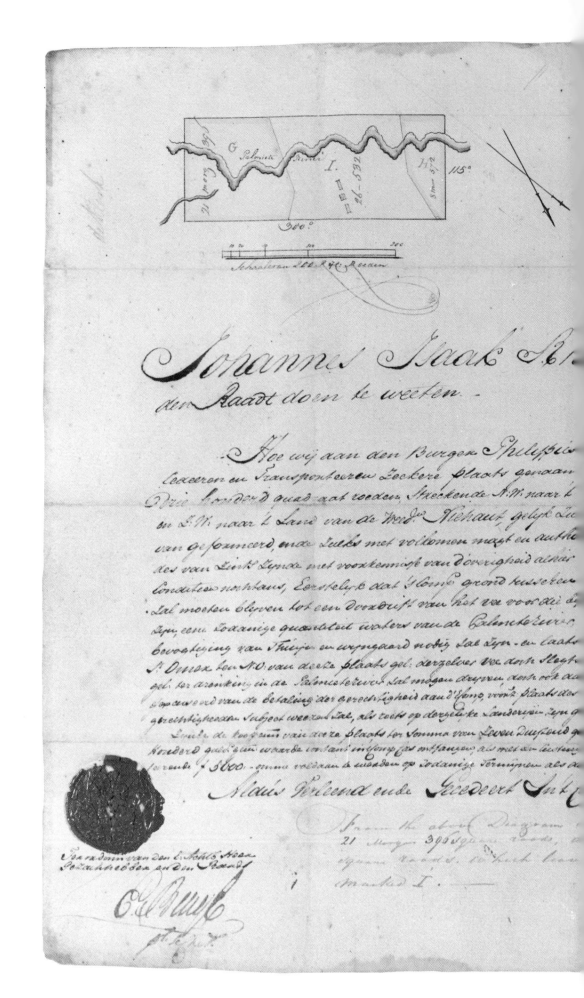

Johannes Isaak Br...

den Raadt doen te weeten. –

Hoe wij aan den Burger Philippus
leaceren en Transporteeren Zeckere plaats genaan
Drie hoonderd quad-raat roeden, Streckende N.W. naar 't
en Z.W. naar 't Land van de Wed.r Niehaut, gelyk Zu
van geformeerd, ende Zulks met volkomen magt en auth..
des van Zirk Zynde met vooxtenniße van d'overigheid alhui
Conditen nochtans, Eerstelyk dat 't lomß grond tusschen
Zal moeten blyven tot een doordrift van het va voor die d..
Zyn, een Zodanige quantiteit waters van de Calonteherivi...
bevoatezing van Thuÿjn en wÿngaard nodig, Zal Zyn - en laats
St. Onrex ten N.O. van deete plaats gel: derzelves ve dock Sleyt
gel: ter aronkung in de Palonisteherivier Zal mogen dryven, doch ook ..
op aweord van de betaling der gerechtigheid aan d'Ifang, voorts plaats des
gerechtigheeden Subject weezen Zal, als roets op derzelijke Landerijen Zyn ..
Zynde de kopprÿs van deeze plaats ter Somma van Zeven Duysend ...
hoonderd quild. een woarde .... in Ifang fas ontfangen, als met ....
te reude f 3600. omma voldaan te worden op Zodanige termÿnen als ..
Aldus Verleend ende Beedeext Int ...

From the abo.. Diagram ..
21 Morg.. 390 square roode, ..
... square roods. .. reck bear ..
... marked I. –

Ter ordonn van den E: Achtb Heere
Gecaahheebben en den Raadt

C. v. Ruÿk.
p. tufsh...

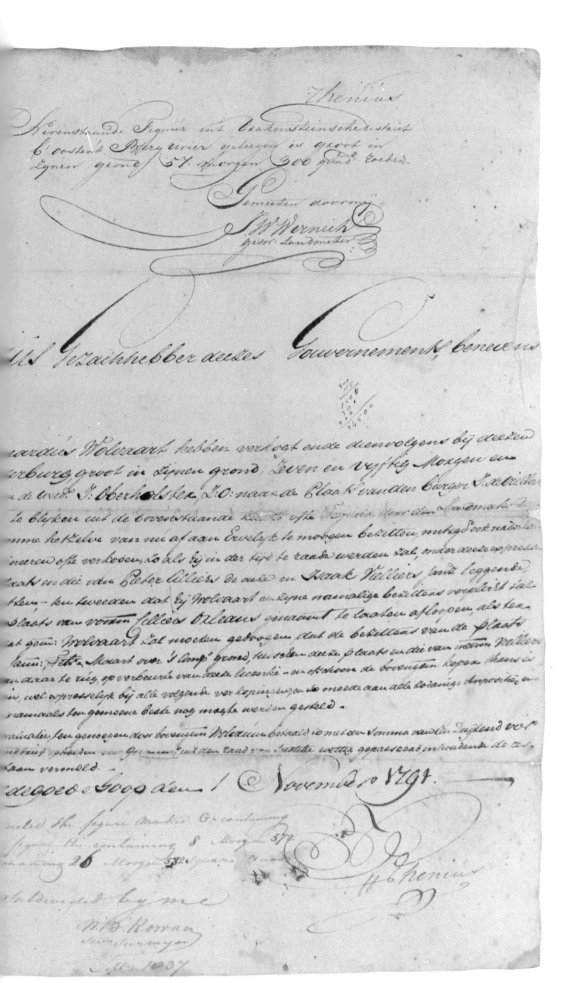

The original title deed granting ownership of the farm Nederburg to Philippus Bernardus Wolvaart. It is clearly dated 1 November 1791 and bears the signature of Acting Governor of the Cape Johannes Isaac Rehnius.

For many years it was believed that Nederburg had been personally granted to its first owner on 1 November 1792 by the visiting Dutch East India Company commissioner, Sebastiaan Cornelis Nederburgh, and consequently named in his honour. This makes a good story, but research undertaken for the preparation of this book has proved unequivocally that the date is incorrect and that the story of the favour to Philippus Bernardus Wolvaart is, alas, no more than a myth.

In the days of Dutch East India Company rule at the Cape it was customary for the governor or his deputy, the secunde, to sign in person two copies of each grant of land. One was filed away with the Company's records and is now among the documents preserved in the Cape Archives; the other was presented to the grantee and handed down from owner to owner each time the property changed hands. At the time of the grant, a hand-written fair copy, which was not personally signed by the governor, was also made for the record. If it pertained to land in the Cape district it was filed in the volume 'Old Cape Freeholds' (OCF), but if it concerned property further inland it was filed in the volume 'Old Stellenbosch Freeholds' (OSF). Today these volumes are kept in the Registry of Deeds in Cape Town and are frequently referred to by conveyancers handling property transactions.

The original error, as far as the Nederburg grant was concerned, was made when the fair copy was misfiled in the OCF volume and not in its rightful place in the OSF volume. This probably occurred immediately after the grant was made. Presumably conveyancers, unable to find the fair copy among the OSF grants, did not think of looking for it in the OCF volume and 'borrowed' the owner's original as this would have provided them with the number and date of the grant and other details required for the preparation of title deeds.

In 1924, when Maurice Pare sold Nederburg to Colonel Robert Adolphus Lyall, an attempt was made to solve this problem by having a *typed* copy made of the owner's grant (which, of course, was in 18th century Dutch) and filing it in the correct place in the OSF volume. Like the owner's copy − but unlike either the fair copy or the original in the Cape Archives − this typed document carries a diagram of the farm as it was originally. It is rubber-stamped, 'Copied from the diagram attached to Title Deed (owner's copy) in favour of P.B. Wolvaart', and this statement is signed by M. L. van der Spuy of the surveyor-general's office and dated 9 June 1924. On its front page, the document bears the endorsement, 'Certified a true copy of the Original this day exhibited to me', a statement which is signed this time by George Denoon, registrar of deeds, also on 9 June 1924. It is interesting to note that this typed copy gives the date of Nederburg's grant as 1 November 1792, whereas all previous title deeds give the date as 1 November 1791. Conveyancers handling transactions subsequent to 1924 apparently referred to this typed copy, which is numbered OSF 27A.

When I began research into the history of Nederburg at the end of 1990 I immediately noticed the discrepancy between the dates, as well as the fact that, when compared with the (relatively recently-discovered) fair copy, there were no fewer than 14 other typing (or language) errors in the typed copy, presumably because the typist could not understand Dutch or decipher the original. This indicated that the date 1792 was also a typing error − and that neither the surveyor-general's representative nor the registrar of deeds in 1924 had scrutinized the document sufficiently carefully, because if they had, the errors and discrepancies would have been apparent. I then compared the typed document with the original grant in the Cape Archives but, because of the scribe's elaborate handwriting, it was not possible to determine whether the date given on it was 1791 or 1792. The only thing to do was to find the 'owner's copy' − if it existed at all.

Nederburg did not have it, nor did the Pare family. Either it must have disappeared or been destroyed, or it was in the possession of the descendants of Colonel Lyall, who had died in 1948. With some difficulty I discovered the address, in Cornwall, England, of his elder son, John, whose immediate and enthusiastic co-operation has made it possible to follow the line of research to its successful conclusion. With the aid of his son, James, John Lyall searched the attic of the family farm at Bonallack and eventually located an old trunk containing a mass of his father's papers. Among them was the missing Nederburg grant, unseen for almost 60 years and bearing the irrefutable date, 1 November 1791. This was an exciting discovery, to say the least, and conclusively established the accurate date of Nederburg's origin.

Perhaps unfortunately, though, it put paid to the story that Commissioner Nederburgh had granted the land as a special favour to Philippus Bernardus Wolvaart. Nederburgh did not arrive at the Cape until 18 June 1792 and, communications being what they were, he could not have been aware of a mere land transaction taking place some seven months earlier. Nor has it been possible to discover any valid reason why he might have wished to 'honour' Philippus Bernardus Wolvaart who, so far as it can be discovered, performed no exceptional services to the Dutch East India Company. It is far more likely that Secunde Johan Isaac Rhenius (whose unmistakable signature appears on both the Archives copy of the document and that in John Lyall's possession), when required to sign a grant of some as yet unnamed and uncultivated land, decided to call it after Nederburgh (the final letter 'h' was presumably omitted from the name of the farm in error) to 'sweeten' him in advance. Nederburgh's brief as commissioner was to investigate the thoroughly unsatisfactory state of affairs at the Cape and Rhenius must have been feeling somewhat uncomfortable at the thought of the can of worms he was bound to open up!

These facts were not known when Nederburg began to plan its bicentenary celebrations for 1992. The actual date is, however, of little consequence when it comes to festivities: the important thing is that Nederburg has been in existence for 200 years, during which time it has had an undisputed impact on social life in South Africa and established a reputation for its products which few wine farms in this country can equal. ∎

THE NEDERBURG GENEALOGY

FIRST OWNER
GRANT OF 1 NOVEMBER 1791
TO PHILIPPUS BERNARDUS WOLVAART
57 MORGEN 300 SQUARE ROODS FREEHOLD

SECOND OWNER
TRANSFER DEED 439 OF 7 SEPTEMBER 1810
P. B. WOLVAART TO WILLEM PETRUS RETIEF (SENIOR)

THIRD OWNER
TRANSFER DEED 20 OF 2 FEBRUARY 1854
W. P. RETIEF (SENIOR) TO W. P. RETIEF (JUNIOR)

FOURTH OWNER
TRANSFER DEED OF 13 May 1881
WIDOW W. P. RETIEF (JUNIOR) TO P. J. HAUPTFLEISCH

FIFTH OWNER
TRANSFER DEED 9102 OF 1 SEPTEMBER 1902
P. J. HAUPTFLEISCH TO H. L. CURREY

SIXTH OWNER
TRANSFER DEED 4819 OF 28 MAY 1918
H. L. CURREY TO M. PARE

SEVENTH OWNER
TRANSFER DEED 4376 OF 30 MAY 1924
M. PARE TO R. A. LYALL

EIGHTH OWNER
TRANSFER DEED 13925 OF 30 DECEMBER 1937
R. A. LYALL TO J. R. G. GRAUE

NINTH OWNER
TITLE DEED 8308 OF 4 JUNE 1954
J. R. G. GRAUE TO NEDERBURG ESTATES (PTY) LTD

TENTH OWNER
1959
NEDERBURG ESTATES (PTY) LTD TO MONIS WINERIES (PTY) LTD

ELEVENTH OWNER
1966
STELLENBOSCH FARMERS' WINERY

IN 1954 MONIS ACQUIRED 50 PER CENT OF THE SHARES IN
NEDERBURG ESTATES (PTY) LTD; J. R. G. GRAUE HELD THE
REMAINING 50 PER CENT. AFTER HIS DEATH IN 1959 MONIS
ACQUIRED FULL POSSESSION OF ALL THE SHARES.

BEFORE NEDERBURG:

WINE AT THE CAPE 1652-1791

The Cape's first Dutch commander, Jan van Riebeeck, planted
vines and produced the original small vintage in 1659. Later, Governor
Simon van der Stel cultivated grapes on his farm at Constantia and,
following their arrival from France in 1688, the Huguenots established
vineyards in the Berg River valley. Wine-production increased steadily but,
apart from the peerless Constantia, Cape wine had found little favour in
Europe or the East by the time Nederburg was established in 1791.

F ew places on earth have been more generously blessed by Nature than the south-western extremity of the continent of Africa. Shaped by the ceaseless pounding of the ocean, its coastline of rugged cliffs and buttresses is interspersed with the wide sweep of silver beaches. Inland, mountains soar skywards, hazy blue in the heat of summer, in winter swathed in a lowering tumult of clouds. Between them lie broad valleys well watered by perennial streams and, in their natural state, clothed in what may well be the richest flora in the world. For centuries before any explorer from Europe set eyes on this remote spot or Sir Francis Drake, sailing by, called it 'the fairest Cape in the whole circumference of the earth', nomadic Khoikhoi peoples grazed their sheep and hump-backed cattle on its indigenous vegetation, but they did not stop long enough in any one place to sow seed or reap crops. It was only in the mid-17th century that the land was cultivated for the first time and then the people who tilled it and garnered its first harvests were strangers from across the sea.

The decision of the Dutch East India Company, based in Amsterdam, to create a vegetable garden at the Cape was an entirely pragmatic one: fresh produce was required to replenish the stores of its tempest-tossed ships on the long haul between their home port of Texel and the Company's rich spice empire in the East. Their directors, the Lords Seventeen, appointed surgeon and senior merchant, Jan van Riebeeck, as commander of the outpost and on 6 April 1652 he sailed into Table Bay with three ships, the *Drommedaris*, the *Reijger* and the *Goede Hoop*. It was he who planted the first vines and pressed juice from their grapes. And it was the Cape's third governor, Simon van der Stel, who, towards the end of the century, expanded and developed its vineyards and made the sweet Constantia wine that became famous in the palaces of Europe. Both Van Riebeeck and Van der Stel were men of vision, and it is to their enterprise, imagination and industry that South Africa's wine industry owes its origins.

Jan van Riebeeck, born in Culemborg in 1619, claimed descent on both sides of his family from the ruling aristocracy of the Netherlands. He was said to be a little man, thickset and sturdy, his skin toughened by North Sea gales and tanned by the sun of the West Indies, his wits sharpened by trading ventures in the Far East. His brief on leaving for the Cape had been to build a fort for the protection of his men, to barter with the local Khoikhoi for meat and to plant fruit and vegetables that would restore scurvy-ridden sailors to health. The Lords Seventeen had no thought of establishing a permanent settlement or of planting anything requiring such long-term planning as vineyards; yet within a month of his arrival Jan van Riebeeck was asking them not only for seeds, berry-shoots and young citrus trees, but for vine cuttings as well.

The Company's directors might not have contemplated planting vines at the Cape, but they were well aware of the virtues of wine. Like all civilized people, they appreciated its finest qualities, but it was for practical reasons that their outgoing ships always carried a good supply on board. Wine, particularly when natural and unfortified, was useful in the treatment of scurvy; besides, it could be added with advantage to the foul drinking water that slopped about in the ships' casks after four or more months at sea. And then, of course, a daily ration made life on board more bearable for officers and crew alike. Commander Van Riebeeck, himself a doctor, knew all this, but his motives in producing wine at the Cape were probably as much for the cheering of homesick hearts in the little mud-built Fort of Good Hope as for the benefit and pleasure of passing sailors.

He was an enthusiastic gardener and a man of prodigious energy so it must have been frustrating in the extreme for him to wait until the end of 1654 before the first vine cuttings arrived from Holland. No details are known of that first shipment, but oenologists think that the plants were five centimetre-long slips taken from young Rhineland vines and that for travelling they were packed in damp soil and sewn up in canvas. The long voyage from one hemisphere to the other could have done them little good; anyway, it was midsummer when they arrived and certainly not the moment for propagating shoots. Not surprisingly, nothing further was heard of them nor of another parcel of vine cuttings that arrived in February 1655. However, when a third consignment reached Table Bay on 22 July of that year, the season for planting was not far off. This time, the

vines took root and a year later Van Riebeeck reported that the young plants were flourishing.

The grape varieties included in that first successful consignment can only be guessed at, but one early 20th-century authority suggested that they were Muscat, Green Grape, Muscadel and French Grape. Another oenologist held that they more probably included Stein, White French or Palomino, Hanepoot and Pontac. One thing is certain, however: from these cuttings slips were taken for later plantings and today their derivatives are among the oldest grape cultivars still grown at the Cape.

The original vine cuttings were struck in the Company's garden, where orange and chestnut trees, tobacco, watermelons and sweet potatoes were already flourishing. Another vine nursery was established in 1657, this time at Rustenburg on the eastern slopes of Table Mountain and overlooking the Liesbeek River valley (in the present-day Rondebosch). Here the first independent farmers, or free burghers, were busily planting their first cornfields and small vineyards. The commander himself had been granted a stretch of ground on the western side of the settlement where Green Point is today, but he soon discovered that it became waterlogged in winter and that in any case the soil was poor and unfit for cultivation. He pointed this out to Commissioner Joan Cunaeus who visited the Cape in 1658 and — in direct contravention of the Dutch East India Company's rules restricting land ownership by officials — obtained permission to exchange his unpromising land for 84 fertile hectares on the far south-eastern bank of the Liesbeek River. Van Riebeeck named his farm, situated in what is today Bishopscourt, Boschheuvel — 'woody hill' — after the forested kloofs on the mountainside above it and it was here, on a blustery, overcast August day in that year, that his 'private agriculturalists and slaves' planted '1 200 rooted branches as well as unrooted cuttings from the cut vines'.

The following summer, the original vine stocks in the Company's garden fulfilled their promise and on 2 February 1659, a fine warm Sunday, Jan van Riebeeck's scribe, no doubt as excited as the commander himself, made an entry in his Journal that was destined to become immortal. 'Today,' he wrote, 'praise be to God, wine was made for the first time from Cape grapes, namely from the new must fresh from the vat. The grapes were mostly Muscadel and other white, round grapes, very fragrant and tasty. The Spanish grapes are still quite green, though they hang reasonably thickly on several vines and give promise of a first-class crop. These grapes, from three young vines planted two years ago, have yielded about 12 quarts of must, and we shall soon discover how it will be affected by maturing.'

CABO DE GOEDE HOOP.

What the commander did discover when, months later, he tasted that wine, no one knows but, judging from descriptions of subsequent vintages, the Cape's first viniculturists had much to learn. What mattered, though, was that the vines had matured and borne fruit and that from them wine had been successfully pressed. There was, indeed, good reason to praise God!

Satisfied though Van Riebeeck must have been at the result of this first small vintage and of his other labours at the Cape, it was his abiding dream to return to the East. After many impassioned appeals to the Lords Seventeen, the longed-for instructions eventually arrived and in 1662 he sailed joyfully for Java. As he watched Table Mountain sink over the pencil-line of the horizon, he was not to know that he would never again set eyes on the compelling beauty of the Cape of Good Hope.

Three years later, Boschheuvel was sold to Jacob

Cornelisz van Roosendael of Amsterdam, a free burgher who, during the ten years that he owned the farm, continued the work Van Riebeeck had begun. He supplied vine cuttings to the farmers, who were becoming increasingly interested in producing wine, and in 1670 was permitted to retail some of his own making. Indeed, canteens where 'strong liquor' was sold were springing up like mushrooms at the Cape and the Council of Policy, alarmed at the temptations they presented to idle burghers, decided to curtail the issue of licences. This led, naturally, to an excess of local wine — a problem that was to beset local farmers for generations — and, in an effort to dispose of it profitably, the Council in India opened the eastern market to individuals by allowing them to export their own wine to Java. This decision was not met with any joy at the Cape, where the farmers were too poor to wait the best part of a year to be paid for their produce. What they wanted was the quick return provided by a market on the spot coupled with the security of a fixed price. Besides, they had little faith in the eastern market. Recently, some wine produced in Company vineyards had been sent as samples to Batavia but, as it had met with scant approval, there was little chance that private sales of Cape wine would have any greater success there.

The situation was relieved only in 1676 when the Council in India despatched an expert named Hannes Koekenberg to improve the quality of Cape wine and to advise farmers. The Company also undertook to provide suitable casks — the poor quality of wine that reached Batavia possibly resulted from the much-used and unhygienic barrels in which it travelled. They also allowed some relief of regulations regarding canteen-keeping and agreed to buy wine from farmers at a fixed price and export it themselves to Ceylon and Mauritius.

In the third quarter of the 17th century, the directors of the Dutch East India Company were confronted by two problems at the Cape. First, how could they maintain a steady and reliable supply of provisions to their ships without incurring too much expense? Second, how could they reduce the costly garrison that had protected the Cape from its enemies during a long war with France yet, at the same time, retain their hold on it while numbers of ships from unfriendly nations were sailing past its shores? The answer to both questions lay in increasing the number of settlers, particularly farmers, and the official they appointed in 1679 to implement their idea proved to be the man who, more than any other, cherished, developed and transformed the early production of wine at the Cape.

Simon van der Stel was born in 1639 in Mauritius where his father, scion of an eminent Dordrecht family, was governor. His portrait shows a swarthy man whose features reveal his oriental origin, for his maternal grandfather, a Dutch sea captain, had chosen as his bride a girl born and bred on the coast of Coromandel in south-east India. Orphaned early in life, Van der Stel completed his studies in Holland, where he absorbed much from the cultural life of the society in which he moved. He learnt to appreciate beautiful things, stimulating company and good wine. He also acquired a love and knowledge of farming, particularly of viticulture, and to put it into practice he bought land where he planted vines for making wine and brandy.

In 1663 Simon van der Stel married Johanna Six, daughter of the influential mayor of Amsterdam. The marriage was apparently not a happy one and it may have been with a degree of relief that he accepted the appointment of commander of the Cape. At all events, he left his wife behind when he sailed from Texel in May 1679, taking with with him instead his sister-in-law, his six children and two young cousins.

The new commander stepped ashore at Table Bay in mid-October and immediately began to familiarize himself with his tasks. Barely three weeks later, he set off across the drifting sands of the Cape Flats, at that season bright with the flowers of early summer, and rode some 50 kilometres eastwards to inspect the outposts of his domain. He camped on an island in the midst of a tumbling river and, with his rare eye for beauty, selected the spot as the site of the first village to be established outside the Cape Peninsula. Perhaps with a touch of conceit, he named it Stellenbosch after himself, little knowing that in time the town that grew up there would become one of the most gracious in South Africa or that the Eerste River valley, cradled between the mountains of Jonkershoek and Simonsberg (also bearing his name), would be renowned as one of the finest wine-producing regions in the Southern Hemisphere.

As soon as he returned to the settlement (many years were to pass before it became known officially as Cape Town), Commander Van der Stel announced that any of the Company's servants intrepid enough to brave the dangers of wild beasts and threats from neighbouring Khoikhoi would be granted land in 'the agricultural colony of Stellenbosch'. Before long, over 30 farms had been marked out and by 1681 both wheatfields and vineyards were flourishing.

By now the settlement was expanding and there were 172 adults and 117 children living at the Cape, as well as 191 slaves, 113 officials and 290 soldiers, with their 70 wives and children. Mindful of his instructions from the Lords Seventeen, Commander Van der Stel was anxious to expand the population yet further. He visited Stellenbosch on several occasions and observed with interest the burgeoning wine industry there as well as that on the Cape Peninsula itself, all the while

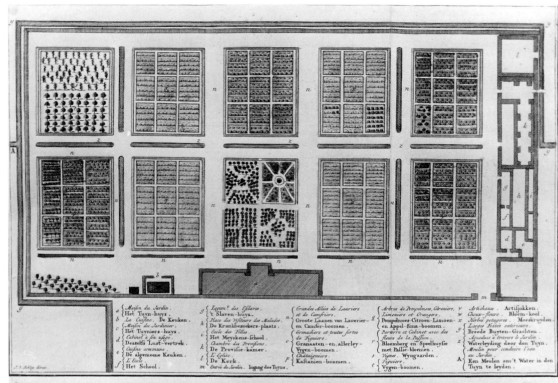

JARDIN DE LA COMPAGNIE AU CAP DE BONNE ESPERANCE. COMPAGNIES TUYN AAN DE KAAP DE GOEDE HOOP.

dreaming of owning his own farm. His hopes were realized in 1685 when visiting Commissioner Hendrik Adriaan van Reede tot Drakestein, Lord of Mijdrecht, granted him just over 760 hectares of land on the Cape Peninsula 'delightfully situated near the foot of a range of pleasant green hills'.

Stretching between Wynberg Hill, by now vine-covered, and the grey boulders of Steenberg, Van der Stel's farm was enormous in comparison with those of the free burghers. It was not only blessed with the most exquisitely beautiful surroundings and protected from the Peninsula's prevailing south-east gales, but the soil proved to be more suitable than any other at the Cape for the production of wine grapes. This was no coincidence, for the commander had analysed earth samples and carried out investigations of the most scientific kind before selecting the precise position of his farm. He named it 'Constantia' (possibly as a compliment to Constantia van Goens, the young granddaughter of a visiting official) and built the simple but spacious house that was to be his home.

Immediately, Simon van der Stel began to plant hundreds of young oaks and thousands of vines, every one of them a living token of his commitment to the land of his adoption; for nothing can demonstrate dedication to the soil with greater intensity than these growing things for which years — even a lifetime — must pass before they or their fruits can reach maturity. Most of the young plants came from the Company's Garden or from the nursery at Rustenburg, but others

were raised from seeds brought from the East and from the Canary Isles. In the fullness of time Simon van der Stel gathered in his first harvest and set his slaves to pressing the wine. With his own knowledge of viticulture, coupled with the expertise of the Company's gardeners, he avoided the mistakes which had resulted in the production, by the other farmers, of unpalatable wine. His vines were spaced well apart and the grapes were gathered only when they were fully ripe and sweetened by the summer sun. No records exist of the wines he made at first, but from the Green Grape, White French, Pontac and Hanepoot he may have made a thin white wine for the supply of passing ships and for his slaves' daily ration. Possibly from pressings of Pinot and Hermitage he produced a better quality red wine that he reserved for his own use and offered to his guests. In late 17th-century Europe, the most favoured wines were sweet, aromatic and bland and possibly it was this type that Van der Stel aimed to emulate. At some unknown date he perfected his formula and began to produce the wine known as 'Constantia', with which his name is still inseparably linked.

No one alive today has tasted Van der Stel's Constantia, but oenologists believe that a red variety was pressed from Red Muscadel grapes with the addition of a small amount of Frontignac, while white Constantia was a smooth blending of White Muscadel with Green Grape. Constantia was probably a full-bodied, liqueur-type wine, low in alcoholic strength, aromatic in bouquet and rich in colour. Known as 'the governor's wine' (for in 1691 Simon van der Stel was promoted to that rank), it achieved a reputation throughout the civilized world that remained unchanged and unchallenged for nearly two centuries.

Simon van der Stel, personally — and not surprisingly — found the wines made locally harsh, an opinion shared by John Ovington, chaplain to James II of England, who visited the Cape in the 1690s. In his book, *A Voyage to Suratt . . .* he wrote of Cape wine: ''Tis Colour'd like Rhenish [wine], and therefore they pass it under that specious Name in *India*, but the Taste of it is much harder and less palatable; its Operations are more searching, and the strength of it more intoxicating and offensive to the Brain.' In an attempt to eliminate these disagreeable characteristics, Van der Stel forbade harvesting until the vineyards had been officially inspected and the grapes pronounced ripe. He urged the farmers to be more careful in their selection of fruit and not to toss grapes of different kinds indiscriminately into the wine-press. He imported new vines and personally supervised their planting at Rustenburg.

Meanwhile, in 1685 — the year in which Van der Stel was officially granted the farm Constantia — an event had taken place half a world away that was to have a profound effect on wine-making at the Cape. This was the revocation by King Louis XIV of France of the Edict of Nantes, an act that ruthlessly deprived all French Calvinists of both their civic rights and their religious freedom. Thousands fled into neighbouring Protestant countries and the United Provinces of the Netherlands thus found itself overrun by penniless refugees, known as Huguenots, for whom it could provide neither work nor shelter. What better, thought the Lords Seventeen, than to send them to the Cape where Commander Van der Stel was crying out for new blood and more farmers? Many were peasants accustomed to life on the land; some were even experienced in the cultivation of the vine.

And so, in April 1688, with the arrival of the first French Huguenots, sea-stained and weary after nearly four months on board the vessel *Voorschooten*, the texture of Cape society was changed, enhanced and enriched. Where formerly there had been only stolid, Teutonic gravity, now there was a subtle, Latin nuance that remains to this day in the names of the Huguenots' descendants — Du Plessis, Marais, De Villiers, Le Roux — and of the wine farms that they hewed out of the wilderness. In his determination to integrate them with the established population, Simon van der Stel settled them cheek by jowl with Dutch and German inhabitants and before long forbade them to worship or study in French. So, within half a century, Pierre had become Pieter and Jacques was Jacob and the Huguenots' language and their allegiance to France were forgotten.

Six months before their arrival, Van der Stel had ridden to the wide, curved valley of the Berg River beyond Stellenbosch and appraised its potential as a farming area. Behind him was Banghoek — fearful corner — so named because of the leopards and other wild beasts that prowled there. To the east was Olifantshoek, a pass trodden over the mountains by elephants, and in the shallow waters of the Berg River, hippopotamus wallowed. Despite these alarming factors this valley, overlooked by rank upon rank of lofty mountains, was — and is — one of the loveliest spots on earth. Honouring the commissioner who had bestowed Constantia on him, Van der Stel named it Drakestein (the letter 'n' crept in almost immediately to make it 'Drakenstein' for ever more), but before long it became known as Le Quartier Français and later as Franschhoek, or French Corner. Farms averaging 60 morgen in size, most of them with a river frontage, were granted to the Huguenot settlers and, with little more than rudimentary tools and their bare hands, they set about transforming the stony mountain slopes into orderly vineyards. Here, in a setting and climate reminiscent of lands fringing the Mediterranean, the Huguenots were to make their mark as wine farmers, for they had brought with them from Europe their skills, their diligence and above all an inimitable French finesse.

Ten years after their arrival, Drakenstein was visited by French traveller, François Leguat. Among those who offered him hospitality was hat-maker, apothecary and vine-dresser, Isaac Taillefert, who farmed at present-day Paarl. He had a garden, wrote Leguat, 'which may very well pass for fine. Nothing there is wanting and all is in so good order and so neat that it may very well pass for Charming . . . He has the best Wine in the Country and which is not unlike our small Wines of Champagne.' This was praise indeed and in sharp contrast to what Leguat had to say about wine-making in general at the Cape — despite the governor's attempts to improve it. 'The Vine,' he wrote, 'bears Grapes two years after it has been Planted, and that in great abundance without Cultivating, insomuch that in some Places a thousand foot of Vineyard will yield six Hogs-heads of Wine. To speak Truth, the Wine is none of the best, being apt to be Green, which proceeds partly from the Peoples not giving themselves the trouble to chuse such Plants as are most agreeable to the Soil and Climate, and partly in that they are not accustom'd to support the Branches with a Vine-Prop . . .'

Simon van der Stel died at Constantia in 1712, 27 years after he had settled there. In 1699 he had been succeeded as governor by his son, Willem Adriaan, who soon showed himself more inclined to pay attention to the development of his splendid estate, Vergelegen, than to his official duties. So outraged were the farmers

TOP
*An early view of Franschhoek
painted in about 1830.*
BOTTOM
*Though a distant relative of the European
grape, this so-called Cape 'wild vine'
(Rhoicissus capensis) is totally unsuitable
for wine production.*

at his personal use of Company money, materials and slaves that they drew up a petition of protest which resulted in his removal from office in 1707. Serious though his misdemeanours were, there is no doubt that Willem Adriaan had acquired from his father a passion for the beautiful and fine things of life, not to mention the luxurious. Vergelegen's vineyards, mantling the matchless southern slopes of the Helderberg 45 kilometres to the east of the settlement, boasted some 250 000 vines — almost half the total grown in the entire colony. One of the complaints brought against Willem Adriaan was that, in addition to cornering the retail wine trade for himself, he was also trying to secure the export monopoly. Certainly, wine was made in Vergelegen's cellars and exported to Batavia by the governor from 'his own demesne'.

From the beginning of the 18th century, records concerning viticulture at the Cape become more detailed. The authorities saw in wine production an excellent opportunity to increase the settlement's inadequate revenue and in 1715 a tax was levied for the first time on every leaguer (the equivalent of 5,82 hectolitres or 150 gallons) pressed locally. As the century progressed, proclamations, regulations, prohibitions and restrictions on wine production were announced with increasing frequency, often with disastrous results and effects. Although at Constantia Jan Colyn continued

Simon van der Stel's tradition of fine wine-making, complaints continued to reach the Cape that the ordinary wine exported to both Amsterdam and Batavia was undrinkable by the time it reached its destination.

Meanwhile, the population was growing steadily and increased numbers of visitors were calling at the settlement, some remaining for months or even longer. Among these was Otto Mentzel, a young Prussian soldier in the Company's service, who arrived in 1732 and stayed for eight years. Long after his return to Europe he wrote an account of life at the Cape, which gives a lively picture of viticulture as he had observed it. He describes the preparation of the soil, the propagation of vine shoots and the transplanting of the young plants. 'The vines,' he writes, 'are all planted in straight lines four feet apart and, when a row has been planted, a passage of at least four or five feet wide is left free between this row and the next, so that one can pass through them in comfort at harvesting time and cut off the grapes without injuring the plants. The vine itself, be it old as it may, is never allowed to stand more than one and a half feet high above the level of the ground . . . The South-East wind does not permit the training of vines on stakes . . . hence they have to be kept as low as possible and trimmed on top when the vines grow too long.' Mentzel describes the pruning of the vines, the harvesting of grapes, pressing and raisin-making. He

mentions the pests that invade the vineyards, worst of which were birds and dogs. 'Dogs,' writes Mentzel, 'which have never been taught by their kind to eat grapes can hardly be kept from them with whips when they get into the vineyards. In the daytime boys do keep them out . . . but during the night, unless they are leashed or locked up, they eat so much that they can hardly stand.' Mentzel also lists the various types of grapes used in wine-making though, he writes, 'nobody will mind my starting with my favourite kind, though it is not pressed nor does it produce any wine. It is the "Haanen-Kloote" (Cock's testicle), but called the "Haanen-poote" (cock's foot) by the ladies of Africa.'

Between 1751 and 1755 – by which time there were 5 510 colonists at the Cape and 6 279 slaves – an annual average of 558 leaguers of local wine was being exported to Batavia but, because of persistently poor quality, this figure dropped to 262 leaguers by 1765. All the while, petty rules and regulations continued to harass Cape wine farmers, but nothing served to encourage them to improve their methods of wine production or, it seems, to introduce any new varieties of grapes. Dutch Rear-Admiral Stavorinus, who called at the Cape in the 1770s, was somewhat more generous in his assessment of locally-produced wines than were most visitors from Europe. 'Next to the genuine Constantia,' he wrote, 'the wines called muscadel, and

TOP
Stellenbosch in 1710 before a disastrous fire swept through the village, destroying half of its buildings.
BOTTOM LEFT
One of the first farms established along the Berg River in the Paarl valley.
BOTTOM RIGHT
A section of a map of the Cape (circa 1695-1710) on which appear the names of several farmers in the Paarl valley.

steen-wine, are esteemed the best. There is a sort which in taste resembles Madeira, but which is neither so strong, nor so racy.'

Nevertheless, during the second half of the 18th century, the Cape prospered as it had never done during the early days of the settlement and by 1783 there were 4,2 million vines growing in Drakenstein alone. Remote, now, in both time and space from the Europe of their origins, farmers of a proud new generation had grown up, their roots as firm in the soil as the vines they cultivated. In a statement of stability, they transformed the unsophisticated dwellings of their forebears into gracious houses, nobly gabled, roofed with mole-brown thatch, and shaded by now mature oaks. On the Peninsula, Van der Stel's Constantia, extensively altered by squire Hendrik Cloete in the 1790s, was among the most splendid, but others with equally lovely names were to be found in the Drakenstein valley. Among them, along the eastern reaches of the Berg River, lay La Provence, L'Ormarins and Plaisir de Merle while, towards the west, on the sunset-facing slopes of Klein Drakenstein, clustered Languedoc, Calais, Orléans and St Omer. It was in this latter area, towards the end of the century, that a hitherto uncultivated stretch of *fynbos* was planted with vines for the first time and a new house was built. Its gable, one of the finest in the land, bore the name 'Nederburg'. ∎

CHAPTER ONE

PHILIPPUS BERNARDUS WOLVAART 1791-1810

*Barely six years after he acquired a stretch of wilderness
in Klein Drakenstein in November 1791, Philippus Bernardus
Wolvaart produced his first leaguer of wine from the
vineyards he had planted there. By the time he sold Nederburg
in 1810, it had become a flourishing farm of
63 000 vines, enhanced by one of the Cape's most
beautiful homesteads.*

*Johannes Isaac Rhenius (1750-1808),
acting governor of the Cape from June 1791
until July 1792. His signature
appears on the document granting Nederburg
to Philippus Bernardus Wolvaart.*

eated in the Castle of Good Hope on the first day of November in the year 1791, Acting Governor of the Cape Johannes Isaac Rhenius took up his quill pen and, with an elaborate flourish, appended his signature to the document placed before him. By doing so, he granted ownership of the farm Nederburg, lying between the Berg and Palmiet rivers in the district of Drakenstein, to one Philippus Bernardus Wolvaart. Until now the land, measuring 57 morgen and 300 square roods, had been no more than a stretch of fynbos belonging to the Dutch East India Company, though the farms surrounding it — each roughly the same size — had by this time been cultivated for almost exactly a hundred years.

At this time, Acting Governor Rhenius was beset by serious problems. The Dutch East India Company, prosperous traders in the East for nearly two centuries and rulers of this remote southern outpost since 1652, was rapidly losing both its wealth and its power. At the Cape settlement, intractable burghers, appalling mismanagement and escalating expenses — not to mention corrup-

tion in high places — had made conditions untenable during the regime of the previous acting governor, Cornelis Jacobus van der Graaff. His personal accounts were enormous — he had maintained 60 carriage horses, among other things — and since his recall six months earlier, matters had certainly not improved. Now Rhenius had received the news that in a last-ditch effort to save the situation, the directors of the Company, the Lords Seventeen, had appointed Sebastiaan Cornelis Nederburgh and Simon Hendrik Frykenius as commissioners-general to investigate the problems in their overseas possessions and that an enquiry into the state of affairs at the Cape was set down for some time during the following year. Anxieties regarding the commissioners' impending arrival must have been uppermost in Rhenius's mind as he contemplated Wolvaart's request for land at Drakenstein and it may be that he saw in it an opportunity to make a favourable impression on the visitors. Possibly it was for this reason that Wolvaart, unlike other, earlier farmers, who had been granted land free of any commitment other than tithes

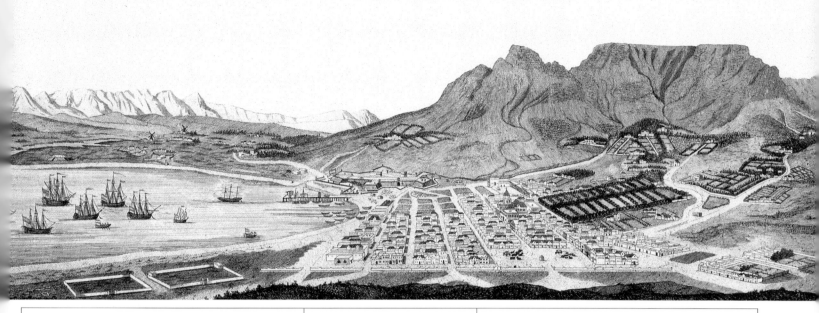

TOP
Table Bay in the late 18th century.
BOTTOM LEFT
Governor Cornelis van der Graaff –
notorious for his extravagances.
BOTTOM CENTRE
Rixdollars were the unit of
currency at the Cape during the rule of
the Dutch East India Company,
though Wolvaart probably paid for
Nederburg in paper money which was
introduced in 1784.
BOTTOM RIGHT
Commissioner Sebastiaan Cornelis
Nederburgh (1762-1811), in whose honour
the newly-granted farm in Klein Drakenstein
was named.

on produce and the settlement of survey costs, was required to pay the sum of ƒ5 600 (guilders) to the Council of Justice before he could call Nederburg his own. Granted, this was a relatively low price for the land and possibly no more than a gesture on Rhenius's part to show that at least some small effort was being made to improve the deplorable condition of the Cape's coffers.

Then, there was the significant choice of the farm's name. Wolvaart's scrawled signature indicates that he was a man of scanty education and, living in a remote spot out of touch with the goings-on in the settlement, he was hardly likely to have had much interest in the commissioners' anticipated arrival. A far more likely reason was Rhenius's frantic hope of ingratiating himself with the important visitors by calling the farm after the younger but more senior of the pair. No one knows to what extent Sebastiaan Cornelis Nederburgh (the final letter 'h' in his name was omitted from that of the farm in the grant and in all subsequent transfer deeds) appreciated the compliment. Significantly, in view of the state of affairs at the Cape at this time, certain

records of the local ruling body, the Council of Policy, for the years 1787 until 1794 are missing from the Cape Archives, leaving the researcher no alternative but to speculate. However, contrary to claims made in the past, it is certain that the commissioner, personally, could not have granted the farm that bears his name to Wolvaart, for by the time he arrived at the Cape in July 1792 the relevant documents had been signed and sealed for eight months and more.

Nederburg lies on the gentle lower slopes of the lofty Klein Drakenstein range facing the setting sun and, across a wide valley, the humped boulders of Paarl Mountain. The earliest known inhabitants of the area were nomadic Khoikhoi, seasonal visitors who, each spring, brought their stock to feed on the valley's indigenous vegetation; and it was with cattle-bartering in mind that Dutchman, Abraham Gabbema, first explored it in October 1657. Gabbema, a man in his early twenties, had risen within a matter of months from the lowly position of midshipman in the Company's employ to that of secretary of the Council of Policy. Now,

TOP
Veteran draughtsman Johannes Schumacher painted this watercolour of neatly expanding Stellenbosch at the turn of the 18th century.
BOTTOM
The old Dutch Reformed church in Stellenbosch where the infant Philippus Bernardus Wolvaart was baptized on 12 October 1749.

with instructions from the commander, Jan van Riebeeck, he was leading a party of 15 white men, four trusty 'kaapmen', or Peninsular Khoikhoi, and nine pack-oxen into this area hitherto unknown to the settlers. On their third day out from the shores of Table Bay, the party had discovered a broad river that they named 'the Great Berg' because of the towering mountains that overlooked it. Next day, as they followed its course, they passed a high ridge crowned by twin granite domes that glittered like jewels in the early morning dew, and to this Gabbema gave the name 'Diamandt ende Peerl bergh'. The Dutchmen watched with wonder as hippopotamuses disported themselves in the river; saw 'horse droppings' — evidence of zebra; met a rhinoceros, which rushed by without touching them; and shot and wounded a lion. They also encountered large numbers of Khoikhoi who, somewhat grudgingly, provided them with seven cows, three calves and 41 sheep. 'There are fine lands for cultivation,' wrote Gabbema in his report on the expedition, never dreaming of the fruitful orchards and vineyards that clothe the valley of the Berg River today.

Other expeditions were to follow, some of them accompanied by the Cape's first land-surveyor, Pieter Potter, who made maps and recorded events in his journal. Usually the explorers had instructions to barter for stock with the Khoikhoi in the area, for at the settlement there was a constant and pressing need for food. Sometimes they passed through the valley on their way northwards in search of the legendary golden city of Monomotapa, while on other occasions galloping adventurers came to hunt down the hippos in the river and to shoot the shy, harmless antelope. Apart from these sporadic intrusions, the valley of the Berg River and the slopes of the mountains brooding above it remained for the time-being the untroubled, age-old habitation of the Khoikhoi.

But development was bound to disturb this idyllic state of affairs. Precisely 30 years after Abraham Gabbema had first pronounced the land good for cultivation, 23 Dutch and German farmers arrived in the area with their families. To each of them Commander Simon van der Stel had granted approximately 60 morgen of land fronting on the banks of the Berg River and on this they were to cultivate crops and breed stock to supply to the settlement. A year later, in 1688, there followed a party of Huguenot immigrants, religious refugees lately fled from Catholic persecution in France, some of them conveniently skilled in the cultivation of the vine. The new farms were no more than patches of veld strung like beads along the valley from below the Berg River's headwaters at Franschhoek to the edge of civilization at Limietberg, now the town of Wellington. The settlers cleared away the vegetation and ploughed the soil; they laid out vegetable gardens, planted cornfields and vineyards and built shelters for their animals and rough thatched houses for themselves. So diligent were they that by 1701, Drakenstein had become the most successful of the Cape's three wine-producing districts — the Cape Peninsula itself and Stellenbosch were the other two. At this stage Drakenstein farmers cultivated less than 600 000 of the colony's total of 1 664 400 vines, yet from their grapes they pressed almost half its entire yield of 1 135 leaguers of wine (a leaguer being equivalent to 5,82 hectolitres or 150 gallons).

After this vintage of 1701, 90 years of ploughing and

reaping, of good harvests and poor, were to pass before Philippus Bernardus Wolvaart took possession of the land that he called Nederburg. New generations had grown up in the area and multiplied and the rough dwellings that their forefathers had built had been transformed into spacious, gracious houses. Philippus Bernardus must have watched them rising above the cores of the original simple dwellings, now a century and more old. He must have seen slaves, oriental in feature and culture, fashioning the curves and scrolls of the gables and introducing, with a quirk of humour, a plaster star here, a bird or a pineapple there. Thatchers would have followed to secure the house against winter gales and to protect it from summer heat, while cabinet makers would have come to install elegant wall cupboards and to hang shutters over small casement windows. Philippus Bernardus must have observed all this industry and, like any young man with a growing family, he would have longed to have a gabled home and a flourishing wine farm of his own.

He was born on 1 October 1749 and baptized in Stellenbosch church 11 days later. His father was German-born Sebastiaan Wolfarth (who sometimes signed himself Seebastian Woolfarth, but the spelling of names was of little consequence in those days) and his mother was a local girl, 20-year-old Regina Barbara van Biljon, daughter of Bernardus van Biljon of Brabant and Maria Waters, first of his four wives. Van Biljon was a man of property who bought and sold land and houses both in Stellenbosch and in Drakenstein and was at one time owner of the farm Coetzenberg, today famous as the university sportsground. His son-in-law was also a man of enterprise: Sebastiaan Wolfarth

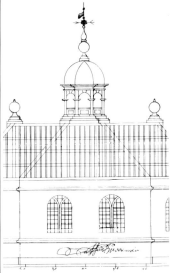

TOP
Paarl nestling under its famous rocks.
The 18th-century homestead sheltered by oaks
may be the old Pastorie.
BOTTOM
The design by Christoffel Meerman for
Paarl's first church. Completed in 1720, it was
here that various members of the Wolvaart
family were married and baptized.

had arrived at the Cape as a humble *stalknecht* (stablehand) in 1730, but within six years could afford to buy the farm De Zoete Inval on the outskirts of the little hamlet of Paarl. By the time he married Regina Barbara on 15 September 1748 he must have been well established and his application for permission to erect a tannery in Stellenbosch a month after the birth of his first son suggests that he was diversifying his interests. Eventually Sebastiaan and Regina Barbara were to have nine children, seven of whom are known to have grown up and married. The three youngest were born at Sebastiaan's last home, the farm Versailles at Wagenmakersvalleij; remnants of the house, much changed, still stand close to Wellington's railway station. Originally granted to Huguenot Pierre Cronier in 1699, Versailles had passed to his stepson, Jean Gardé, who sold it to Sebastiaan Wolfarth on 16 November 1758. According to the *opgaafrol* (census) taken the following year, Wolfarth owned seven adult slaves, five male and two female, and there were ten horses on the farm, 16 head of cattle and 156 sheep. A total of 10 000 vines were in cultivation and from them nine leaguers of wine were pressed in that year. Probably aided by the young Philippus Bernardus, Sebastiaan improved production at Versailles so that by 1765 he had 13 slaves — 11 adults and two children — 13 horses and 100 head of cattle. No mention is made of sheep — he may have sent them to a loan farm somewhere in the 'interior' — but the number of vines had increased to 20 000 and the leaguers of wine to ten.

On 16 April 1766, when their youngest child, Ernst Hendrik, was barely five months old, Sebastiaan Wolfarth and his wife, Regina Barbara, made a joint will. One imagines the six witnesses who signed the document standing round the testator's bedside as he breathed his last for he did, in fact, die only 12 days later. The will contained little more than the usual formalities, but it ensured that Regina Barbara, now 37 years old, would be the 'sole and universal heir . . . of all goods moveable or immoveable'. No doubt this inheritance must have enhanced whatever charms were already hers. Six months had scarcely flown by when Regina Barbara abandoned her widow's weeds in favour of a second outfit of bridal attire. The man who led her up the aisle of the Paarl church on this occasion was Johannes Thomas Rodewald, a Dane from Copenhagen, who had been at the Cape since 1753 when the ship in which he was travelling to the East had been condemned and broken up in Mossel Bay. A son and daughter were born of this marriage and if the subsequent development of Versailles is anything to go by, Regina Barbara's new husband proved a worthy consort. When a census was taken in 1773 they had between them five sons and four daughters living on the farm, which they ran with the aid of eight male and six female slaves. For some reason horses — an essential to every farmer — are not mentioned; cattle had dwindled to a mere 30 head, though the sheep now numbered 300. What is significant, however, is that where Sebastiaan Wolfarth had undoubtedly increased the number of his vines commendably, under Rodewald's hand they proliferated to 30 000, from which 30 leaguers of wine were pressed in that year. By 1790 Johannes Thomas Rodewald had acquired two further male slaves and had raised his vine production to 40 000, though he seemed unable to squeeze a drop more than 30 leaguers of wine from the grapes that they bore.

No one knows to what extent Rodewald's success as a farmer was the result of hard work on the part of his stepsons, for certainly the *opgaaf* counts taken during the years following his marriage to Regina Barbara reveal that Philippus Bernardus and his younger brothers, Sebastiaan, Guilliam and Ernst, were on Versailles. Each of them at first possessed only a single horse and three guns — the latter, since time immemorial, being an essential item of equipment to every self-respecting South African farmer. On the other hand, Rodewald's agricultural skills may have been an inspiration to his eldest stepson, who in 1791 decided to go farming on his own account. By this time, Philippus Bernardus, now 42 years old, had been married to Margaretha Niehout (also spelt Nieuwoudt) since 31 October 1773 and was the father of two sons and two daughters. He must have known Margaretha since his childhood: her father, Gerrit Niehout, was a neighbouring farmer and was also one of the witnesses at the signing of Sebastiaan's last will and testament. Philippus Bernardus and

Treading the grapes on a Cape farm. Wolvaart's slaves would have pressed wine in the time-honoured manner as sketched by Sir Charles d'Oyly.

Margaretha were registered as members of Paarl church congregation, both aged 20, in 1770 and the two families, like so many others at the Cape, were destined to be inseparably linked by a succession of marriages through several generations.

What, one wonders, made Philippus Bernardus Wolvaart decide to buy 57 morgen and 300 square roods of uncultivated wilderness, later to be known as the farm Nederburg, from the Honourable Dutch East India Company? The serious economic problems that had beset the Cape during the previous decade had certainly had disastrous consequences as far as the wine farmers were concerned. Not only had the local currency, the rix-dollar, dropped in value, but the prices of slaves, farming equipment and household articles had risen as much as threefold. Besides, between the years 1776 and 1786 wine production had doubled, but the demand for it had not kept pace proportionately. Attempts were made to export the surplus and when this failed because of the outbreak of war between France on one side and Britain and Holland on the other, desperate farmers, unable to dispose of their wine, broke open their wine casks and allowed thousands of leaguers to run to waste. It was a brave man — or perhaps a foolish one — who would throw in his lot with so unstable an industry at such a time.

However, nothing daunted, Philippus Bernardus Wolvaart went ahead and bought his farm. The grant made to him on 1 November 1791 informs us that it stretched towards the Paarl Mountain to the north-west; and that it adjoined the land of the Widow J. Oberholster to the north-east and the farm of the Burgher I. de Villiers to the south-east. West of it lay land belonging to the Widow J. Niehout. A river, the Palmiet, flowed through Nederburg and the grant obliged Wolvaart to allow his neighbours certain water rights and to permit their cattle to make use of his drift. The Widow Oberholster, formerly Elisabeth Prevot, was owner of the farm St Omer where, according to the *opgaafrol* of that year, she lived with her four slaves, a horse and 32 cattle. No mention is made of vines or other crops. She had married as long ago as 1728 and by 1791 was a great-grandmother. More prosperous was the farmer, Izaak de Villiers, 40 years old, owner of Palmietvlei and married to Anna Roos. He was the seventh of the 20 children of Jean de Villiers, respected master of Boschendal and of various other farms. In 1791 Izaak, who was himself father of nine children, cultivated 40 000 vines and produced 30 leaguers of wine on Palmietvlei. In addition, he owned 15 slaves, 18 horses and 20 head of cattle.

The last of Nederburg's neighbours was the 64-year-old Widow Johannes Niehout on Salomonsvlei. She had been born Anna Minnaar and her husband, who had died in 1785, had been a brother of Gerrit Niehout and therefore the uncle of Philippus Bernardus Wolvaart's wife, Margaretha. Perhaps it was this aunt who encouraged the Wolvaarts to buy Nederburg. An indication of just how close and complicated family relationships were within such a small and confined community as that of Drakenstein, is the fact that the Widow Niehout's brother, Jan Minnaar, had married Anna Catharina Niehout, sister of Johannes and Gerrit and was therefore also an aunt of Margaretha! Another pointer to the friendly terms existing between the families is that when, on 2 April 1790, the Widow Niehout had made a will, she had appointed Philippus Bernardus as one of her executors, the other being the Burgher Willem Weidman, married to her eldest daughter Johanna. In the year that Nederburg was granted to Wolvaart, she was living on Salomonsvlei with another of her three daughters and, with the aid of six slaves, producing 11 leaguers of wine from her 40 000 vines. Clearly the Widow Niehout was a person of some substance and in a position to lend Wolvaart ƒ9 000, an amount which he had apparently borrowed from her at some undisclosed stage and which is mentioned as outstanding in a later will which she signed on 19 December 1800. Significantly, by this stage she had stated, in a codicil, that in his place as executor she appointed another son-in-law, Johan Hendrik Baard, who had married her daughter, Helena, widow of Paul Retief. It is interesting to speculate on whether Wolvaart borrowed this money to buy the land which became Nederburg from the Dutch East India Company — certainly it covers the sum that he was required to pay for it — and then failed to return it to the Widow Niehout within the stipulated time.

And so, as the year 1791 drew to a close, Philippus Bernardus Wolvaart surveyed his new domain and saw that it was good. Behind him, the jagged and gloriously beautiful Klein Drakenstein mountains shimmered under the blazing blue of the summer sky. On the farm lands all round him the vines, in full, green leaf, sheltered the maturing grapes, while in the valley below meandered the unhurried waters of the Berg River. Above it and opposite Nederburg, loomed the granite rocks of Paarl Mountain, glinting and metallic in the brilliant sunlight. Could he have been aware, this son of the southern soil, that all was not well with the rest of the world? Did he know or care that France was in turmoil, its king fearing for his life and its government in disarray? Or that George III of England was undoubtedly going mad? Barely a month after Wolvaart acquired his new farm, one of this world's great geniuses, a young man named Wolfgang Amadeus Mozart, was buried in the frozen earth of a Viennese cemetery with no one but a gravedigger as witness, but no doubt this information would have meant little to a man familiar only

Visiting Dutch clergyman and writer François Valentijn, who visited the Cape four times during the governorships of Simon and Willem Adriaan van der Stel. The methods of vine cultivation that he observed had changed little by the time Philippus Bernardus Wolvaart started farming at Nederburg.

with tunes scraped out on the squeaky fiddles of a slave band. Here at home, things were bad enough. Money was tight and the authorities were indolent and corrupt. The fortifications at the Cape had been closed down and the Swiss and German mercenary soldiers who were supposed to have been protecting the settlement from its enemies had sailed away to Europe. Undoubtedly their departure was regretted: it hit the canteen owners severely, for the soldiers had been welcome frequenters of the settlement's numerous taverns and their loss was therefore also a serious blow to the wine farmers. But perhaps even these disturbing thoughts were brushed away by Philippus Bernardus Wolvaart as he turned his mind to the immediate task of clearing the soil so that by the time the winter rains came the new young vines could be planted. And, in any case, things were bound to have improved by the time they would be bearing.

The farming methods he employed would have differed little from those followed at the Cape a century earlier. In those days of tardy and uncertain communications, new ideas being put into practice by agriculturists in Europe were slow to reach or be adopted at the other end of the world. Indeed, crop cultivation and wine production during the governorships of Simon and Willem Adriaan van der Stel, as described by Dutch clergyman François Valentijn, were similar to what was observed by German soldier and teacher, Otto Mentzel, 50 years later; and these, in turn, scarcely differed from the practices recorded by Dutch Rear-Admiral Stavorinus when he visited the Cape in the 1770s.

The good farmer — so wrote Marnitz in his famous work *A Geographical-Topographical Description of the Cape of Good Hope* — pruned his vineyards in August, leaving two or at the most three buds on each branch 'to put forth new tendrils or shoots' when the sap began to rise. Cultivation and manuring around the vines took place immediately afterwards, although, cautioned Marnitz, this should be done only every third year or the taste of the wine would be spoilt. Meanwhile, the cuttings that had been removed at pruning would have been covered up and laid together in the ground as close as possible to a small stream. With the advancing spring, roots and shoots would begin to sprout and, after two years, the now established young vines would be ready for removal from their nursery and planted out in the vineyard. But, said Marnitz, 'he who lays out the vineyards and has previously dug the soil thoroughly, cleaned it of weeds and stones and manured it, does not plant the shoots that have taken root at random'. With caterpillars and 'suckers' successfully destroyed and the grass hoed to prevent it from becoming too luxuriant and sapping the vines, nothing else needed to be done in the vineyard, according to Marnitz, until harvest time. 'The first fruit,' he

said, 'may be confidently expected in the second or third year after transplanting, but in the three succeeding years the plant is the most fruitful.'

There are no documents to indicate how Philippus Bernardus Wolvaart set about planting his vineyards, but one can assume that he followed the time-honoured methods described by Mentzel, aided, of course, by slave labourers. According to the *opgaaf* taken in 1792, when he started clearing the ground at Nederburg, he employed two male and two female slaves; the following year the demands of his new property led him to acquire two more males. There is nothing to indicate whether he had the additional assistance of Khoikhoi labour in these early years but, in any event, it must have been hard work for there were also 300 sheep, ten draught oxen and six horses to look after. Then there were domestic duties to be fulfilled. Obviously a home for his family would have been a priority, for by the time Wolvaart became owner of Nederburg, Margaretha had borne him four children – George Sebastiaan, Johanna Maria, Philippus Bernardus and Regina Martha had been baptized, respectively, in 1774, 1776, 1777 and 1783. At some time in the last decade of the 18th century, a site for the Wolvaart's new house was chosen, the foundations were laid beside a useful little stream and the sun-dried bricks laid above them in the traditional H-form of a country gentleman's homestead. Encircled by a broad stoep paved with Batavian tiles, it was surrounded by young oaks destined to outlive by well over a century the family that would live there.

TOP
The Strooidak church in Paarl as the Dutch artist Johannes Cornelius Poortermans painted it in the mid-19th century. The oldest Dutch Reformed church in South Africa, it was completed in 1805.
BOTTOM
The kindly dominee, Robert Nicolaus Aling, from whom Wolvaart's mother, Regina Barbara van Biljon, sought advice regarding her daughter Catharina Dorothea.

In the valley west of Nederburg, and within easy reach of it by cart or on horseback, lay the little town of Paarl. It had grown slowly and was described by various travellers who visited it as being a picturesque village containing only a handful of houses straggling along a single tree-lined street, as well as a large mill and a thatched church. It was this church, completed in 1720, that was the local centre of social as well as religious life: it was here that farmers and their families met one another at services on Sundays and at the three-monthly sacrament of *nachtmaal*; it was here that they gathered at weddings, baptisms and, less happily, at funerals. The dominee during the closing years of the 18th century was the Reverend Robert Nicolaus Aling, a burly and genial German who, among other things, appreciated the wonders of nature and the virtues of good wine. Father of six daughters and one son, he died in 1800 aged only 49 and his is one of the oldest graves still to be seen in the old Paarl churchyard.

It was Aling who, with the support – one trusts – of the church elders, had to deal with a problem that was of much concern to the Wolvaart family at this time. In March 1794 (according to the church records, which have existed since 1714) Regina Barbara van Biljon, mother of Philippus Bernardus and by now widowed for the second time, hurried from her farm at the Wagenmakersvalleij some 20 dusty kilometres distant to visit Dominee Aling, clearly in a state of great agitation. She confessed to him that her daughter Catharina Dorothea, 30 years old and unmarried, was pregnant by

her brother-in-law, Jacobus Redelinghuys, and had fled in shame to her brother, Sebastiaan, and his wife, Maria, who ran sheep on a loan place in the remote Bokkeveld. The Widow Rodewald (by which name Regina Barbara would now have been known) urged Aling to inform the dominee at Tulbagh church of Catharina's presence in the area so that he could, if possible, baptize the child as soon as it was born. Despite the mother's disgrace, it was unthinkable that her baby, in an age when death in infancy was no uncommon occurrence, should be denied the benefit of the sacrament.

Redelinghuys, who farmed at Sonqua's Drift on the Berg River some 55 kilometres north of Paarl, seems to have got off scot-free. He had married Catharina's 23-year-old half-sister, Debora Helena Rodewald, on 25 April 1792 and their son, Johannes Hermanus, was born (after a respectable lapse of time) in June the following year. It is likely that Catharina, as the elder, spinster sister, had kept house for Debora Helena during her accouchement and, as a little simple arithmetic shows a difference of just about nine months between the birth of the Redelinghuys baby and the expected arrival of Catharina's, one is tempted to suspect that Jacobus had whiled away the long and cold winter evenings very comfortably in her company. At all events, the church in Paarl, no doubt at the urging of the warm-hearted Aling, eventually took pity on the luckless Catharina Dorothea and allowed her to bring the child back in September for its baptism. She was christened Maria Catharina Wolvaart, her first name possibly be-

ing a gesture of gratitude on Catharina's part to her sister-in-law for taking her into her humble household during her time of distress. Mother and child then returned to the Bokkeveld where, five years later, Catharina Dorothea married a certain Andries Salomons 'van Cabo de Goede Hoop' and, with him, passed into obscurity.

All the while, despite domestic anxieties, Philippus Bernardus Wolvaart's labours (he was by now 47 years old) were beginning, literally, to bear fruit, for by the time the census of 1796 was taken and he had been on Nederburg for just over four years, there were 20 000 vines growing in his vineyards and the trampling feet of his slaves had pressed from their grapes the first leaguer of Nederburg wine.

It is likely that the grape varieties that Wolvaart planted were those most often in cultivation at the time – Hanepoot, Muscadel, Steen and Green Grape. His method of extracting juice from them must have been similar to that described by Stavorinus, in his *Voyages to the East Indies*, published in 1778. He writes: 'The pressing of the grapes is performed in a more simple manner here than in Europe. The slaves gather them, and put them into a vessel, the bottom and sides of which are bored full of holes; this is set in the inside of a larger one, upon a crosspiece of wood laid at the bottom of the latter; this outside vessel has a spigot and faucet, through which the juice, as fast as it is pressed out, runs into a tub placed beneath. The grapes being heaped up, in the inner vessel, to the brim, three or four slaves,

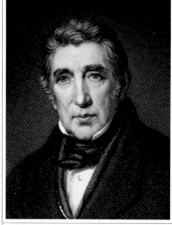

after having washed their feet in a tub of water standing at the side, get upon the fruit, and holding themselves fast by a rope fixed to the ceiling, trample upon it, and squeeze out the juice as long as they are able. In the mean time the must that runs out is put into large high vessels to ferment . . . The trodden grapes, before they are further pressed, are put upon a coarse strainer, made of rattans, on which they are rubbed with the hand, till the husks go through it; the stalks remaining behind, which are thrown away as they are supposed to make the wine austere and bitter. The husks are then put into the fermenting vessel, which the next morning is in full fermentation; during this process the thick parts subside, and the must grows clear, when it is barrelled off, being first filtered through a wicker basket. The grounds remaining in the fermenting vessel, are afterwards put into a square vessel pierced full of holes, and placed in a larger one with a spigot and faucet at the side; at the top there is a screw of wood, or metal, by means of which the last drop of juice is pressed out from the husks. From the dregs and husks that remain over from the last pressing, brandy is distilled. No yeast is used for accelerating the fermentation.'

Meanwhile, time had certainly not stood still either at the Cape or in the wider world. In the year that Philippus Bernardus Wolvaart pressed his first wine an event occurred that was to change the character of the far-flung settlement for all time. This was the arrival in Simon's Bay on 11 June of a fleet of nine British warships under the command of Rear-Admiral George Keith Elphinstone, the troops on board being led by Major-General James Henry Craig. Their purpose was to prevent the French, with whom Britain had been at war for the past two years, from occupying the Cape, a halfway station to the East which England, then a powerful mercantile country, regarded as indispensable. With the intention of taking over from the Dutch with as little trouble as possible, Craig brought with him a letter from the Dutch Prince of Orange, then in exile in England, bidding Governor A.J. Sluysken to admit the British peaceably. The negotiations failed and there followed the battles of Muizenberg and Wynberg at which all the local forces — half-hearted in their resistance and divided in their loyalties — were completely routed in a campaign lasting three brief days. With the signing of articles of capitulation at Rustenburg in the suburb of Rondebosch on 16 September 1795, the rule of the Dutch East India Company at the Cape came to an end

TOP
Life on Cape farms in the early 19th century was extremely unsophisticated. Here a scantily clad slave child waves away the flies while the housewife (also barefoot) concocts something in a small dish. She probably spent the night under a kaross on the crude kadel (left). Her husband's powder horn, hat and jacket hang against the wall.
BOTTOM
General Jan Willem Janssens, (1762-1838), military commander and governor at the time of the second British occupation.

and the first period of British administration began.

These events could not fail to affect the Cape wine farmers. When the heavy ox-wagons trundled back to Paarl after disposing of produce at the Cape market, they brought accounts of soldiers and sailors (British this time) once more crowding the streets and entertaining themselves rowdily in the numerous canteens. This was good news for the farmers and raised hopes — soon to be fulfilled — for an increased demand for their wine. Following the usual laws of economics, by 1797 the price, a mere 25 rix-dollars a leaguer before the invaders arrived, had risen to a very satisfactory 60 rix-dollars, despite the abysmal quality of the wine. It seems that this was of little concern to those roisterers who consumed it with such gay abandon at the canteens, yet to anyone with a refined palate Cape wines were, in general, distasteful, to say the least.

In his work, *Travels in South Africa*, John Barrow, private secretary of Lord Macartney, Britain's first governor at the Cape, had some critical observations to make on both the production and the quality of the local product. 'Most of the wines,' he wrote, 'have either a thinness and a slight acidity, or, for want of a proper degree of fermentation, and from being pressed when over ripe, acquire a sickly saccharine taste.' Cape brandy, in his opinion, was even worse: 'This article is here in general very bad indeed,' he writes, 'evidently owing, in a great degree, to the manner in which it is manufactured. In order to get as much spirit as possible, the materials thrown into the still are of the grossest kind . . . the apparatus is bad; the conducting of the process is committed to the hands of a slave, who has little knowledge of, and less interest in, the business he is commanded to perform: he falls asleep; the fire goes out; a rapid blaze succeeds to make up for loss of time; the spirit carries over with it a strong emphyreumatic flavor which it never loses . . .'

Yet, on 4 July 1797, this same John Barrow, when writing from Paarl to Lady Anne Barnard (who acted as hostess to Lord Macartney and herself made many shrewd comments about life at the Cape) had this to say about Paarl: 'Everything here flourishes with the greatest luxuriance. The oaks are large, straight & tall . . . Walnuts, Chestnuts, Almonds, Oranges and in short all sorts of fruit are in abundance . . . but the chief produce is the Vine, and I can assure you that the Wine here is altogether different & infinitely superior than at the Cape . . .'

But any joy that Philippus Bernardus Wolvaart may have experienced in knowing that his wines were 'infinitely superior' to those produced in the cellars of Constantia would have been clouded by the death of his wife, Margaretha, on 27 November 1798. She was 48 years old and during 25 years of marriage had borne him four children, all of them – perhaps surprisingly, in view of the times – still alive when she died. The eldest, George Sebastiaan, was by then 24 years old and the youngest, Regina, was just 15. Late 18th-century domestic records are faded, brief and businesslike: no word on Margaretha's death notice indicates whether she died as a result of illness or accident, whether her end was lingering or sudden or even where it occurred. It may be that she breathed her last in a small dwelling at Nederburg which has, in recent years, been enlarged into sophisticated reception offices, for the building is thought to be even older than the homestead itself. It was possibly the Wolvaarts' home at first and it may be from here that Margaretha's mortal remains were taken to some unknown, untraced plot of ground to be buried. She never saw the large house which Philippus Bernardus Wolvaart built for his family, for it was not com-

pleted until two years after her death. On settling at Nederburg his first task would have been to erect such necessary outbuildings as a wine cellar, stables and slave quarters; only once these essentials were completed could he concentrate on creating a house that could compete in grace and grandeur with any of the splendid dwellings built by neighbouring farmers over the past half century.

And the finished Nederburg homestead did indeed have all the finest attributes of what is commonly known as Cape Dutch or Cape vernacular architecture – beautiful proportions under a sleek thatched roof, fine yellowwood shutters, beams and doors, and floors laid with warm red Batavian tiles. Of course, like most late 18th-century Cape houses, its glory was its gable, in which playful convex-concave outlines surged to their zenith in a pediment of disciplined, classical beauty. It bears the date 1800 and – a rare feature – the name of the house inscribed above a garland of foliage. If Margaretha had lived to see Nederburg completed, Philippus Bernardus would almost certainly have paid her the compliment of entwining her initials with his in a romantic monogram fashioned from whitewashed plas-

ter on the centre of the gable — but that was not to be.

Not many years before Philippus Bernardus Wolvaart started building his house at Klein Drakenstein, another farmer on another wine farm some 70 kilometres away was renovating — with the aid of two of the most distinguished craftsmen the Cape has ever known — a house originally built a century earlier. The farmer was Hendrik Cloete, the craftsmen were architect Louis Michel Thibault and sculptor Anton Anreith, and the farm was the incomparable Groot Constantia. And, all the while, as they worked under Simon van der Stel's burgeoning oaks, wine that was to become a legend was maturing under the thatch of Groot Constantia's silent, shadowy cellars. Governors, travellers and connoisseurs alike praised it and by the end of the 18th century it was being drunk by kings and nobles at banquets in the palaces of Europe.

But Constantia was not the only wine to be exported, although free trade for wine growers did not as yet exist. Alas, the bulk of Cape wines to reach foreign shores was of a very different character and quality. For the most part these wines were blended, a little of good quality being mixed with a large quantity that was in-

ferior and highly fortified, the combination being further 'doctored' when the casks reached Britain. No records exist to indicate whether any of Nederburg's pressings were included in these highly adulterated exports, which a British member of Parliament described as being 'suitable only for tipplers and bargemen'. By the time Philippus Bernardus Wolvaart was adding the date to Nederburg's gable, he was producing 25 leaguers of wine from his grapes each year, so it is possible that some of it — much mixed — was reaching the hostelries of London's East End.

For six years he remained a widower and in that time the oaks with which he had surrounded Nederburg must have grown steadily taller. When, in 1804, he did decide to remarry, his choice fell on Margaretha's cousin, 47-year-old Anna Niehout. Anna was a daughter of Nederburg's neighbour, the Widow Johannes, and herself a widow but, as far as can be traced, childless. Her previous husband, a German settler named Casper Müller, had farmed in the area before setting up practice in Paarl as a surgeon. He had died scarcely a year before Anna married Philippus Bernardus but, at a time when eligible women at the Cape were in such

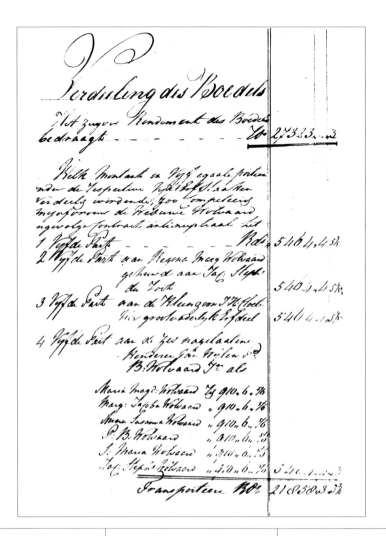

A page from the will of Philippus Bernardus Wolvaart. His estate was worth almost 28 000 rixdollars which, in 1840, would have been equivalent to about £25 500.

short supply, widows did not have to wait long to find new husbands. With Anna beside him, Wolvaart worked hard at developing Nederburg yet further while the events of history, at home and abroad, continued to roll on.

Once more, the Cape was in the hands of the Dutch. In 1803, in terms of the Treaty of Amiens, Britain had been obliged to hand it back to the Netherlands, then known as the Batavian Republic, in the persons of General Janssens and Commissioner De Mist. In faraway Paris, only two days before Philippus Bernardus and Anna made their nuptial vows, Napoleon Bonaparte had snatched the crown from the Pope in a ceremony in Notre Dame Cathedral and crowned himself emperor. But, despite these dramas, life seemed to change little for the Cape wine farmers. The youthful German physician and naturalist, Martin Hinrich Karl Lichtenstein, could have had Nederburg and its owners in mind when he described the farmers living in the Berg River valley in the early 19th century. 'Although according to European ideas,' he wrote, 'they cannot be accounted rich, for none are great capitalists, yet they have abundance of every thing which can render the physical life pleasant and comfortable. This appearance of plenty contributes equally with the aspect of the country itself, where the slopes are ever clothed with verdure, where farms, with their clean white-washed houses, their vineyards, their orchards, and their avenues of oaks . . . are strewed everywhere around . . .'

Early in 1806, barely three months after Nelson's victory at the Battle of Trafalgar, the British were back. Determined to prevent Napoleon's ally, Holland, from interfering with her trade, Britain dispatched a fleet of 61 ships, together with over 6 000 troops, to take possession of the Cape. They sailed into Table Bay on 4 January and, after a skirmish on the dunes behind Blaauwberg beach, most of General Janssens' motley collection of militia and mercenaries made an ignominious dash for the hinterland, leaving the remainder of the forces to capitulate to General David Baird at Papendorp.

Like every other emotion experienced by Philippus Bernardus Wolvaart, his reaction to the news of the second British occupation will never be known. What is on the record is that by 1808, 63 000 vines were growing on Nederburg and that they were producing 40 leaguers of wine and four of brandy. One male and two female 'Hottentot' labourers supplemented 19 adult slaves — 14 adults and five children — and although the census states that everything on the farm was devoted to wine and fruit trees ('Alles tot wijn en boomvrugte') Philippus Bernardus Wolvaart also owned 57 draught oxen, 75 breeding cattle, nine horses and three four-wheeled wagons. All this conjures up a picture of relative prosperity and security, so it is with a degree of surprise that we discover that in 1810 he decided to sell the farm. Perhaps he had tired of hard manual labour — he was by now 60 years old. At all events, on Thursday and Friday 19 and 20 April he held an auction of his possessions ('alle Sodanige Goederen en Effecten') at Nederburg and, as it was a 'vendue' sale, it must have been an occasion for all and sundry in the Drakenstein district to meet and take part in what Lichtenstein described as 'the revelry going forwards'. 'For,' as he writes, 'how great soever may be the number of guests, the purchaser must feast them all, and this, if he be a man of generous spirit, he does very handsomely. Here . . . they laugh, they joke, and throw aside all restraint. Sometimes wine is also busy among the company . . .' The secretary to the local drostdy acted as auctioneer, or 'venduemeester' and knocked down hundreds of items, ranging from a lump of lead and bundles of thatch to oxen and wagons. There are no fewer than 12 pages listing the items sold, the prices paid for them and the purchasers' names. They reveal that Philippus Bernardus and Anna were simple, country folk who used metal spoons and forks, had a large number of drinking glasses of various kinds and slept on feather beds. Their family and neighbours — the Minnaars, Niehouts, De Villiers and Oberhol-

When Wolvaart sold Nederburg in 1810 he held a sale of his possessions. The articles listed on the reekening *provide an interesting insight into the manner in which he and his family lived.*

sters — were there in force. Petrus Hauptfleisch bought a horse and some curtains; Sebastiaan Wolvaart Junior was the purchaser of a number of items, including two wagons and 20 wine casks, while his brother, Philip, took over the family four-poster bed. The takings of the vendue amounted to 3 010 rix-dollars, less expenses and commission of just under 200 rix-dollars, and one hopes that it more than covered the cost of the food and drink for so large a crowd.

Philippus Bernardus and Anna then moved into the town of Paarl, where they bought a plot of land. Anna died in her 68th year on 22 February 1825 and, presumably to comfort himself in his old age, 82-year-old Philippus married for the third time on 2 June 1832. This time his bride was Elisabeth van Reenen, aged 49, widow of one Willem Joubert and mother of his four children. Philippus Bernardus died on 11 June 1840, having outlived all his children with the exception of Regina, now Mrs Jacobus Stephanus du Toit. He had reached the great age of 90 years, 8 months and 10 days and left an estate worth ƒ27 323. For a man who, in 1765 at the age of 16, had owned only one horse and three firearms and had applied for exemption from military duty on the grounds of weakness of the chest and a knee injury, he had not done badly at all.

■

CHAPTER TWO

THE RETIEFS, FATHER AND SON 1810-1881

Proprietors of Nederburg for 71 years,
Willem Petrus Retief and his son enlarged the farm and
planted 93 000 vines. In 1838 they had to adapt
themselves to the emancipation of their slaves; in the 1860s
their vines were struck by the fungus disease
Oidium tuckeri and they had to bear the financial consequences
of Britain's withdrawal of special tariffs.

n 6 September 1810 '*zeeker plaats ofte Hofsteede genaamd Nederburg*' was transferred to Willem Petrus Retief for the sum of *f*35 782 — five times more than Philippus Bernardus Wolvaart had paid for it 19 years earlier. There are three possible reasons for this phenomenal increase in price. In the first place, the Dutch East India Company, which usually granted land to farmers free of charge, had probably charged Wolvaart only a nominal sum for Nederburg. Secondly, there had been a tremendous rise in the cost of living during the intervening years. And thirdly, one must bear in mind the considerable development that had taken place on Nederburg which, at that stage, still consisted of 57 morgen and 300 square roods. Wolvaart had acquired no more than a stretch of wilderness at the beginning of November, 1791; in 1810 he handed over to his successor a farm planted with 63 000 vines and an unknown number of fruit trees, besides an *opstal* consisting of two dwelling houses and several outbuildings.

Retief had been among the large crowd that had attended the vendue sale at Nederburg earlier in the year and had bought, among other things, a quantity of wine.

Nederburg's new owner belonged to a well-known family of Huguenot descent. François Rétif, great-grandfather of Willem Petrus, was a French vine-dresser who had been born in 1663 at Mer, a small, strongly Protestant town near the River Loire in an area known for its wine production. After the revocation of the Edict of Nantes in 1685, François and his sister, Anne, fled to Holland, where they remained for some time before sailing for the Cape in 1688. Not long after his arrival, François was granted a farm in the Wemmershoek valley between Franschhoek and what became the village of Paarl. Named La Paris, it adjoined the farm L'Arche d'Orléans, whose owner, Pierre Rousseau, wooed and married Anne Rétif. François waited until 1700 to marry and chose as his bride Maria Mouij, not yet 15 years old and 22 years his junior. Another French

refugee, she had arrived at the Cape with her family only six months earlier. Over the following 20 years, she was to bear François nine children, the sixth of them being Paul who, in his 29th year, married Dorothea Melius. Their eldest surviving son, also Paul and born in 1749, married, first, Maria Louisa Joubert and, after her death in 1790, Helena, youngest daughter of Johannes Nieuwoudt (or Niehout) and sister of Philippus Bernardus Wolvaart's second wife, Anna. Willem Petrus Retief, born on 3 September 1785, was the fourth child of the younger Paul and Maria Louisa Joubert and therefore the stepson of Philippus Bernardus Wolvaart's sister-in-law! Complicated relationships of this kind were common in the days when the population of the rural areas of the Cape was small and families lived in close proximity to one another. Willem Petrus Retief would have been familiar with Nederburg through his stepmother and may even have offered to buy it when he heard that Wolvaart had decided to give up farming.

PAGE 34: TOP
Nederburg as it appeared to the missionary John Campbell in 1813. This is the first known depiction of the homestead.
BOTTOM
A Cape farmer dressed in his best. No likenesses of Willem Petrus Retief have been discovered, but he may have looked something like this.
PAGE 35: TOP
Crossing the Berg River in 1811. This, particularly in winter, was the most serious hazard in the journey to Cape Town.
BOTTOM LEFT
An early 19th century farmer's wife dressed for church.
BOTTOM RIGHT
Du Pré Alexander, Earl of Caledon (1777-1839), governor of the Cape at the time when the elder Willem Petrus Retief bought Nederburg.

Willem Petrus Retief had been brought up on a farm and, as with other farmers' sons, knew no other way of life. He was born on 3 September 1785, probably on his father's wine farm, Frederiksburg, near the village of Simondium in the Drakenstein valley. His mother died when he was only four years old and as his father married Helena Nieuwoudt (then a young widow) only six months later, the responsibility of his upbringing would have fallen on her. He was only 21 when, on 18 August 1806, he led 19-year-old Hester Germina de Wet up the aisle of Paarl's Strooidakkerk, which had been opened during the previous year. She was the daughter of Heemraad Frans de Wet and his wife Elisabeth du Toit and a direct descendant of the famous soldier and adventurer, Olaf Bergh. Two sons were born to Hester in quick succession — Paul Johannes and François Jacobus — but she died on 5 December 1808, less than three months after the birth of the second child. Willem Petrus mourned the death of

his young wife for two years before choosing a new bride to take on the care of his little boys.

Hester's successor was Maria Elisabeth Haumann, 20-year-old granddaughter of Eduard Christiaan Haumann, eccentric owner of the beautiful and historic farm, Stellengift. Now Simonsvlei, it lies between Frederiksburg, which Haumann had in fact once owned, and the town of Paarl. Maria herself lived near Franschhoek on the farm Laborie (now La Bri), which was owned by her father, Pieter Eduard Haumann. It may be that Nederburg was a wedding gift to her, for Willem Petrus signed the transfer deed the day after their marriage in the Stellenbosch church on 6 May 1810. Within a year, as was to be expected in those days, the first child of this union – another son, Pieter Eduard – was born. Then followed Willem Petrus, born on 3 November 1812, Johannes Hendrik, born on 4 June 1814, and Eduard Christiaan Paulus, born on 10 March 1816. Daniel Pieter, born on 7 December 1817, lived only 13 months, and six months after his death – on 27 July 1819 – Magdalena Agatha arrived. No doubt this child, their only surviving daughter, was particularly precious to Willem Petrus and Maria, especially as the three babies that followed – a girl and two boys – were all destined to die in infancy. By the time the last child was born – he died aged five days and unbaptized on 12 December 1824 – his mother was 34 years old and had borne nine children in 14 years of marriage. Despite the sorrow of losing four of them, Nederburg's homestead at this time must have rung with the noisy voices of a lively young family for there were

PROCLAMATION.

By His Excellency Lt. General Sir JOHN FRANCIS CRADOCK, Knight of the Moſt Honorable Orders of the Bath and Crescent, Colonel of His Majeſty's 43d Regiment of Foot, Governor and Commander in Chief of His Majesty's Castle, Town, and Settlement of the Cape of Good Hope in South Africa, and of the Territories and Dependencies thereof, and Ordinary and Vice Admiral of the fame, Commander of the Forces, &c. &c. &c.

WHEREAS it is neceſſary to call the ſerious attention of the Cultivator, the Merchant, and the Farmer of this Colony, to the ſubject of the Wine Trade; a confideration, above all others, of the higheſt importance to its opulence and character.

The beneficent intentions of the Government to promote this Branch of Commerce to its utmoſt extent, are entirely defeated by the practices that prevail, whether in the view of the original preparation of the Wine, as, in many respects, erroneous and negligent, or, of its improvident and thoughtleſs exportation, without concern as to its quality or age. The object ſeems alone, to make a little profit for the moment, without regard to the future; and, by ſuch proceedings, this valuable, and, in His Majeſty's Dominions, unrivalled Article of Commerce, is upon the point of being ſacrificed.

The Colony, from theſe cauſes, has already loſt the demand from South America; and unleſs Government interpoſe its powers, the bright proſpects opened by the capture of the Iſles of France and Batavia, will be equally cloſed, and the Settlement will have to lament, for ever, her blindneſs and perſeverance in a falſe courſe.

It is an undoubted fact, and it ſhould make the pride, as well as the wealth of the Inhabitants, that this Colony can produce as excellent Wine of various ſorts, as perhaps any Country in the World. If therefore the Cultivator and Merchant be but true to their permanent Intereſts, and will abandon the petty profit of the moment, to the infinitely greater advantage of futurity, equally within their power, what the Colony has ſuffered in the depreciation and diſeſteem of its Wines, may be repaired; and confidence and reputation being reſtored, every avenue to its exportation will be re-opened and enlarged.

Having thus demanded, in authority, from the Settlement, a ſerious and lively attention to their own Intereſts, I hereby promiſe the moſt conſtant ſupport and patronage on the part of Government, and that no means of aſſiſtance ſhall be left unattempted to improve the cultivation, and every encouragement given to benefit induſtry and adventure to eſtabliſh the ſucceſs of the Cape Commerce in this her great and native ſuperiority.

In the courſe of this year, premiums and rewards will be given by Government, for the production of the beſt Wines.

As ſoon as this important ſubject ſhall have received due confideration, the neceſſary Regulations will be eſtabliſhed and declared, and an Office of Taſter of Wines be inſtituted to ascertain the quality of Wines for exportation.

In the mean time, all perſons wiſhing to export Wine, can alone have permiſſion by making ſpecial application to Government, and a temporary order will be given for its inſpection and approval.

And that no one may plead ignorance hereof, this ſhall be publiſhed and affixed as uſual.

Given under my Hand and Seal, at the Cape of Good Hope, this 19 day of Dec. 1811

seven children tumbling about in it, six of them boys.

At this time, in the hub of things at Cape Town, there was much concern among the authorities regarding the state of the wine trade. Britain, isolated from her European neighbours by prolonged war with France, saw the Cape as a potential 'wine cellar' for the United Kingdom if only the quality of the local wine could be improved – always excepting, of course, the rare and prized Constantia. Captain Robert Percival, who had visited the colony during the first British occupation, had sharply criticized both local wines and the farmers who produced them. In his work, *An Account of the Cape of Good Hope*, he wrote: 'The defects in Cape wines proceed from the avarice of the planter on the one hand and his extreme indolence on the other . . . The planters go on in their old and rude way, equally inattentive to private advantage and the public good. Though the quantity of wine made at the Cape is considerable, yet it is still little esteemed from its poorness and insipidity . . . In India no Englishman would buy it, nor would a Captain of an East Indiaman think it worth room in his ship.' And as for Cape brandy – well, it was 'awful stuff, with a strong resemblance to Irish whisky, only harsher and more fiery'.

Things had not changed by the time the Dutch finally relinquished the Cape in 1806 and Percival's opinion continued to be endorsed by most people of any sophistication during the early years of Britain's second administration. Accustomed to the finesse and nuances of French wines, the English found the ordinary product of the colony utterly unpalatable yet, at the

same time, there were those, even then, who had faith in the Cape's potential as a great wine-producing region. Among those determined to encourage the local wine industry was the first British governor, Du Pré Alexander, Earl of Caledon. In a letter of 21 March 1810 addressed to the Earl of Liverpool, then colonial secretary in London, he wrote: 'My Lord, I send you eight kinds of the common wines and some Cape brandy with their prices, and if it be the pleasure of His Majesty to encourage the growth of wine in this Colony for the supply of the Navy or for Home Consumption, and to reduce the duty to that upon the home-made wines and spirits, I have little doubt of this Colony becoming in a few years competent to supply any demand that may arise.'

But it was Lieutenant-General Sir John Francis Cradock, appointed governor in September 1811, who made the first positive move to stimulate the Cape wine industry. His proclamation of 19 December of that year did not mince matters when it stated: 'The beneficent intentions of the Government to promote this Branch of Commerce to its utmost extent, are entirely defeated by the practices that prevail, whether in the view of the original preparation of the Wine, as, in many respects, erroneous and negligent, or of its improvident and thoughtless exportation, without concern as to quality or age . . . It is an undoubted fact,' he went on, 'and it should make the pride, as well as the wealth of the Inhabitants, that this Colony can produce as excellent Wine of various sorts, as perhaps any Country in the World.' Sir John then 'demanded' the wine farmers' 'serious and lively attention to their own interests', in

PAGE 36: TOP
Oupa tells a tale. Pipe-smoking and coffee-drinking, the farmer's family gathers round while chickens forage for crumbs on the kitchen floor and slaves prepare a meal.
BOTTOM
A proclamation issued by Governor Sir Francis Cradock with the intention of improving the quality of Cape wines.
PAGE 37: TOP
A familiar sight on Cape Town's old jetty, wine barrels wait to be loaded on board for export.
BOTTOM
Sir John Francis Cradock (1762-1839) proved a far-sighted governor. He resolved the problem of land tenure and made a serious effort to encourage farmers to produce good wine.

return for which he assured them of the government's support and patronage in attempting to improve every aspect of the wine industry. Further, to ensure that only wine of the highest quality would be exported, he announced the creation of the post of official wine-taster.

The first incumbent, a Mr William Caldwell, assumed his responsibilities on 3 January 1812 – one imagines with a degree of nervousness, even surprise, since he had previously held the office of postmaster-general. His chief duty was to examine all wines intended for export and to put his official stamp only on those casks whose contents met certain standards of age, strength and quality. But the wheels of bureaucracy have always ground slowly and before anything had been done locally, parliament in Westminster had announced the good news, in 1813, that preferential tariffs were to be allowed for ordinary Cape wine sent to the United Kingdom. This step was taken because, in the first place, Napoleon had effectively prevented the wine-producing countries of Europe from exporting by blockading their seaports; and secondly, because of Britain's sympathetic attitude to her colonies. At all events, it proved the most important single stimulus for the Cape's wine industry during the 19th century. Soon afterwards a 'general advertisement' was distributed among the wine farmers, informing them that the time was ripe for the introduction of Cape wines into general use abroad, but that this could not be accomplished 'without the total abandonment of the present system conducted as it is under a false principle and full of error throughout'.

Captain Robert Percival had certainly not been the

Cape's only critical visitor: almost every literate traveller had commented on the haphazard manner in which viticulture was practised. Now, detailed instructions were given to the farmers regarding the methods they were expected to adopt. For example, continued the 'advertisement', vines should be planted further apart and trained onto espaliers of bamboo or reed; vineyards should be scrupulously weeded; young shoots and leaves should be removed to give the ripening grapes sufficient air and sunlight and, above all, the greatest possible care should be taken in gathering in the harvest and preparing the grapes for pressing. Farmers could send their wine to Cape Town after the first fermentation, after which the wine merchants were expected to store it for at least 16 months before separating it into four different qualities and blending it. As an incentive, gold medals were to be awarded to farmers both for the number of vines planted and for the quality of various types of wine they produced.

Certainly, the authorities' encouraging approach had the desired effect. Farmers throughout the wine-growing areas began energetically extending their vineyards; row upon row of vines were planted and before many years had passed, the busy feet of slaves had trampled thousands of extra leaguers of wine from green grapes and red. At *nachtmaal* and vendu sales this fresh breath of life blowing through the wine industry must have been the chief topic of conversation and Willem Petrus Retief on his new farm at Nederburg would have been in the thick of it all. According to a census taken in 1813, within his first three years there he increased the number of vines under cultivation from the 63 000 that Philippus Bernardus Wolvaart had left behind to 80 000. This he achieved with the aid of only eight slaves — six males and two females — and a 'Hottentot'

couple, whereas Wolvaart's labour force in the year he gave up farming had consisted of 13 male and six female slaves (including three young girls) as well as two 'Hottentot' women.

From 1814 onwards the official wine-taster kept records of all export wine brought into Cape Town. As one opens the dusty old volumes in the Cape Archives and reads the faded, spidery scrawl covering page after page, it is easy to picture the ox-wagons lumbering across the windswept, often impassable drifting sands of the Cape Flats — a journey of up to four days — to bring their burdensome loads from Drakenstein and Stellenbosch to the seaport. All the familiar farm-names are listed in the records — among them La Motte, L'Ormarins and La Provence in the Franschhoek valley and, beyond Simonsberg on the far side of Stellenbosch, Blaauwklippen, Meerlust and Vergenoegd. The wines brought in for export included Madeira — pale, high-coloured, old-straw-coloured, pale deep and yellow; and there were several types of Muscadel, as well as 'very old' Steen, Pontac and others. Nederburg's first entry is dated 19 October 1814, when W.P. Retief sent four-and-a-half leaguers of eight-month-old Green Grape wine to the merchant C. Brink in Cape Town. Within a month he had sent 16 more leaguers of the same type of wine to the same address and continued to deliver wine, always Green Grape, to Cape Town for at least the following ten years. On occasions the consignment consisted of as many as ten leaguers; on others he sent only one. His neighbours, Philip and George Sebastiaan Wolvaart, sons of Philippus Bernardus, were also delivering wine to Cape Town, but in much smaller quantities.

These were prosperous days for the wine farmers. Not only was there a strong army and navy presence at

the Cape, but from 1813 onwards Britain's demand for Cape wine increased and other new overseas markets opened up. Then too, after the Battle of Waterloo in 1815, St Helena, where Napoleon paced up and down like a caged tiger, began to order substantial quantities of wine from the Cape. To keep pace with this increasing demand, frantic farmers expanded their vineyards further and yet further again. In 1810, there had been 16,9 million vines growing at the Cape, from which a total of 10 400 leaguers of wine were pressed; by 1824 the number of vines had increased to 31,9 million and the quantity of wine to 16 183 leaguers. More than half the vines grew in Drakenstein and from their grapes more than half the total of the Cape's wine was produced. In 1813, when preferential tariffs were introduced, 200 leaguers of wine were sent abroad; in 1824 a total of 6 672 leaguers were exported. The price of wine also increased dramatically: only 60 rix-dollars a leaguer at the turn of the century, it rose sharply to between 135 and 185 rix-dollars after 1813. (The currency at the Cape had not yet changed to sterling.)

If the wine-taster kept any accounts of the amount of money paid to each farmer for the wine he brought to town, they have not been preserved, so there is no way of telling how much cash reached the pockets of Willem Petrus Retief. It is certain, though, that like many other farmers allured by the increasing demand for wine, he enlarged his vineyards during these years, for when a census was taken in 1825 no fewer than 93 000 vines were growing at Nederburg. From them, seven male slaves trampled 78 leaguers of wine and three of brandy – a substantial quantity, most of which was loaded in casks onto Willem Petrus's five wagons for transport to Cape Town. A total of 56 draught oxen and 18 breeding cattle, in company with nine horses, grazed on Neder-

burg's pastures, and five pigs rooted among acorns fallen from trees planted nearly 30 years earlier by Philippus Bernardus Wolvaart. Five female slaves and their four children no doubt performed sundry domestic duties in the house, where four of the Retief sons and their sister Magdalena Agatha still lived. In one of the several outbuildings reposed a two-wheeled vehicle (perhaps a Cape cart – the census returns record that it was kept 'for pleasure') and in it Willem Petrus and his wife, Maria, could go bowling along the dusty road to call on friends in Paarl or to attend divine service at the Strooidakkerk on Sundays.

At this time, Retief entered into an agreement with four of his neighbours as a result of which, on 15 April 1826, they were granted, on perpetual quitrent, 403 morgen 436 square roods of undivided, commonly-held land. According to the grant, it was bounded by the farms Ambagts Valley, Orléans, Nederburg, Knolle Valley, Palmiet Valley, Hartebeestkraal and Salomons Valley and it was subject to the condition that 'the present and future proprietors . . . [shall] be obliged to suffer at all times the inhabitants of the Paarl to cut wood upon the land and to convey it from thence; without, however, their being allowed to unyoke the oxen which they may have occasion to use on the land or to let such cattle graze upon the same'. For what purpose the five co-owners required the land is not known but, like the inhabitants of Paarl, they may have gathered wood there and even grazed their cattle on it. It is interesting to note that at this stage, despite the wording of the perpetual quitrent grant, Willem Petrus Retief did not actually own the land between Nederburg's original acres and the boundary of this property although, as was the accepted custom of the time, he may well have 'appropriated' it and converted it into a vineyard.

Land tenure in South Africa

*

Land could be owned in two ways in the early days of colonization: leasehold and freehold. Later, during the 18th and early 19th centuries, the systems of quitrent and erfpacht were introduced and operated for sporadic periods. Eventually leasehold, which entailed payment of an annual levy but no right of disposal, fell away, leaving freehold as the prevailing system.

Registration of freehold land conferred on the owner unrestricted rights of use and of alienation. Rural areas granted in freehold were relatively small with vacant, ungranted land often separating farms. It was here, beyond the surveyed original freehold, that illegal expansion of farming activities — such as the planting of vines — became common practice, creating a most unsatisfactory state of affairs. Eventually, in 1813, Governor Sir John Cradock sought to resolve this chaos by the introduction of perpetual quitrent tenure to augment freehold, with both systems co-existing as forms of land ownership. The illegally occupied areas were ordered to be surveyed and then granted as equitably as possible as perpetual quitrent land. An annual levy (quitrent) was demanded for its use. It may well be that Philippus Bernardus Wolvaart and the elder Willem Petrus Retief had been cultivating the area surrounding the original Nederburg farm for years before it was officially granted in quitrent.

Today, freehold and quitrent are obsolete terms. Land is referred to merely by its erf number in the case of urban areas and, in rural areas, by farm numbers.

Michiel van Breda (1775-1847) was founder of the first agricultural society established in southern Africa.

PAGE 41: TOP
Nederburg as it was surveyed in 1830. The rectangle in the centre of the diagram represents the farm originally granted to Wolvaart in 1791. The irregularly-shaped area surrounding it is the perpetual quitrent land acquired by the elder Willem Petrus Retief in 1831.

BOTTOM
The problem of producing superior quality wine and brandy was of constant concern to farmers, scientists and administrators — as indicated by this pamphlet issued by a committee appointed by Governor Lord Charles Somerset in 1826. It remained unsolved until cold fermentation was introduced in the 1930s.

During the years that the winelands of Drakenstein continued to flourish, the wine-taster's post in Cape Town was held by several incumbents, all of varying degrees of incompetence. Caldwell, for one, admitted that his knowledge of the gauging of casks was limited and asked, with little success, for an assistant who was better qualified for the task. Disagreements arose between the wine-taster and the authorities and although Lord Charles Somerset, appointed governor in 1814, enforced strict measures of control, before long complaints from Europe concerning the shocking quality of Cape wines began to pour in. Eventually a commission of inquiry was held; its findings indicated that because of the demand from abroad for Cape wines, local farmers and wine merchants were concerned with producing quantity rather than quality. And naturally, since it was quantity that mattered, the farmers made little effort to implement the new agricultural standards and methods laid down in 1812. The merchants, too, adopted their own questionable systems of blending the wine while it was undergoing the requisite 16 months' maturation in their keeping, thus hastening its steady downward slide. They probably had little respect for the wine-taster, who may have simply passed and approved every cask submitted to his office. The result was disastrous. Far from improving its image, the Cape wine industry at this period tarnished its reputation almost beyond redemption (as subsequent centuries have shown) and, not surprisingly, the post of wine-taster was abolished in July 1826. This, from the researcher's point of view, if for no other reason, is a pity for it meant that no further records were kept of the quantities and types of wine produced by Nederburg and other farms for export.

Meanwhile, in March 1825 the local wine trade had been dealt a severe blow by legislation passed by parliament in London. This reduced the preferential duties on Cape wines and so narrowed the gap between their landed cost in Britain and that of wines imported from elsewhere. From now on Cape wines had to compete with those produced in France and other European countries not only in standard but in price — both of which proved impossible. The loss of privilege, coupled with the unacceptable quality and over-production of Cape wines, led, inevitably, to an enormous surplus and an accompanying sharp drop in price. Even at home, people were averse to drinking the local product and no host of any standing would consider offering his guests anything but the French wine and brandy that were being liberally imported. Many farmers who had mortgaged their land in order to finance the plantings of new vineyards were ruined, especially as the price of 30 rix-dollars per leaguer barely covered the cost of transport to market. In fact, there were some who were so desperate that they broke open their casks and allowed

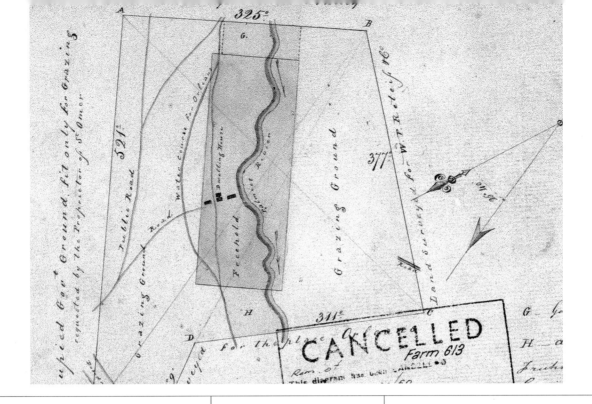

the unwanted and undrinkable contents to run away into the ground. Numerous though the cases of insolvency were at this time, none of them involved Willem Petrus Retief. There is no way of knowing how he disposed of the 90 leaguers of wine and five of brandy that he produced in 1831, but he must have retained his faith in the future of farming for on 24 January of that year he increased Nederburg's original extent of 57 morgen 300 square roods by the acquisition of a further 222 morgen 472 square roods. This considerable area was granted to him on perpetual quitrent, provided that he paid an annual sum of £1 to the civil commissioner of the Drakenstein district and 'that all roads and thoroughfares as also the water courses running over the lands hereby granted' would remain free and undisturbed as they had been formerly. The newly-acquired land was an irregular shape surrounding the original Nederburg and, according to the perpetual quitrent grant, it extended 'S.S.E. against the land surveyed for Knool (sic) Valley, S.W. against the land surveyed for W.P. Retief & Co., W. & N.W. against the land surveyed for Orléans, N. & N.E. against unoccupied Government land requested by the owners of St Omer'. The land 'surveyed for W.P. Retief & Co.' refers to the area acquired by the five neighbours in 1826 and the fact that Retief had now gained legal possession of the intervening ground makes it seem more likely than ever that he had for some time been cultivating it or at least grazing his stock there.

The 1830s were a period of change and disturbance in South Africa. The cataclysmic *Mfecane*, or scattering of hundreds of thousands of people from Zululand in the

VERHANDELING

OVER HET

MAKEN VAN **BRANDEWYN,**

EN

DE VERBETERING

VAN DEN

Gewonen Kaapschen Brandewyn;

MET EENIGE

INLEIDENDE AANMERKINGEN.

OVERHANDIGD AAN HET WYN COMMITTEE,
Op den 23sten Maart 1826,

DOOR

P. H. POLEMANN.

—◆◆—

KAAPSTAD:
GEDRUKT TER GOUVERNEMENTS DRUKKERY.

1826.

years following King Shaka's rise to power in 1816, continued for a decade after his death in 1828 — but perhaps not even its ripples were felt by the Retief family far away at Nederburg. Of much greater concern to Willem Petrus and his fellow Klein Drakenstein farmers was something a good deal closer to home: the anticipated emancipation of slaves. On 28 August 1833 the bill by which all slaves in the British dominions were to be set free received the assent of the reigning monarch, King William IV. At the Cape, 1 December 1834 was fixed as the day on which the slaves were to be emancipated, but all those over six years of age had to pass through a four-year period of apprenticeship before they were granted their final liberation. As compensation to the slave-owners, the British government voted a total of £20 million, of which the Cape was to receive £3 041 290.

To most of the Cape farmers, their slaves were not only their chief capital investment, but the very basis upon which their social structure existed. In a practical sense the end of slavery meant little — it would, in fact mean fewer mouths to feed at a period when times were bad — but it was a threat to the farmers' way of life and symbolic of British domination. The abolition of slavery was not the only cause of the mass migration — the Great Trek — of the Boers to the unknown hinterland during the 1830s, but it certainly contributed to it. Perhaps most famous of those who left the Cape was Willem Petrus Retief's second cousin, Piet Retief, five years his senior and, like him, a great-grandson of the Huguenot settler, François Rétif. Piet Retief spent his childhood on the farm Welvanpas in the Wagenmakersvalleij not far from Nederburg but, after farming near Stellen-

The register of slaves owned by the elder Willem Petrus Retief at Nederburg between 1817 and 1819. It is interesting to see that they came from as far away as Bengal and Mozambique.

bosch for several years, moved to the Eastern Cape in 1813. From then on Willem Petrus Retief could have seen little of him, but one wonders how he felt when he learnt of his second cousin's murder at the hands of the Zulu chief, Dingaan, in February 1838.

Meanwhile, in the months before emancipation, district officials known as field cornets travelled great distances from farm to farm assessing the value of slaves. A meticulous system of classification had been drawn up and the farmers, often scarcely literate, were completely baffled by the complicated forms – in English – which they were required to complete. When the last calculation had been made it was estimated that the Cape's 38 427 slaves were worth £45 281 738. 5s. 10d. – a sum far beyond any the slave-owners could hope to receive. To make matters worse, claimants were required to travel to London to collect their compensation or, if this proved impossible as in most cases it did, they were to put their interests into the hands of agents. The plight of the colonists was supported by the urgent recommendations of the governor, Benjamin D'Urban, but the British Treasury, in which the actual payment was vested, turned a deaf ear to his appeal. Many a naïve farmer was duped into granting his power of attorney to an unscrupulous agent or persuaded to sell his claims at an appallingly low price. As a result, when at last the slave-owners did receive their compensation (and in some cases this was not until December 1840) they were paid much less than their legal right and many got as little as one-third of their original claim.

TOP
The register of slaves owned by the elder Willem Petrus Retief at Nederburg between 1817 and 1819. It is interesting to see that they came from as far away as Bengal and Mozambique.
BOTTOM
Piet Retief, a second cousin of the elder Willem Petrus. They must have known each other from childhood as Piet Retief grew up in the Wagenmakersvalleij outside present-day Wellington.

Among those who were hard hit was Willem Petrus Retief of Nederburg. When the field cornet visited him on 13 February 1834 to obtain the required information, he must have found the obligation to obey the bureaucratic command and stop work in the midst of grape-harvesting exceedingly irritating. The records of that visit show that Retief owned 21 slaves at the time – 12 men, four women over 16 years old and five little girls. Some of them – for instance old Esau (born in Mozambique 68 years before), 61-year-old Jephta and Sara, now 59 – had lived on Nederburg for at least 17 years, probably longer, and all the children had been born there. Europa, Asia and America, all now in their forties, had come to the Cape from Mozambique many years before. In addition to labourers, the slaves included a thatcher, a butler, a gardener, a wagon-driver, a coachman and a carpenter, while one of the women was a cook and two were housemaids. Nothing has been traced to give an indication of how Willem Petrus Retief treated his slaves or of how they regarded their master; certainly his name does not appear in any of the recorded cases of ill-treatment of slaves, although on one occasion he was chastised for failing to report, within the prescribed time, the death of a slave child. In a memorial to Governor Lord Charles Somerset dated 1 September 1824, Retief begged to be relieved of the fine of 26 rix-dollars, explaining that the 'neglect' had arisen because 'he had laboured with fourteen persons in his house under a severe sickness' at the time. He did not mention that less than two weeks before he submit-

ted this memorial his youngest son, two-year-old Tiel-man Jacobus, had died.

The total value of the slaves on Nederburg in 1834 was assessed as £2 064. 10s. The most highly prized was 22-year-old locally-born Antony, whose price stood at £187. 10s., while Sara and Damon, born in Bengal 65 years before, were considered worth no more than £2 and £7. 10s. respectively. At £18 15s., even little Roset, four years old, must have had some potential. Four years were to pass before Willem Petrus Retief received his payout from the British Treasury: the compensation amounted to £785. 2s. 7d. — just over one-third of his claim.

The census taken in 1839, the year after the slaves received their final independence, reveals that by then the domestic situation on Nederburg had changed somewhat. Heading the list of *huisgezinnen* is Willem Petrus Retief junior, now 27 years old, his wife Anna Magdalena Mostert (whom he had married, when she was 17, on 7 November 1835) and their two young sons (later they were to have seven more as well as a daughter). Next follows Willem Petrus senior with his wife Maria Elisabeth and their only daughter, still unwed. Also living on Nederburg were Jan Hendrik Retief, his wife Elisabeth de Wet and one son, besides two of the elder Willem Petrus's as yet unmarried sons, Pieter Eduard and Eduard Christiaan. A household of such a size — 12 in all — suggests that Nederburg homestead must have been bursting at the proverbial seams, but almost certainly some members of the family would have been

TOP
A canteen in Dorp Street, Cape Town. Besides being exported, Nederburg's wines were sold locally in taverns such as this one.
BOTTOM
The proud Plantagenet, Lord Charles Somerset (1767-1831). Like British governors before and after him, he attempted to improve the quality of locally-produced wine.

living in the original small dwelling or *jonkershuis*. Working for Willem Petrus junior were two 'apprentices' — as former slaves were still termed — one male and one female — with their two children, while Willem Petrus senior employed four male apprentices and one female who had between them seven children. The picture in 1839 is a very different one from that presented by a census taken four years earlier, when 16 adult apprentices lived on Nederburg with their ten children. Now, in 1839, the Retiefs, father and sons, employed only ten labourers — probably the adult apprentices and some of the older children — but no 'Hottentots' or prize negroes (blacks rescued from ships trading illicitly in slaves and forcibly apprenticed at the Cape for 14 years). This census is the first to record the area of land under cultivation: this was a mere 15 morgen, on which 80 000 vines were growing — 10 000 fewer than those growing on Nederburg in 1835. On the remaining area of *weiland*, four horses (11 had died of the dreaded horse-sickness during the previous year) and 39 head of cattle were grazing.

The last census to reflect the situation at Nederburg was taken in 1844. It indicates that by this stage the only child of Willem Petrus Retief senior remaining on the farm was the younger Willem Petrus, who by now had fathered five sons. From this period onwards the running of the farm appears to have been shared by the two Retiefs, father and son, who in 1844 were producing between them 28 leaguers of wine and two of brandy — a very meagre amount compared to the 78

leaguers of wine and three of brandy produced from grapes culled from Nederburg's 93 000 vines in 1825. What led to this decline in prosperity is not known. It is certain that Drakenstein wine farmers were feeling the lack of labour that followed the emancipation of slaves and at times were so short of workers that they were unable to complete the grape harvest in time. It may be, too, that the elder Willem Petrus, now nearing 60 years old, was becoming less active, though ten years were to pass before he let go the reins altogether.

Title deeds drawn up on 2 February 1854, when Willem Petrus Retief was in his 69th year, show that on this date his farm was divided into three portions and sold. Perhaps in anticipation of this, it had been surveyed and subdivided by the sworn surveyor, W.B. Rowan, as long ago as 1837. Now an area measuring 8 morgen and 572 square roods of freehold land and 52 morgen and 107 square roods of perpetual quitrent land (61 morgen and 79 square roods altogether and including at least one building) was sold to Daniel Jeremias de Klerk for £500 sterling. Another portion, consisting of 21 morgen and 396 square roods of freehold land and 64 morgen and 579 square roods of perpetual quitrent (86 morgen 375 square roods altogether) was sold to Retief's son Pieter Eduard; and the remaining portion of 26 morgen and 532 square roods of freehold land and 105 morgen and 386 square roods of perpetual quitrent (132 morgen 338 square roods altogether) was sold for £1 375 sterling to Willem Petrus Retief junior. Allowing for a few dis-

crepancies in measurement, as often happened, these three areas add up to the original 57 morgen and 300 square roods freehold granted to Philippus Bernardus Wolvaart and the 220 morgen and 472 square roods perpetual quitrent acquired by the elder Retief in 1831. Nederburg's homestead and *opstal*, the domestic and working heart of the farm, stood on the portion bought by the younger Willem Petrus, which became farm No. 610 in the district of Paarl. For him, 1854 must have been a year of considerable importance, as it was, indeed, for the history of South Africa. In addition to the conclusion of the Bloemfontein Convention, by which the Republic of the Orange Free State came into being, it saw the implementation of representative government at the Cape Colony – in fact, the election for the first Legislative Council was held less than a month before Nederburg's new title deed was drawn up.

Filed with the title deed by which Willem Petrus Retief junior became master of Nederburg are certain conditions drawn up on 23 December 1853 – indicating that the farm was in fact sold several months before transfer took place. These conditions laid down that the elder Retiefs should continue to live in the homestead for their lifetime, and that Willem Petrus senior should retain the front portion of the wine cellar for his own use as well as a stable for his horses and the uppermost walled garden. Besides, two rows of orange and naartjie (*lamoen en nardges*) trees, a row of fig trees and ten rows of vines were to remain the property of the

elder Retief and his wife, Maria Haumann, and they could make use of whatever crops had been sown and fenced. They were to keep the eight-day clock, two brandy stills and the bellows that kept the fire going. Important, too — as it always is in Africa — was their claim to have and hold as much water as they needed from the Palmiet River.

The following years were not easy ones for the Cape wine farmers. The Cape of Good Hope Agricultural Society, founded in 1831, did its best to encourage the industry by holding shows and presenting awards, but the fact remained that overseas both consumers and merchants held a pretty poor opinion of Cape wines — so much so that it was not uncommon to see inn signboards inscribed: 'Here at least no Cape wine is drunk'. Things in Drakenstein began to improve after the new hard road across the Cape Flats was completed, so reducing the time and hazards of travelling between the winelands and Cape Town. Then, in the late 1850s, there was a welcome upturn in the industry: merchants overseas turned once more to the Cape for their wine supplies when an outbreak of powdery mildew (*Oidium tuckeri*) devastated the vineyards of Europe. During the years between 1853 and 1859, Cape wine farmers' exports enjoyed boom conditions during which exports increased tenfold and prices rose from 67 to 82 rixdollars a leaguer. (Wine prices were still quoted in the Dutch currency.) Alas, their prosperity was short-lived. The fateful fungus found its way to South Africa, where it was first noticed at the beginning of November 1859

PAGE 44: TOP
The town of Paarl seen against the Drakenstein mountains, as it appeared to the English painter, George French Angas, in 1845.
BOTTOM
The happy slave on emancipation day, 1 December 1834. Slaves went barefoot, so the first thing they invariably did on gaining their freedom was to acquire shoes — no matter how tattered they might be.
PAGE 45
The Commercial Exchange, home of the Cape Town Chamber of Commerce. Its members did everything in their power to prevent the British government from abolishing the preferential tariffs which Cape wines enjoyed until the 1860s.

and by the end of the ensuing grape harvest had virtually laid waste the vineyards of the western Cape.

In January 1860, the colonial botanist, Carl Wilhelm Ludwig Pappe, undertook an inspection of the winelands and discovered that the vineyards of Paarl had been particularly seriously affected by powdery mildew although, as he reported, 'vines planted on elevated or sloping ground, and being exposed to a free current of air, have either escaped infection or suffered less'. It may be that Nederburg, benefiting from its position on the west-facing lower slopes of the Drakenstein range, suffered less severely than its neighbours situated in lower, more sheltered positions. In his completed report, which included an assessment of each individual farm, Pappe wrote of Nederburg: '...60 000 vines. This [farm] I have not seen . . . but learn from good authority, that the mildew has made its appearance on the Steendruif grape.' However, research undertaken while the disease was at its worst in Europe, had proved the efficacy of treating vines with flowers of sulphur, and by the end of the harvest the *Oidium* had been brought under control.

Hardly had the farmers recovered from this scourge when, in 1860, they received the devastating news that the British government, under Prime Minister Lord Palmerston, had entered into a trade agreement with France which drastically reduced the import tariff on French wines. Worse was to come, for the following year the preferential tariffs which Cape wines had enjoyed since 1813 were abolished altogether. For the Cape wine trade, this was the most bitter blow of all — and

one from which it did not begin to recover for over a century. On the basis of quality alone, the local product could not hope to compete with French wines. Farmers in Paarl and elsewhere gathered together at meetings to protest against the new legislation and to draw up petitions, but their appeals to the British government went unheeded. Within a few years exports of wine from the Cape ceased entirely.

The Cape economy was, in fact, in a parlous condition. Stringent steps, such as the cancellation of public works and the retrenchment of civil servants, did little to alleviate the situation, and by 1866 the financial crisis eclipsed every other problem the government was facing. The wine farmers suffered particularly severely at this time, for the price they received (between £2.10s. and £3. 10s. a leaguer) barely covered their expenses. The one relieving factor, as far as Drakenstein farmers were concerned, was the connection of the railway from Cape Town via Paarl to Wellington in 1863 — a service which reduced their transport costs considerably.

In 1866 — at a time when things could not have been much worse at the Cape — some children were discovered playing with a 'pretty pebble' on the arid south bank of the Orange River. The pebble turned out to be a diamond and so — despite initial scepticism on the part of the authorities — South Africa's great industrial revolution began. From all corners of the earth fortune-hunters flocked to the diggings and — since adventurers are almost without exception thirsty men and not particularly discriminating when it comes to liquor

TOP
Turning the first sod of the railway between Cape Town and Wellington, 1 March 1869.
BOTTOM
Under the premiership of Sir Gordon Sprigg (1830-1913), during the late 1870s, the Cape government attempted to boost the State treasury by levying extra excise duties on Cape brandy.

— they soon expressed a welcome new demand for Cape wines. A minor boom resulted and the price of wine rose to £12 a leaguer in 1874. Willem Petrus Retief the elder did not live to enjoy these good times for he died at Nederburg, in his 80th year, on 30 January 1865. His wife, Maria Elisabeth, outlived him and, of the original quiverful of 11 children, only three sons survived.

Little remains to hint at the personality of Nederburg's second owner. We know that, like his father Paul Retief, he served the local church as elder and deacon for many years. The liquidation and distribution account drawn up after his death shows that he must have taken an interest in Afrikaans culture for he subscribed to *De Zuid-Afrikaan*, the newspaper that acted as the mouthpiece of the Afrikaans people. It shows, too, that his coffin cost £5. 10s. and that Drs Zeederberg and Fismer were owed £31. 15s. and £22 respectively. His total assets amounted to £3 581. 14s. 1d. — a substantial amount in those days — of which Maria Elisabeth received her widow's portion of £1 703. 11s. 10d. The balance of £1 878 2s. 3d. was divided between Maria Elisabeth, Willem Petrus's three surviving sons and the children of the three sons who had predeceased him — each of whom received £215. 10s. 3d.

One of the surviving sons was the younger Willem Petrus, who now became master of Nederburg in every sense of the word. He was 52 years old and in his prime, though no records have been traced to indicate whether, under his hand, the fortunes of the farm or the family prospered. It is reasonably certain, however, that this second Willem Petrus Retief was a man of some stature in his community for, like his father and grandfather before him, he served as elder and deacon at the Paarl Dutch Reformed church over many years and was also elected to the board of the Paarl Bank, established in 1852. One wonders how he was affected by the emerging Afrikaans language movement which, at this time, had its origins in Paarl — more particularly on the farms in the Dal Josafat area, a mere stone's throw from Nederburg and undoubtedly well known to him.

The 1870s were not easy years for the farmers of Paarl — nor, indeed, for anyone connected with the Cape's liquor industry. In an effort to boost the State treasury, the government under Sir Gordon Sprigg proposed to levy extra excise duties on Cape brandy, but this led to a veritable outcry on the part of the farmers. Already burdened with a wine surplus, they maintained that the increased cost to the consumer would lead to a drop in sales. A group from the Paarl area initiated a

TOP LEF

A report made in January 1860 by the government botanist, Dr Carl Wilhelm Ludwig Pappe (1803-1862), on the outbreak of Oidium tuckeri in Klein Drakenstein. TOP CENTRE

Couched in grandiloquent terms, this advertisement in a local publication attempts to persuade 'captains of ships' and others to buy Cape wines.

TOP RIGHT
The Paarl valley was the scene of the
Afrikaans language movement. This
statement of unity by Die Genootskap van
Regte Afrikaners in 1875 has the
Bible as its heart and is symbolically
surrounded by the produce — both animal
and vegetable — of the land.
BOTTOM

By the 1870s, Cape farmers were becoming more sophisticated, as this scene in the voorkamer of a Paarl house shows.

move which resulted in the establishment in Cape Town in June 1877 of a united body of farmers known as the Zuid-Afrikaansche Wijnbouwersvereeniging. Expressing their dissatisfaction through the Press, appeals to parliament and protest meetings (one of the liveliest was held in Paarl in June 1878) the wine farmers eventually succeeded in getting what they wanted: almost complete exemption from the excise duty.

The younger Willem Petrus died at Nederburg on 4 January 1881 at the age of 68 years. How far he was involved in the protest activities in Paarl is not known but, as a farmer and an Afrikaner, it is unlikely that he could have been unaffected by them. He was outlived by his widow, Anna Magdalena, and seven surviving sons. Anna Magdalena herself died, at the age of 65, on 30 September 1882. During the intervening 20 months that she was a widow, Nederburg was sold, and so passed out of the possession of the family that had owned and occupied it for 71 years.

CHAPTER THREE

THE YEARS OF

PETRUS JACOBUS HAUPTFLEISCH 1881-1902

By the time Jacobus Petrus Hauptfleisch bought Nederburg,
the Cape government no longer kept statistical records, so little is
known of the development of the farm at this time.
An inventory taken in 1887, however, when Hauptfleisch went
insolvent, provides a revealing picture of the farm and insight into
Hauptfleisch's lifestyle. An outbreak of *Phylloxera vestatrix*
was the possible cause of his insolvency.

O n 7 May 1881, barely four months after the death of her husband, Anna Magdalena Retief sold Nederburg and moved into Paarl. The new owner was Petrus Jacobus Hauptfleisch, who paid £3 800 for the farm — almost treble the price the elder Willem Petrus Retief had charged his son for it 27 years earlier. To raise the required amount, Hauptfleisch obtained from the widow Anna Magdalena a mortgage of £1 500, on which the rate of interest at the time was six per cent.

The land transactions in which Nederburg's various owners have been involved over two centuries may, with justice, be described as a conveyancer's nightmare. When Hauptfleisch bought the farm it still basically comprised the 46 morgen and 398 square roods (26 morgen and 532 square roods of freehold land and 91 morgen and 466 square roods of surrounding perpetual quitrent land) which Willem Petrus Retief the younger

The dreaded Phylloxera vestatrix,
scourge of vineyards throughout Europe
and the Cape during the two closing
decades of the 19th century.

had bought from his father in 1854, but by now the fifth share of the 403 morgen and 436 square roods of grazing ground that the elder Willem Petrus Retief had acquired with four neighbours in 1826, had become one-fourteenth. This was the result of numerous sales and subdivisions negotiated by the original co-owners and their successors, and before transfer of the Retiefs' fraction could be effected, the Court had to appoint Anna Magdalena executive dative of her father-in-law's estate. She was then able to make a declaration that he had sold it to his son during the lifetime of both men. There also appears to be a discrepancy between the 91 morgen 466 square roods of perpetual quitrent land mentioned on the transfer of 1881 and the 105 morgen 386 square roods on that of 1854, but this and other discrepancies may be accounted for by inaccurate surveying, which was not unusual in those days.

Nederburg was the only home Anna Magdalena

TOP
Grape-picking was a back-breaking job before farmers adopted the system of trellising vines.
BOTTOM
Winter activity at Paarl in the closing years of the 19th century. This is the time when fields and vineyards are fertilized and prepared for spring burgeoning.

Retief had known since she had crossed its threshold as a 17-year-old bride over 45 years earlier. Her ten children had been born under its thatched roof and the two whom she lost in childhood had probably died there. No mother or widow could have left such a home without pangs of nostalgia – and as evidence of this there is included in the transfer deed to Petrus Jacobus Hauptfleisch the 'special condition' on which Nederburg was sold to him. In the words of the document: 'the Seller reserves the sole and exclusive right for herself and relatives to the Burial ground on the farm . . . and also the right of extending the enclosure to the extent and in the direction indicated on the day of sale and of effecting the necessary repairs thereto from time to time and for these purposes the stone building material on the adjacent portion of the farm may be used.'

Presumably Willem Petrus the younger was among the Retiefs laid to rest in the little burial ground and it was not long after his death that two new graves were dug there. Anna Magdalena, in her 66th year, died in Paarl on 30 September 1882, to be followed less than a fortnight later by her eldest son, a third Willem Petrus Retief, aged 47. She left household furniture and 'claims' – including money lent to three of her sons and Hauptfleisch's unpaid mortgage (plus interest) – to a total value of £3 000. Six of her sons were left to mourn her, several of them farmers like their father. Descendants of some of these Retiefs live in Paarl to this day; others have moved to the Orange Free State and Natal. Anna Magdalena's seventh child, Jacobus Arnoldus, born in 1850, came to a tragic end when, in

an effort to rescue a labourer who had fallen into a wine vat, he was overcome by the fumes and died himself. But this happened on 15 February 1896, many years after his mother's death.

Nederburg's new owner, Petrus Jacobus Hauptfleisch, belonged to a family that had been in the Wagenmakersvalleij for several generations. In 1734 his great-great-grandfather, Johan Georg Hauptfleisch of Breslau in Silesia, arrived at the Cape as a soldier in the service of the Dutch East India Company. However, he soon afterwards abandoned his military career, first to become a schoolmaster and then to follow the calling of a surgeon, though his qualifications – if any – for such a profession are unknown. In 1736 Johan Georg Hauptfleisch chose as his bride Marie-Elisabeth Migault, whose father, François Louis Migault, had also forsaken soldiering in favour of teaching. Among Migault's pupils was 16-year-old Marie Magdalene (daughter of Etienne Niel, original owner of the incomparably beautiful Franschhoek farm, La Dauphiné), whom he wooed and married in 1719. They settled in Table Valley and, no matter that Migault instructed the local children in the Christian religion (as well as in Dutch and French), he was so flagrantly libertine in his behaviour that the God-fearing little community had him summarily deported to Holland after Marie Magdalene's death only a few years later. Marie-Elisabeth was the elder of the two virtually orphaned Migault children, but fortunately an aunt left her a substantial bequest, so she did not enter the estate of matrimony with Johan Georg Hauptfleisch empty handed.

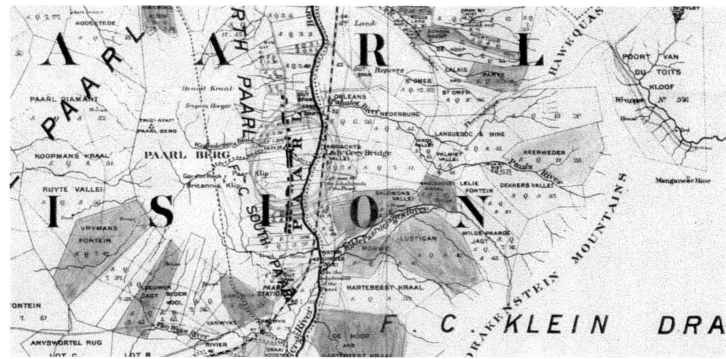

All this was ancient family history by the time their descendant, Petrus Jacobus, future owner of Nederburg, was born in 1845. Not quite so remote was his connection with the Retiefs. His grandmother, wife of David Carel Hauptfleisch, was Martha Elisabeth Retief, sister of Piet Retief of Voortrekker fame and second cousin of Willem Petrus Retief the elder. What is more, Petrus Jacobus's father Georg Stephanus, eldest child of this union, married his first cousin, Helena Susanna Hauptfleisch, which made their children great-nephews on both sides to Piet Retief. Thus, some rather complicated reasoning leads one to conclude that Petrus Jacobus Hauptfleisch was a third cousin once removed of the younger Willem Petrus Retief, from whose widow he bought Nederburg! Tenuous though this blood relationship might have been, the fact that the families lived within the same geographical area meant that they must have known one another as neighbours if not as kith and kin.

The little town of Wellington, built round the church that served the farmers of the Wagenmakers-valleij, had been in existence for only five years when the infant Petrus Jacobus Hauptfleisch was baptized there by Dominee A.F. du Toit, its first minister. It was to the same church that he brought 22-year-old Francina Carolina Brink for their wedding on 16 April 1869. They were to have three sons, George Stephanus, Jan Gotlieb and Jacob le Roux, and later they adopted a daughter, Anna Hauptfleisch, obviously a relative.

Steeped in a tradition of wine farming, Hauptfleisch would have known that in the year before he bought Nederburg the Cape government had carried out a statistical survey which revealed that 20 000 acres (8 100 hectares) of land in the colony had been devoted to wine farming and that on them no fewer than 60 million vines were growing. During the following five years, there was a considerable increase in plantings, so that by 1886 there were at least 70 million vines at the Cape. At this time, wine growers and merchants were claiming that the production of Cape vineyards surpassed that of any other wine-producing country in the world. The yield was estimated to be 1,5 leaguers per

1 000 vines — the equivalent of 86,5 hectolitres per 10 000 vines, which was the average number grown on one hectare of land in Europe. This, so claimed the Cape's wine producers, was a record of which anyone, anywhere, could justly be proud. Connoisseurs in Europe were not so sure. Quantity might be something to boast about but alas, for the Cape wine industry, quality was quite another matter. Baron Carl von Babo, an Austrian authority on viticulture appointed to supervise the experimental wine estate established by the colonial government at Groot Constantia in 1885, reported that the wines 'with a very few exceptions, have in common a disagreeable and strong brandy taste. Such wines have been mixed with so much brandy that they cease to be wines; they are liqueurs . . . In consequence of the addition of other substances, they acquire a taste which does not improve them.' So, after more than a century and despite the authorities' periodic efforts to improve their standard, Cape wines were still regarded with repugnance by all civilized wine drinkers in Europe. The days when the sweet wines of Constantia were

TOP
The happenings of the outside world, such as the visit to the Cape in 1901 of the Duke and Duchess of Cornwall and York, were of little concern to wine farmers of the Boland grappling with the ravages of Phylloxera.
BOTTOM
Paarl Rock, which overlooks and dominates both town and valley.

acclaimed by kings and princes were long forgotten.

But even in the vineyards of Europe things were far from well. The culprit was a minute greenish-yellow insect that in the ten years following 1875 completely devastated one-third of France's vineyards. This was *Phylloxera vestatrix*, a member of the aphid family introduced to Europe in 1861 with vines imported from North America, its natural habitat. This creature infests the roots of vines and, by sucking moisture from them, causes galls to form on the leaves and nodules on the roots so that the entire plant eventually rots. So virulent was its attack on the vineyards of Europe that between 1870 and 1880 it had invaded Austria, Portugal, Germany, Spain, Switzerland, Italy and Russia. As the infestation progressed, Cape wine farmers looked towards the Northern Hemisphere with growing apprehension and in 1880, in an attempt to keep the invader at bay, the government decided to ban the importation of all foreign plants. Four years later, when the epidemic was continuing unabated in Europe, the Scanlen-Merriman-Rhodes cabinet, in an extraordinarily short-

TOP LEFT
Although there is no record of Petrus Jacobus Hauptfleisch having entered wine at the Paarl Show, the show would doubtless have been an important event on his calendar.

TOP RIGHT
Huguenot Bridge outside Paarl. The erection of bridges over the Berg River towards the end of the 19th century made transport of produce much easier for farmers on the east side of the town.

BOTTOM
Henry Collison, one of Cape Town's leading wine merchants during the 19th century, was proud to advertise that his products had won medals at a variety of exhibitions in Europe.

PAGE 53: TOP
Looking over wintry vineyards towards Paarl Rock at the end of the 19th century.

BOTTOM
The popularity of bicycles in turn-of-the-century Paarl made scenes such as this one in Lady Grey Street a familiar sight to Hauptfleisch.

sighted move, relaxed these regulations. The response was a furore in parliament, followed by a vote of censure which led the cabinet to resign — in fact, as a political wag put it, 'the ministry went out on a bug'. The fears of the farmers were to be realized only too soon.

One day in January 1886 — the year in which gold was to be discovered on the Witwatersrand — someone casually strolling through 'Mr Kotze's vineyard in Mowbray' happened to notice some sinister blisters on the burgeoning vine leaves. There was no doubt about it, said Dr Louis Albert Péringuey, zoologist at the South African Museum who examined specimens brought to him, this condition was evidence of the dreaded *Phylloxera*. In what seemed the twinkling of an eye the disease swept through the wine farms of the Peninsula and then made its relentless way inland. Commissions and inspectors were appointed and various methods were tried in an attempt to eradicate the pestilence. Eventually it was realized that the only remedy was wholesale burning of infected vines and their replacement by imported American rootstock naturally immune to the insect's ravages. With heavy hearts, farmers uprooted entire vineyards and smoke from 22 million smouldering vine stumps hung heavy in the air from Constantia to Paarl and over the mountains of the western Cape as far inland as Tulbagh and Robertson. One after another entire farms were laid waste and one after another their owners went bankrupt.

To begin with, the Paarl area escaped the scourge of *Phylloxera*. Then, in the summer of 1890-1891, it

reached the Drakenstein valley and swept through it like wildfire, devastating almost every vineyard in its path. It is hard to say to what extent Nederburg was affected. A divisional council map of Paarl dated 25 January 1895 shows that by that late stage in the epidemic Nederburg and its neighbours, Languedoc and Orléans, had not yet been proclaimed *Phylloxera*-infected, though the government inspector noted in his report that they were likely to be 'declared' shortly. *Phylloxera* or not, before the disease had reached its worst in the Drakenstein area, Petrus Jacobus Hauptfleisch was already in severe financial straits for the records show that on 12 December 1887 he went into voluntary liquidation. On the same day his property was attached, meaning that he could not 'dispose of, remove, conceal, or receive any part thereof, with intent to defeat this attachment' without running the risk of imprisonment 'with or without hard labour' for five years or of being transported for up to seven.

It seems that Hauptfleisch, distressed by his financial insecurity, had decided that his best course was to choose voluntary liquidation. Notice of this, dated 15 December, appeared in the *Government Gazette*, authorized by J. Hofmeyr, Master of the Supreme Court. It stated that 'by order of the Honourable Mr Justice Smith' Hauptfleisch's estate had been placed under sequestration and called upon his creditors to appear in the office of the resident magistrate of 'the Paarl' on 20 and 27 of that month. Nobody turned up at either of these meetings, but apparently Hauptfleisch's creditors

were present at a third called on 24 January of the following year. Two trustees, Jozua François Petrus Perold and Jacob Isaac de Villiers, had been appointed and their report reveals that Hauptfleisch's assets at that time consisted of a 'certain farm called "Nederburg" situate at Klein Drakenstein in this division and valued at £1 500 and of moveable property such as fustage, cellar & farming utensils, live stock, household furniture and a quantity of wine together of the value of £260. 15. 6'. His debts amounted to £2 196, 'thus leaving a deficiency of £435. 4. 6'. The report continues: 'The Insolvent has offered to take over all the assets of his Estate for the sum of £1 730 — namely: for the farm the sum of £1 500 — and for the moveable assets the sum of £230 — which offer is herewith submitted for the information of creditors,' but he applied to be allowed to retain his furniture and to trade on his own account. In view of his offer, the trustees had delayed advertising the assets for sale by public auction until they received instructions from the creditors in this respect.

Hauptfleisch ascribed his plight to 'the general depression and the depreciation of his assets in consequence for which he originally paid about £4 000'. There is something very puzzling about Hauptfleisch's insolvency. Even taking into account the prevalence of *Phylloxera* and a possible deterioration in the condition of the farm, it is unlikely that Nederburg's value could have dropped from the £3 800 that he paid for it in 1881 to the mere £1 500 at which it was assessed in December 1887. Besides, in itself this latter figure is significant

as this was the amount borrowed from the widow Anna Magdalena Retief. On her death five years earlier the mortgage for the same sum was ceded to Hauptfleisch's mother's sister, the widow Susanna Maria Magdalena Retief. According to the schedule of his liabilities, Hauptfleisch had not only failed to redeem any part of the £1 500, but had not even paid the interest due on it. His other debts ranged from £1 owing to a Mr Hoffman to £330 due to the Wellington Bank.

At the meeting held on 24 January 1888 Hauptfleisch's creditors adopted the trustees' report: they agreed that he should be allowed to take over his landed property for £1 500 and his moveables for £230. He was also granted the unusual concession of being allowed to 'trade in his own name and for his own benefit'. As is customary in insolvency cases, the account and plan of distribution framed by the trustees remained for inspection in the office of the Master of the Supreme Court from 28 April until 19 June. It reflects insolvency expenses of £65. 3s. 4d. plus £1 680 (£1 500 capital and £180 outstanding interest) owing to the widow Retief. Hauptfleisch's assets were the £1 500 declared value of the farm and moveable possessions worth £230; once these amounts had been realized and the insolvency expenses paid, there was a credit balance of £1 665. 3s. 4d. which would be 'awarded in preference' to the widow Retief, leaving her with a deficiency of £14. 16s. 8d. The Wellington Bank and remaining creditors were far less fortunate as the 'bottom line' — literally — of the

Slavery might have ceased 60 years ago, but treading the grapes was still practised when Petrus Jacobus Hauptfleisch owned Nederburg. This drawing by Sir Frank Brangwyn was made in 1891.

PAGE 55: TOP
Taking their turn in the queue, wagons wait to off-load their freight for export from Table Bay docks. Masts, outlined like tall trees against the bulk of Table Mountain, indicate that steamships were not yet in command of the oceans.

BOTTOM
Main Street, Paarl, in the 1890s. Wagons trundling Hauptfleisch's annual vintage to town must have made many a journey down this, the longest main street in South Africa.

liquidation and distribution account reads: 'We [the trustees] do hereby certify that there are no more assets available wherewith to meet the deficiency to Creditors as above set forth or any part thereof.'

The documentation in the Cape Archives of Hauptfleisch's insolvency is detailed, yet it leaves one wondering why Nederburg was valued at only £1 500 when it was almost certainly worth considerably more (as is clear from the sum for which Hauptfleisch sold it in 1902). It seems that despite his financial insecurity, Hauptfleisch's creditors considered that his position was not irredeemable. The largest sum was owing to the widow Susanna Retief, but she showed a degree of complaisance regarding the eventual outcome of the situation by allowing the assessed value of Nederburg to cover only just the amount for which it was mortgaged. Family feeling, too, may have played a part in what appears her amenable attitude. Also of significance is the failure of the creditors to attend the first two meetings. They must have been aware of Hauptfleisch's position and had they been really concerned they would certainly have put in an appearance. In any event, the amounts involved were relatively insignificant and none of them, including the Wellington Bank, was a 'secured creditor' — that is, one, such as the mortgagor, who is paid out before any others are considered. Possibly the bank, realizing that in the future its services might be required by Hauptfleisch, to its advantage, was willing to bide its time.

Jacobus Petrus Hauptfleisch did not part with his farm as might have been expected. On 24 July 1888, just seven months after he was declared insolvent, a 'certain place called Nederburg situate in the Division of the Paarl . . .' was transferred to him from his own insolvent estate for the sum of £1 500. And there he remained, master of his own vineyards and orchards, for nearly 14 years.

To anyone anxious to know how Nederburg's owners conducted their domestic lives in the past, the most interesting of the documents relating to Hauptfleisch's insolvency is the inventory of his possessions drawn up on 21 December 1887. The official appointed to undertake this lengthy task in the heat of Paarl's midsummer was one Musgrove J. Tomkin, messenger of the court of Paarl's resident magistrate, who bequeathed to posterity four closely written foolscap pages which give a vivid picture of Nederburg just over a century ago. One pictures Tomkin, no doubt clad in suit complete with waistcoat — the civil servant's unofficial uniform in those days — as he bowled along the dusty road in his pony-trap and alighted under the leafy oaks to inspect the exterior of the house before the sun rose too high in the sky for comfort. His inventory shows that in the farmyard he found the usual trappings of a Cape *opstal* — discarded harness, spades, forks, ladders and an iron wheelbarrow. Nearby, grazing in the open, were four cows and their calves, 'said to be the property of Messrs George and John Hauptfleisch, sons of the Insolvent',

while two brown horses and one grey — also said to belong to George — snorted impatiently in the stable. Inside the cool, thatched cellar — once his eyes were accustomed to the shadowy gloom — Mr Musgrove J. Tomkin took note of a variety of wine containers: eight fermenting tubs, eight casks, one hogshead, one brandy still (complete) and seven buckets. In addition to these relatively small vessels, there were also five vats, each of the capacity of six leaguers (35 hectolitres) and another slightly smaller one. Curious to relate, all these containers were empty, though there was in the cellar one giant vat containing about seven leaguers of wine (just under 41 hectolitres) and a barrel of vinegar. Why, one wonders, were most of the wine casks empty? Was this because the bulk of the previous summer's vintage had been sold off in October (the usual month for disposing of eight-month-old wine) or had the vineyards indeed been decimated by *Phylloxera*? Also in the cellar was a wine-treading tub complete with its stand and receiving vessel. Mr Tomkin made note of a wine pump and a wine dip, a copper raisin kettle, several brass taps and a wooden funnel. Two 'reed forms for fruit drying' indicate that other crops besides grapes were being cultivated on Nederburg at the time.

Stored in the wagon-house, as Mr Tomkin observed, were a mule wagon and a Cape cart (there had also been an open cart outside), besides a single-furrow iron plough and two vineyard cultivators. This outhouse was obviously the farm 'dumping-ground' for it contained a wooden door-frame, numerous pieces of wood of various lengths, and more spades and shovels, as well as picks. In the wagon-house, too, were 24 fruit baskets and five for grapes; ox-yokes, wagon-jacks, more pieces of harness and a variety of oddments borrowed from a variety of people.

Then Mr Tomkin moved on to the homestead itself. When its splendid *bo-en-onder* front door was opened to him, he was confronted by an interior very different from that created by Philippus Bernardus Wolvaart 87 years earlier. At some stage in the 19th century its beautiful proportions had been lost when the carved wooden screen or *porte-de-visite* dividing the *voorkamer* from the *agterkamer* was replaced by a wall from floor to ceiling. In the stunted front room the first object of which Mr Tomkin took note was a brass spit-toon (*sic*)! It was in company with two tables, and ten cane-seated 'American' chairs (the quotation marks are Tomkin's) and a folding easy chair. How, one wonders, was there room in this cramped space for a rosewood harmonium — and who played it? Who arranged flowers in the large ornamental vase and embroidered the 'fancy-work' on the two antimacassars that obviously caught Mr Tomkin's eye? The dining room, or *agterkamer*, contained a set of three dining-tables (covered with oilcloth) and six black chairs, an armchair, two footstools, a sofa somewhat surprisingly upholstered in coloured chintz, two ottomans, a Dutch eight-day pendulum clock, various lamps and — again — a 'spit-toon'! But most interesting of all, Mr Tomkin's inventory mentions here Nederburg's exquisitely carved *muurkas*, as it had been originally built into the back wall of the *agterkamer*. Before this room was physically closed off from the *voorkamer*, the wall-cupboard faced the front door and was thus the focal point for every visitor entering the house. Restraining bureaucracy would not permit a mere messenger of the court to comment on the beauty of the *muurkas* or to describe the gleaming stinkwood and yellowwood of which it was made. Carved at some unknown date by some unknown person — no doubt a master of joinery in the days of Philippus Bernardus Wolvaart — this was certainly the most elegant article of furniture in the house. What Tomkin does tell us is that on the shelves, protected by glass doors, stood 'two decanters and sundry articles of glass and crockery ware'.

Behind the diningroom was the back sittingroom. Crammed into it were no fewer than eight black chairs, two ottomans, a table (and cloth), a small clock and a work-box — probably containing the coloured threads used for embroidering the antimacassars. On its left was the kitchen which, naturally, was dominated by a cooking range, though it also contained a deal table, a cupboard, a baking-trough, numerous pots and pans, buckets, a set of scales, a lamp and a kettle. There were two

In the late 19th century, picks and shovels were necessary adjuncts to the manuring of vineyards during the winter months.

more kettles (one tin and the other copper) in the pantry where the shelves, believe it or not, had been knocked up out of the remains of the *porte-de-visite*. There were boxes and grocery canisters in this small room, a paraffin stove, a coffee pot and a coffee mill, but no mention is made even of the whiff of fresh bread baked in the kitchen range. Mr Tomkin recorded no joints of home-smoked ham suspended from the reed ceiling (after all, Christmas was only a few days away), no jars of watermelon *konfyt* or preserved figs jostling one another on the shelves, no spicy *soetkoekies*, crisp *oblitjies* or syrupy *koeksisters* — indeed, none of the delicacies with which every self-respecting Cape housewife would proudly fill her pantry. But perhaps these delights were beneath the (official) notice of Mr Tomkin and not really regarded as assets when a matter as serious as insolvency was being considered.

More to the point was the furniture in the three bedrooms. In the first, on one side of the *voorkamer*, there was a 'teak four-post bedstead' with a mattress and four pillows. There was a washstand with jug, basin and slop-pail as well as a tin bath, a tin water jug and a towel horse. Two brass candlesticks stood on the 'toilet table', no doubt to throw light onto the 'toilet glass'. In the back bedroom there was another four-poster, merely 'wooden' this time, with its mattress and four pillows, as well as a clothes press and a writing desk. The furniture provided in the second front bedroom appears somewhat basic, perhaps because Hauptfleisch's two younger sons slept here — the eldest, George Stephanus, had probably left home by this time. It consisted of an iron bedstead (with mattress and pillows) and a wooden stretcher (also with mattress and pillows). Seating was provided by an ottoman and ablutions were performed at the usual washstand with the aid, no doubt, of a toilet glass hung above a toilet shelf.

Detailed though the inventory is, it is from the omissions rather than from what is included that we gain a glimpse into the lifestyle of Petrus Jacobus Hauptfleisch and his family. Unless Petrus Jacobus Hauptfleisch had prudently removed any treasures he still owned in anticipation of Mr Tomkin's arrival, Nederburg could boast no silver, pride of many a Cape Dutch household, and very little glassware. True, the list does include 'one lot of knives, one lot of forks and one lot of spoons' (all in the kitchen), but these were almost certainly made of tin. There could have been no great quantity of cups and saucers or plates, for the *muurkas* appears to be the only place where crockery was kept. And before the days of built-in cupboards, how many garments could be stored in a few ottomans that must also accommodate spare blankets — if any? Granted, there was an angora goatskin on the *voorkamer* floor and 'one piece of matting' in the diningroom, but when Petrus Jacobus

MASTER'S NOTICES.

Notices and Declarations of Insolvency.

Master's Office, Cape Town,
15th December, 1887.

NOTICE is hereby given that the Estate of PETRUS JACOBUS HAUPTFLFISCH, of Kleinrakenstein, in the District of the Paarl, has, by order of the Honourable Mr. Justice SMITH, dated the 12th of December, 1887, been placed under Sequestration in the hands of the Master of the Supreme Court, and that all Persons having any claim upon the said Estate are required to attend two Meetings of Creditors, to be held before the Resident Magistrate of the Paarl, at his Office, Paarl, the first Meeting to be held on Tuesday, the 20th of December, 1887, at 10 o'clock precisely, for the proof of Debts; the second Meeting on Tuesday, the 27th of December, 1887, at 10 o'clock precisely, also for the proof of Debts, and for the election of a Trustee or Trustees who shall administer the said Estate.

J. HOFMEYR,
Master of the Supreme Court.

Insolvent Schedule C.

Particulars of the Moveable Property, Stock in-Trade, etc , etc. *of Petrus Jacobus Hauptfleisch of Klein Rakenstein in the Paarl Division*

Description of Property.	Valuation.
1 Small Table	3
1 Bedstead with bedding	5 - -
1 Washhandstand & dressing Table	1 10 -
1 Looking glass	- 5 -
1 Iron bedstead with bedding	5 - -
1 Wooden Stretcher	1 10 -
1 Wash hand stand	- 7 6
1½ dg American chairs	2 10 -
1 Set Dining Tables	2 - -
1 Dutch Clock	2 - -
1 Small Table	- 5 -
1 Large do	- 7 6
1 Small press	

Hauptfleisch rose from his bed on cold winter mornings to supervise activities in the dairy, he — like most of his kind in those days — had to step onto a floor all but bereft of cover. Someone had made an attempt to beautify the austere second front bedroom with 'one lot of small pictures', but nowhere, in any corner of the house, was there a single book — not even, it seems, the ubiquitous family Bible. And what of the firearms that were so essential to every farmer's existence? Perhaps they were so much part of Hauptfleisch's being that Mr Tomkin did not even try to identify them separately.

No known records indicate to what extent Petrus Jacobus Hauptfleisch managed to rehabilitate himself or to develop Nederburg after his insolvency, but he continued to live there — and presumably to farm — for 14 more years before deciding to move elsewhere. During these years, wine farmers of the Cape were hard put to it to restore their *Phylloxera*-ravaged vineyards. Between 1891 and 1894, just under 700 000 American vine cuttings were imported and distributed among the farmers by the government. They were propagated locally and within 13 years over 19 million grafted vines had been replanted in the Cape Colony. This was the period that saw the mushrooming of the gold-mining town of Johannesburg and the rush to it of thousands of adventurers all bent on grabbing for themselves a share of its glittering wealth. It was the understandable demands of these 'foreigners' — *Uitlanders*, as they were called — in Paul Kruger's unsophisticated republic, coupled with the ruthless ambition of the British, that led to the outbreak of war in the Transvaal in October 1899. Petrus Jacobus Hauptfleisch has left his chroni-

TOP LEFT
On 16 December 1887 the Government Gazette published this notice, dated the previous day. It had been inserted by the Master of the Supreme Court and advertised the insolvency of Petrus Jacobus Hauptfleisch.
TOP RIGHT
The inventory of Hauptfleisch's possessions, from both inside and outside the Nederburg homestead, presents a lively picture of the lifestyle of his family.

cler nothing to indicate whether his allegiance lay with the staunchly British Western Cape where his family had lived for generations, or with the Afrikaner nation to which he belonged by heritage, but like so many of his kind his loyalties were in all probability sadly divided. The war ended on 31 May 1902 and within six months of the signing of the Peace of Vereeniging, Nederburg had changed hands once more.

Petrus Jacobus Hauptfleisch spent his last years in the home of his son, Jan Gotlieb, first on a farm at Agter Paarl and then in a house in the town's long Main Street. His wife, Francina Carolina, had died aged 59 in 1907, but Petrus Jacobus was destined to outlive her for 18 years, dying, aged 85, on 7 November 1925. About £2 240 and his modest possessions — a clock and a pocket watch, a few articles of furniture and a large portrait of his wife — were bequeathed to his adopted daughter, Anna (now Mrs Labuschagne), his two elder sons and their children. No mention is made in his will of the youngest son, Jacob le Roux Hauptfleisch, though no death notice for him can be traced before 1925, so it seems he survived his father. Only an obituary appearing in the *Paarl Post* of 14 November 1925 gives us what is barely a glimpse into the personality of Nederburg's fourth owner. 'Oom Pieter,' it reads, 'was vriendelik van aard en algemeen bekend. De overledene genoot goede gezondheid en is bezweken aan de zwakheden van de ouderdom.' ['Oom Pieter was friendly by nature and widely known. The deceased enjoyed good health and passed away as a result of the infirmities of old age.']

■

CHAPTER FOUR

A POLITICIAN AT NEDERBURG:

HENRY LATHAM CURREY 1902-1918

Harry Currey, the first of Nederburg's three English-speaking
owners, had been private secretary to C. J. Rhodes for nine years before he
entered politics and became a member of Merriman's last Cape
Cabinet before Union. Currey never lived at Nederburg; he bought it as a
holiday home for his children and in the hope that one of his sons
would choose wine farming as a career.

Handsome and urbane, courteous and witty — yet always sheltering a secret sadness — Henry Latham Currey, Nederburg's fifth owner, gave the impression throughout his long life of being every inch an English gentleman. And that, indeed, was what he was, even though he had been born and bred in South Africa and was, in fact, one-quarter 'Cape Dutch'. It was part of his philosophy never to incur debts of any kind and so, when he acquired Nederburg on 2 September 1902, he handed over to the fortunate Petrus Jacobus Hauptfleisch £5 000 in cash.

Harry Currey, as he was known to everyone, first saw light of day on 13 January 1863 in the home of his maternal grandparents, Ewan and Aletta Christian. Their house, which stood on the corner of Church and St George's streets in Cape Town, was double-storeyed and sizeable enough to accommodate the large Christian family. Surrounded by a high *stoep*, red-tiled and tree-shaded, it was famous for its elaborately decorated ceilings painted early in the century by Italian-born Antonio Chiappini. Ewan Christian, of Manx origin, had first arrived at the Cape in 1797 as a 13-year-old midshipman in the Royal Navy but was sent back to England the following year with the despatches announcing the sudden death of his kinsman, Rear-Admiral Hugh Cloberry Christian, commodore of the Cape station at Simon's Town. For 18 dreary northern winters, Ewan cherished memories of the charms and blue skies of the Cape and, as soon as the wars with France were over, joyfully returned to make it his home. Once in Cape Town, he quickly established himself as a merchant and met and married Aletta Johanna Hendrina Schultze, a local girl of German-Dutch descent. Ewan Christian's affairs prospered and in the house opening onto St George's Street he and Aletta were able to bring up their nine offspring in comfort and the greatest possible respectability.

The youngest of these children was Mary Margaret, born in 1839. The story goes that one day in 1858, as she stepped out of her carriage in bonnet and crinoline, she was spied by a young man, at that time a total stranger, named John Blades Currey, who fell instantly and irrevocably in love with her. Employed at that time as a clerk in the civil service, John Currey had come out to the Cape eight years earlier to visit two of his brothers who were farming at 'the Knysna'. He had been granted a year's leave from Oxford where he was an undergraduate, but on Christmas Day a few months after his arrival, war broke out on the eastern frontier for the eighth time and John Currey, 21 years old and lusting for adventure, shouldered his gun and rode off to join the colonial forces. By the time arms and assegais had been finally laid down, South Africa, as is its wont, had claimed him physically and spiritually as its own and all ideas of furthering his studies were abandoned. On 26 January 1860 John Blades Currey married Mary Christian in St George's Cathedral, to which — although it was a mere stone's throw from her parental home — she had been driven in glittering splendour attended by a dozen bridesmaids. As their first connubial home, John had rented the farm, De Hoop op Constantia, once part of Simon van der Stel's historic estate; and here, after he had ridden the daily 15 miles to his office in the old Supreme Court building and home again, he tended the old-established vineyards. The wine he produced was of such excellent quality that at the Cape of Good Hope Agricultural Show held in September 1863 he was awarded two splendid silver cups, one for the best white wine of the 1862 vintage and the other for the best red wine of any age. But John Currey's joy in farming was destined to be short-lived. Within four years the dreaded fungus, *Oidium tuckeri*, had virtually destroyed the vines of De Hoop op Constantia; and this, combined with the British government's withdrawal of preferential tariffs allowed to colonial wines, followed by a newly-imposed duty, put paid to the young Curreys' hopes of making a fortune from wine farming. In 1864 they abandoned De Hoop op Constantia and moved

PAGE 58: TOP
The historic farm, De Hoop op Constantia, where Harry Currey's parents spent their early married life.
BOTTOM
A plate from a dinner-service bought at an auction on Cape Town's Parade by Currey's grandfather.
PAGE 59: TOP
A cartoon which appeared in a Kimberley newspaper in 1875. It lampoons John Blades Currey who, as secretary to the government of Griqualand West, aroused the intense dislike of the diggers whose unruly lives he attempted to regulate.
BOTTOM
A sauce spoon from the Curreys' blue dinner-service.

into the Christians' Cape Town house with their two young children, May and Harry.

Throughout his youth, Harry Currey was to be deeply influenced by the character and career of his father. A devoted husband and a tender and loving parent in private, in his public life John Blades Currey affected a persona that was snobbish in the extreme and almost laughably pompous. He was inordinately ambitious yet his extraordinary ineptitude prevented him from realizing any of his many dreams. In 1867 he was entrusted with introducing the first diamond to be discovered in the Cape — the 'Eureka' of over 21 carats — to the *cognoscenti* of Europe but, far from being impressed with South Africa's mineral-producing potential, geologists, gemologists and Press alike laughed John Currey to scorn, declaring that the Eureka was nothing more than a freak. When, five years later, he was appointed secretary to the government of the newly-created crown colony of Griqualand West, John Currey saw himself on the way to a full governorship — with a title to boot — but these illusions melted away when a rebellion by the diggers in Kimberley (for which he, personally, had chosen the name to flatter the current colonial secretary in London) involved the Imperial government in expenses upwards of £28 000. An undeserving scapegoat, John Currey found himself ignominiously retrenched on half-pension. There followed nine years of austerity in Cape Town, during which several little Currey siblings made their appearance and their father scraped together some sort of living by contributing articles — all of them extremely perceptive and well written — to local as well as London newspapers.

Then, in 1884, a seeming paradise opened up before John Blades Currey when he was appointed manager of the London & South Africa Exploration Company with its local headquarters in Kimberley. The years that followed were undoubtedly the happiest in his life — but also the most indulgent. Improvident to a degree, he lived extravagantly, entertained lavishly and saved not a penny. He spared his family no luxury: during Queen Victoria's diamond jubilee year, he took a flat in London's Half Moon Street and hired a horse bus so that his daughters could see the sights. But once again disappointment was in store for the unfortunate John Blades Currey. One day in 1899, just before the outbreak of the South African War, a telegram arrived from his old friend, Cecil Rhodes, then in London, with the news that De Beers Consolidated Mines had bought out the London & South Africa Exploration Company and that he was to be deprived not only of his job but of all his many 'perks', from the house he lived in down to the bed in which he slept and the horse on which he rode. Fortunately, Rhodes, remembering the

Curreys' kindnesses to him when he was young, poor and sick during Kimberley's early days, appointed John Blades steward of his Groote Schuur estate and provided him and his six daughters with the house, Welgelegen, that stood on it for their lifetime.

So, for the ten Currey children, including Harry, life was either a feast or a famine. There was sufficient money to allow him four years at an English public school — Kings School in Canterbury, one of the oldest in the country — but not enough to pay for a university education even though, of all the Currey offspring, he was the most scholarly by nature. No doubt vowing that, unlike his father, he would never indulge in wanton extravagance — for throughout his life he was to be extremely careful with money — Harry left school before his 17th birthday and returned to his home in the Cape Colony at a time when his father's finances were at their lowest ebb. Opportunities at the Cape in January 1880 for a young gentleman of his kind were few and far between, so Harry Currey did what at that time and in his circumstances was the obvious thing and joined the civil service. A post was found for him as a clerk in the office of the general manager of telegraphs, Mr (later Sir James) Sivewright, at the salary of five shillings for each working day, a sum that to him seemed not far short of a fortune. During the 18 monotonous months that followed, Harry painstakingly recorded the number of telegrams that his office received, trans-

mitted and despatched each day. It seemed that the tedium would never end but at last his diligence was rewarded in June 1881, when he was appointed private secretary to the commissioner of Crown Lands and Public Works. This post was held by none other than John X. Merriman, his father's close friend and from Harry's childhood days his own personal idol. From then on, according to the memoirs of Harry Currey's daughter, Audrey, John X. Merriman was to Henry Latham Currey what Gamaliel had been to Paul.

Yet his career in the office of Crown Lands and Public Works was to last only three years and was succeeded by what proved the most exciting, important — and eventually the most distressing — years of his life. On a July day in 1884 (by which time Merriman had been appointed treasurer-general and Harry had a new taskmaster), he looked up from his desk to see Cecil John Rhodes, then member of the House of Assembly for Barkly West, striding into his office. Rhodes, whom Currey had known since his parents' earliest Kimberley days, brought the news that he was about to leave for Bechuanaland (now Botswana) to conduct a commission of enquiry and that he wanted Harry to accompany him as private secretary for the duration of the project. Harry, of course, jumped at the offer, little knowing that the post would later become permanent and that for the following nine years he was to work with and for Rhodes in terms of the greatest amiability and intimacy.

In 1886 he was to accompany Rhodes on his first visit to dust-swept Ferreira's Camp, as Johannesburg was then known, only a few months after the discovery of gold on the Witwatersrand. At that time Rhodes's partner, Charles Dunell Rudd, was in London forming the Consolidated Gold Fields of South Africa, which was to take over their interests on the Reef; when they offered Harry the post of secretary to the new company at a salary of £450 a year, it seemed that he was stepping onto the gold-paved streets of El Dorado itself. Rhodes and Rudd, as joint managing directors of Consolidated Gold Fields, showed their confidence in the young man they had employed — Harry was just 24 years old — by giving him their full power of attorney, and for months at a time he was left in Johannesburg in supreme command of their affairs. 'It was,' as he was to write many years later with typical understatement, 'a very enjoyable period of my life.'

In July 1890, when Rhodes became prime minister of the Cape Colony, Harry Currey returned to Cape Town and from there ran the operations of both the Consolidated Gold Fields of South Africa and the British South Africa Company, founded by Rhodes with Alfred Beit in 1889. Rhodes had just acquired the Groote Schuur Estate and he invited Currey, as his private secretary, to live with him and to run the bachelor household. For this he was given an allowance of £250 a month — an immense amount of money in those days

TOP
Vineyard activities in Paarl during Harry Currey's ownership of Nederburg.
BOTTOM
Harvesting grapes in the Paarl valley. A rare photograph taken early in the 20th century.

and some indication of Rhodes's scale of entertainment. Soon after this Rhodes, accompanied by Currey, visited London. They stayed in the Westminster Palace Hotel where Harry had to arrange a tight schedule of appointments with politicians, financiers, newspapermen (and women) as well as with society luminaries, and where such famous personalities as the Duke of Abercorn and Lord Rothschild were regular callers. But to Harry the most interesting visitor of all was undoubtedly the Irish politician, Charles Stewart Parnell, for whose Home Rule campaign he hurried to the bank, on Rhodes's instructions, to cash a cheque for the enormous sum of £5 000 — the first half of an amount promised for the cause. Rhodes gave Currey another bewildering instruction during this visit. He was told to go to Maples' famous store and order the household furniture for his mansion at Groote Schuur. With the aid of a sympathetic salesman, Harry, who was completely out of his depth with such a commission, took about half an hour to choose what was required and had it shipped out to the Cape. Interior decorating was never one of Harry Currey's strong points, so perhaps it was fortunate that all these tables and chairs, beds, sofas and wardrobes — undoubtedly of the best quality but somewhat uninspired in taste — were fated to be reduced to ashes in the fire that destroyed Groote Schuur in 1896.

On 8 August 1891 Harry Currey announced his engagement to 20-year-old Ethelreda, daughter of Charles

TOP
Edwardian fashions were hardly suitable for Paarl's mid-summer heat.
CENTRE
Cecil John Rhodes, whom Harry Currey served as private secretary for nine years.
LEFT
Sedgwick's, whose name is associated with the wine industry to this day, placed this advertisement in The Cape Almanac *of 1902.*

Aken Fairbridge, lawyer, member of the Cape House of Assembly, bibliophile and scholar. 'How well I remember that evening at Groote Schuur,' an old friend wrote to Harry many years later, 'when you announced to Rhodes that you were engaged and he went off the deep end at the idea of losing you.' But Harry himself had no thought at that stage of leaving Rhodes's employ, though perhaps, in Rhodes's reaction to the news, he should have seen the writing on the wall as far as their relationship was concerned. Meanwhile, he blithely continued with his job completely unaware that his particular paradise was the habitation of at least one fool. He and Ethel were married in St Paul's Church, Rondebosch, on 23 February 1892, and after the ceremony, when Rhodes stooped to congratulate the bride, Harry heard him whisper to her, 'I am very jealous of you, you know.' Did he, at that moment, feel a twinge of anxiety for the future?

Insidiously, after this, a subtle tension began to develop between the two men. Not many months after the wedding, Harry was astonished to learn that Rhodes's brother, Ernest, a recently retired army officer with no business experience whatsoever, had been appointed managing director of Gold Fields in Johannesburg. An even greater shock was the peremptory order to leave Cape Town forthwith and return to the company's office in what had become the Golden City. Harry's

association with Rhodes's brother in Johannesburg was brief and bitter. Only too soon was he to realize that Ernest Rhodes, perhaps stung by jealousy, was determined to make the younger – and brighter – man's position untenable. Currey, ever a proud man, felt forced to resign and immediately went to Cape Town to discuss the situation with Cecil Rhodes. He confronted the great man in the prime minister's office, but throughout the interview Rhodes steadfastly continued to hold his newspaper in front of his face and responded to Harry's urgent questions with nothing but a series of grunts. Dejected beyond words, Harry Currey decided that his only recourse was to sue Rhodes and Rudd for wrongful dismissal. The outcome was a settlement out of court and Rhodes's payment to Harry Currey of £3 000.

And so the happy and intimate relationship that had existed between Cecil John Rhodes and Harry Currey for nine years was broken for all time. They never spoke a word to each other again, not even on a voyage to England which they made in the same ship. Within Harry Currey's own family the story goes that in the blazing heatwave of March 1902 he tried to see Rhodes as he lay dying in his thatched cottage by the sea, but that Rhodes's two close friends, Leander Starr Jameson of 'the Raid' infamy and Sir Charles Metcalfe, turned him brusquely away. Certainly, never again in his life did Harry Currey willingly mention the name of Cecil John Rhodes. Bitterness was, perhaps, his besetting sin.

Possibly because of his personal integrity, Currey never amassed a fortune, as many others did, during those early days on the goldfields. Nevertheless, wise investments made while he was employed by Rhodes, swelled by the £3 000 he was paid in settlement, enabled him to support himself and his family in relative comfort for the remainder of his life. Yet, financial security was scant compensation for the hurt he had suffered. Plagued by insomnia and denied employment by all who supported Rhodes – the prime minister's reputation had not yet been wrecked by the débâcle of the Jameson Raid – Harry Currey, with Ethel ever loyal at his side, left South Africa in order to read for the Bar at the Inner Temple in London. Here their two eldest children were born – Ronald Fairbridge in October 1894 and Audrey Mary in July 1896. Harry, now 'a barrister learned in the law', returned to the Cape with his family and took chambers in St George's Street, but the years that followed were scarcely productive professionally. It may be that he was not suited to the law; perhaps, too, the Cape had not forgotten the unhappy ending of his relationship with Rhodes. An even greater contribution to his lack of success was the unpopular stand that he took on the outbreak of the South African War in October 1899. While he most certainly was not anti-British, he was passionately convinced that the war was

TOP
Skilled coopers at work in Paarl at the time when Harry Currey owned Nederburg.
BOTTOM
Branches from Nederburg's ancient oaks hide the front gable with its graceful swan's neck pediment. This photograph was taken in 1910.

TOP
*John X. Merriman, prime minister
of the Cape Colony, in pensive mood.
He was Harry Currey's mentor and idol.*
BOTTOM
*A silver goblet awarded to Harry Currey's
father in 1863 for wine made by him at
De Hoop op Constantia.*

a ghastly blunder and that it should never have been allowed to happen. In this he shared the opinion of John X. Merriman, who had declared that it was both 'unjust and unjustifiable' and foresaw the legacy of bitterness that it was to leave.

Ethel Currey, meanwhile, found her loyalties wrenched apart for, to her own family, Harry's attitude was anathema. One and all, the Fairbridges, particularly Ethel's clever sister Dorothea, were ardent supporters of the British cause. In fact, there was more than a little truth in the rumour that Dorothea Fairbridge was for years passionately, but of course discreetly, in love with Governor Lord Milner. As far as her family was concerned Harry was clearly pro-Boer and that, at the Cape, with its Jingo propensities, simply would not do. There were others who shared the Fairbridges' opinion of him and for the war years at least, Harry and Ethel found themselves shunned by many of the leading lights in Cape society. Young as they were, the Currey children — there was now a third, John Mackarness, born in October 1898 — could sense the social chill in the air and were completely bewildered by it, for to them their father represented all that was noble and upright. But public opinion was not to deter Harry from the career he had by now decided to pursue. By the time the war ended on 31 May 1902 he had made up his mind to forsake the law and, like his mentor Merriman, to launch out into the squally sea of politics.

But there was another — and happier — respect in which Currey was to play follow-my-leader at this time. In 1892, as a solution to the problem of finding an occupation secondary to politics, John X. Merriman had bought and resuscitated the beautiful but almost derelict wine farm, Schoongezicht, outside Stellenbosch. Perhaps his disciple had dreams of inheriting his mantle in more ways than one, for ten years later prospective parliamentarian, Henry Latham Currey, turned part-time farmer, set his sights on the lovely lower slopes of the Klein Drakenstein mountains and bought Nederburg.

From the beginning, it seems, he had no intention of living there. Before he parted from Rhodes in 1893 he had bought seven acres of what had once been free-burgher land stretching from Camp Ground Road in Rondebosch almost to the railway line. Here, in what had been a plantation of 'umbrella' pines, the Curreys built a solid, unimaginative house to which they gave the equally unimaginative name of 'Pinewood'. This was to be their home for over 30 years; Nederburg's main purpose, for the time being, was to provide country holidays for the children. Even if Harry Currey, personally, never lived there, there was always the possibility that one of his boys might take up wine farming. A third son, Harry Philip — known as Phil — was born in September 1902 and dreams of a future for him in wine farming gave Currey an added incentive in buying the farm. If, to begin with, any fruit or wine were forthcoming and proved profitable, well, that would be an added

bonus. Harry Currey was no gardener, let alone a farmer. In this respect he certainly bore no resemblance to John X. Merriman, who not only made Schoongezicht's exquisite house his home, but developed the farm's orchards and vineyards so that it became a significant producer of fruit and exporter of wine. Harry, on the other hand, left the tilling and the pruning, the harvesting and the wine making, to a manager named W. S. de Villiers, who lived in the cottage — once the *jonkershuis* — near the old stable and earned £100 per annum plus 3 per cent of the farm's gross income. For the rest, Harry was content to bundle his family into a train bound for Huguenot station when he could snatch a few days away from electioneering or parliament and drive up to his farm in a pony-trap, giving no more than a cursory thought to the burgeoning of Nederburg's acres or to its economic success.

By now, his family aside, politics had become Harry Currey's *raison d'être*. After a successful by-election in 1902, three months before transfer of Nederburg was passed in his favour, Currey took his seat in the House of Assembly as member of parliament for the constituency of George. He represented the South African Party — or 'S.A.P.' — which had come into being in 1898 when a coalition was formed between the Afrikaner Bond M.P.s and the liberal independents, and in standing for its tenets once more made public his loyalty to John X. Merriman. Political upheavals and economic depression beset the Cape at this time and when

TOP
Cape Town celebrates the establishment of the Union of South Africa in 1910. The choice of Louis Botha as prime minister dashed Merriman's hopes of appointment to this office.
BOTTOM
Harry Currey's silver Vesta case. The matches were stuck on the corrugated reverse side.

an election took place in 1904 it was the Progressive Party, led by Dr Leander Starr Jameson, that came into power. Currey was once more returned to parliament as member for George, as he was at the elections of 1908. On this occasion Jameson's party was defeated at the polls and when the new prime minister, John X. Merriman, formed a new government, his cabinet included Henry Latham Currey as Minister without Portfolio.

His first task was scarcely a pleasant one. He was given the responsibility of retrenching large numbers of men from the civil service in an attempt to rescue the Cape from the financial Slough of Despond into which it had been sinking ever deeper since the end of the South African War. On the horizon loomed the union of the two former Boer republics and the two British colonies and as Merriman was determined not to bring the Cape into it insolvent, drastic measures had to be taken. Civil servants had their salaries slashed by 5 per cent and it fell to Harry Currey to decide which of them could remain and which had to be dispensed with. He found this an utterly odious duty; besieged in his office and in his own home by incensed people deprived of their livelihood, he sought refuge from the strain in the peace and tranquillity of Nederburg.

The homestead that he had bought was rare not only in its graceful proportions and craftsmanship, but because it was one of the few of its kind that had never been 'Victorianized'. Unlike many houses in Stellenbosch and Paarl — and perhaps because in those days it

LEFT AND RIGHT
*Etched glasses belonging to the
Currey family.*
CENTRE
Posed against a fashionable art nouveau
*background, the Currey children —
Audrey, Philip, Ronald and John (in sailor
suit) — in about 1906.*
PAGE 67: LEFT AND RIGHT
*Stemmed glasses belonging to the
Currey family.*
CENTRE
*Deil's awa wi' th' exciseman.
A* Cape Times *cartoon lampooning
Merriman, prime minister of the Cape
Colony, when he supported the Wine
Licences Amendment Bill in 1909.*
BOTTOM
*John X. Merriman and flowergirl
Nancy Currey at the wedding reception of
Audrey Currey and John Brooke on
23 April 1918.*

was so remotely situated — Nederburg during the 19th century had never lost its thatch to the doubtful charms or practicalities of a corrugated-iron roof, nor had any deal-framed plate-glass windows replaced its original shuttered casements. In more recent days, the owners of many of the old country houses had taken to stripping the fine old brasswork from their doors and even removing the cupboards from their walls in order to sell them to the *nouveaux riches* of Kimberley or Johannesburg — but Nederburg had never suffered this fate. True, when Harry Currey first saw the house he realized that certain unlovely changes had been made to its interior, but all these he soon set to rights, salvaging the remnants of the original teak *porte-de-visite* screen from the pantry shelves into which they had been converted and restoring it, rebuilt, to its rightful place between *voor-* and *agterkamer*. All this was extremely pleasing to Harry Currey's sister-in-law, Dorothea Fairbridge, who at that time was appealing, through the Press and in books that have become sought-after Africana, for the preservation and appreciation of the old houses of the Cape. In an article that appeared in *The State* in November 1911 she writes that Nederburg's homestead was 'hidden

amongst its oaks' and mentions 'a tiny garden' between two of the gabled wings where 'Banksia roses and Isle of France grow riotously'.

Little is known of the state of the farm itself when Harry Currey bought it. Dorothea Fairbridge tells us that there were large fruit orchards at Nederburg where naartjies and apples, peaches and apricots grew in abundance. These may have been planted by Petrus Jacobus Hauptfleisch to replace *Phylloxera*-ravaged vines, or perhaps they were established later on the instructions of Currey. Certainly he was stimulated not only by Merriman's enterprise at Schoongezicht but also by the work of Harry Pickstone, pioneer of the fruit industry and founder, with Cecil Rhodes, of the Rhodes Fruit Farms. As for Nederburg's vineyards, one can only speculate on how they were cultivated during Currey's period of ownership. At this time the 'bush' or 'low head' system of viticulture that had been practised at the Cape for over two centuries was being replaced at many Cape farms by the trellising method that was becoming popular in South Africa for the first time, but it is unlikely that Harry Currey adopted it at Nederburg. Well-known viticulturist, C. J. Meyer, maintained, in

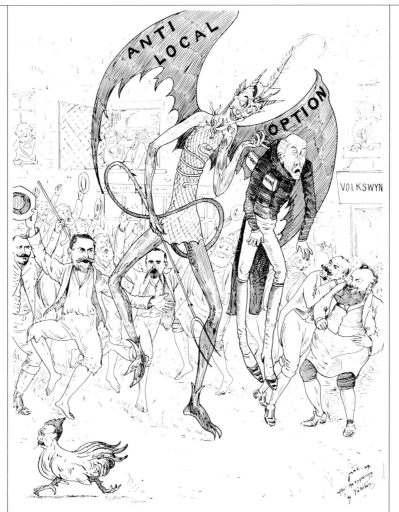

the *Agricultural Journal* of September 1902, that a trellised vine could be expected to produce double the quantity of grapes grown on a bush vine, while the yield of wine per trellised acre averaged from a third to double, or even treble, that of a similar area under bushes. In addition to an increase in quantity, claimed Dr Meyer, there was also an improvement in the quality of wine produced from trellised vines.

It is true that Harry Currey was always fascinated by a new theory of any kind, but preoccupation with other matters and his frequent absences from Nederburg may have led him to overlook Meyer's advice. There is no one alive today who knows whether Mr de Villiers was instructed to train Nederburg's vines onto trellises or to say whether there was a marked improvement in the wine they produced. Not that Harry Currey had any pretensions to being a connoisseur, though perhaps his palate was more sensitive than he cared to admit. In his memoirs, written three years before his death, he tells a story that is worth repeating.

'A few years ago I was on a visit to Hermanus,' he wrote, 'when a very rich man with an entourage of secretaries, grooms, horses and a motor car arrived with his family. One evening the secretary came to me and said, "Today is Mr W.'s birthday and he will be very glad if you will come to his rooms and drink his health. He has some remarkably fine port to offer you." I availed myself of the invitation.

'In due course a bottle covered with dust and cobwebs was brought in in a wicker "cradle". The cork was drawn and the glasses filled without the bottle being moved. We all wished Mr W. good luck and I tasted the wine. It seemed to me horrible – but for my sins I was first approached for my opinion of the priceless old port. I know nothing whatever of wine but as I really could not, even with every desire to be polite, say that I liked it I said that I thought that it was "somewhat corked". It sounded, under the circumstances, a safe comment to make.

'"Bring another bottle!" ordered our wealthy host. The same game was played. Another bottle covered with dust and cobwebs was brought in lying in a wicker cradle and into another lot of glasses the contents were poured.

'Fortunately another guest was appealed to for his opinion and he expressed himself very forcibly for he

Fairmead.
Rondebosch.
17th May 1918.

My dear Mr Merriman

I was sorry to miss you yesterday but I had to go up to the Mount to lunch. I wanted to tell you that I have sold Nederburg to Maurice Faure whose wife is Namita daughter of the late Judge Smith. I am very sorry to part with the place but de Villiers is in fact and has been for some time past a resident pensioner. The present prospects under his guidance were not very attractive because as time goes on he is sure to become a still more lazy. You will say why not sack him and get another fellow. Had I done so I would have been boycotted by every man and woman – white and black – in the valley. Faure can start with a free hand. Moreover neither Ronald, nor John nor Phil are likely now to take to that walk in life. I hope that Faure who took de Villiers to the farm and acted on his advice will make a good thing out of it – for we are both distantly connected with the Brookes and I don't want any family weeping and wailing.

That Jew who bought the Baptist Church from the old Trustees behaved uncommonly well in handing it back to the Congregation at the price he paid for it. I don't know that every Christian or even every Baptist would have under the circumstances abandoned such an obviously good chance of making a small commission on the transaction.

Yours as always
Harry Currey.

said, "I think it is a d . . . d thing worse than the first bottle!"

'Our kindly host was almost struck dumb but managed to turn to me and say, "You think the wine is corked?"

'"Yes," I feebly assented.

'"Bring the corks here," he ordered; and on a silver salver the corks were brought to him. I thought our host was suddenly taken ill, so knocked-out did he look. And no wonder — for the corks were stamped "Schoongezicht", showing of course only too plainly that the butler had drunk (or sold) the wonderful port and refilled the bottles with our local product.'

This, of course, does not say much for the wines produced at Schoongezicht at that time, though probably those pressed in Nederburg's cellars were very little better. Philip Currey used to recall with amusement the wry face that his father invariably pulled when obliged to fulfil his seasonal duty of tasting the new wine.

Where that wine was sold or how it was disposed of is yet another unsolved mystery, for no records of Nederburg's dealings during these years have been traced. Certainly Harry Currey could not have chosen a more unpropitious moment than 1902 to buy a wine farm. True, the battle against *Phylloxera* had been won at last and by 1904 there were 78 million healthy vines in full production in the south-western Cape. But a plenteous harvest, instead of improving the farmers' financial situation, gave rise once more to a most urgent problem of over-production and under-consumption of wine. As a result a commission of enquiry was appointed and evidence that it heard from farmers during April and May 1905 established that 'beyond a doubt the wine and brandy industry [of the western Cape was] . . . in an alarming state of depression'. The commission made several recommendations, the most important of which was 'the establishment of co-operative central cellars on a small scale at the commencement, with Government aid, as a means of securing a uniform good quality of Cape Wine and Brandy, and of laying fresh foundations for the prosperous development of the industry'.

The outcome of the commission's findings was the passing of Act No. 43 of 1905, by which the government made £150 000 available for loans to finance the establishment of small co-operative wine cellars. Meetings were held in all the main wine-producing districts; Wellington took the initiative in February 1906 by founding the Wellington Co-operative Winery and others soon followed. Yet, during the following two years, things went from bad to worse and in 1907 only £2. 10s. was paid for a leaguer of wine, just half the price paid for the same quantity in 1905. Harry Currey, struggling with the financial blizzard that had struck the civil service, must have been only too keenly aware that the wine industry was in an equally desperate situation. Even if his own experience at Nederburg had not convinced him of this, the vociferous campaigning on behalf of Cape wine farmers by a Progressive Party member of the Cape Parliament's Legislative Council, one Charles William Henry Kohler, would have made it perfectly clear to him.

On 24 March 1909 Kohler, himself a prominent farmer from the Drakenstein valley, published an open letter drawing attention to the plight of the farmers of the western Cape. He called upon them to present their grievances to the government in person and on Wednesday 14 April thousands of farmers from all the wine-producing regions, their wives and children — as well as sympathetic store-keepers who had shut up shop for the day — converged on Cape Town's newly-built City Hall, each protester distinguishable by the green ribbon in his buttonhole. Kohler delivered an impassioned address and a motion was passed that 'this great meeting . . . declares the wine industry to be in an alarming serious condition [sic], and that unless serious legislative action is forthwith taken, in which we urge the Government and the Opposition to combine, the great national industry will be ruined'. The farmers then marched to the House of Assembly and the resolution was handed to Prime Minister Merriman personally. He received it with his customary graciousness but, with the Cape in such a parlous financial position, there was little that could be done at that stage to help the farmers. One can only imagine the ambivalence with which both Merriman and Currey viewed this incident and the pain which it gave them to turn the farmers away. Kohler, however, continued to sound his battle-cry of 'co-operation' for he was convinced that only by combining their efforts into one giant co-operative union could the wine farmers hope to prosper and the industry improve both its products and its image.

On 31 May 1910 the Union of South Africa came into being. Its first prime minister was Louis Botha, not John X. Merriman, as Harry Currey and many others had devoutly hoped. This, as Currey's eldest son Ronald was to write much later, was Merriman's 'fall from greatness, and Harry Currey fell with him'. Ten members of Merriman's pre-Union cabinet became members of the new Union cabinet; four were chosen as administrators of the four provinces, but Harry Currey, Merriman's faithful lieutenant, was passed over. 'The price of loyalty to his chief,' commented Ronald Currey, 'had proved a stiff one.'

Meanwhile, the wine industry continued on its descent towards disaster just as inevitably, it seemed, as Europe was sliding into war. On 4 August 1914, when hostilities began, Harry and Ethel Currey were in England on a visit to Ronald, who was about to take up the

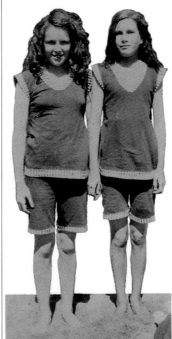

PAGE 68
Harry Currey's letter to Merriman telling him of his decision to sell Nederburg. Merriman had been farming successfully at Schoongezicht outside Stellenbosch since 1892.
PAGE 69: TOP
All dressed up to go swimming in the Palmiet River. Girl Guides from Rondebosch enjoyed camping holidays at Nederburg during the First World War.
BOTTOM
Seated outside Pinewood, their Rondebosch home, Ethelreda Currey with her youngest child, Nancy Margaret.

Rhodes Scholarship awarded to him two years earlier. They had planned a holiday in the Austrian Tyrol with Audrey, who had been at school in Wiltshire for the past four years, but the outbreak of war changed all that and a good deal besides. Ronald's scholarship was put on ice while he was commissioned in the Argyll and Sutherland Highlanders and the rest of the family hastily returned home in the last ship to sail for the Cape without a convoy to escort it.

To Ethel Currey the First World War was unrelieved, prolonged anguish. Both Ronald and John fought with the British forces in France throughout the four years (Ronald was to be awarded the Military Cross and Bar) and in 1916 13-year-old Phil arrived in England to start his training as a cadet at the Royal Naval College at Osborne. Tortured by an excessively active imagination, Ethel knew no peace throughout that time; even the calm and beauty of Nederburg could not allay her terrible fears for her three boys. The two Currey daughters — Nancy Margaret, very much the *laatlammetjie*, was born in 1910 — remained at home and Audrey whiled away the time by organizing the local Girl Guides. It was part of her task to take them camping and during those grim days Nederburg provided the backdrop for many hilarious holidays. But if Nancy was still a child, Audrey had by now grown up and on 23 April 1918 she married John Brooke, Anglican rector of Rondebosch, a widower 23 years her senior. Less than a month later — on 17 May — Harry Currey was to write to Merriman: '. . . I have sold Nederburg to Maurice Pare whose wife is Nanita [sic] daughter of the late Judge Smith. I am very sorry to part with the place but De Villiers is, in fact, and has been for some time past, a resident pensioner. The present prospects under his guidance are not very attractive because as time goes on he is sure to become still more lazy. You will say why not sack him and get another fellow. Had I done so I would have been boycotted by every man and woman — white and black — in the valley. Pare can start with a free hand. Moreover, neither Ronald, nor John nor Phil are likely now to take to that walk in life . . .'

And so, on 28 May 1918, Harry Currey parted with Nederburg where so many happy holidays had been spent. He said — though this was probably no more than an excuse for poor farming — that its soil was unsuitable for wine grapes. On the other hand, for the rest of their lives his children — Ronald the headmaster and classicist, Audrey the poetically-inclined clergyman's wife, John the sheep farmer with an abundance of wit, Phil the rear-admiral and grower of superb roses, and Nancy, who never did anything in particular — spoke of its vineyards and orchards, its oaks and its mountain streams with wistful nostalgia. From their point of view, it seems, its wines were barely worth mentioning. ∎

CHAPTER FIVE

MAURICE PARE:

A SIX-YEAR INTERLUDE 1918-1924

Born in London in 1883, Maurice Pare lived and worked
in the Seychelles before settling at the Cape and buying Nederburg.
During the six years of his ownership, he witnessed the
emergence and growing strength of the K.W.V. and became a
financial victim of the collapse of one of the smaller wine co-operatives.
Despite his inexperience, Pare produced wine that was highly
commended at the Paarl Show.

*Maurice Pare: a photograph
taken some years after he left Nederburg in
1924. As manager of the South African
Fruit Growers' Co-operative Exchange,
he was to maintain an interest in the fruit
industry until his death in 1946.*

Complex family relationships are not the prerogative of the Cape's inhabitants of Dutch and French origin. They also exist among those of British descent and are indeed found throughout much of what was long ago the 'settler' community. This was the case with the Curreys and Maurice Pare, the man who became Nederburg's owner six months before the end of the First World War. A matter of weeks before Pare acquired the farm, Harry Currey's elder daughter, Audrey, had married the Reverend John Brooke; his sister, Lucy, was the wife of Maurice Pare's brother, another Harry whose name, in full, was Henry Alfred. News of Harry Currey's intention to sell Nederburg must have filtered through family channels to Maurice Pare, who was farming beyond Ceres at the time but was anxious to find a suitable property closer to Cape Town. At all

events, he bought Nederburg for £5 700, giving Harry Currey a profit of £700 on the price he had paid for it 16 years earlier. And this, considering the undoubtedly run-down condition of the farm, was a sum that was not to be sneezed at.

In 1918 the brothers Harry and Maurice Pare had been in South Africa only a short time. Of somewhat remote French ancestry, they could trace their lineage as far back as the eminent 16th-century surgeon, Ambroise Paré, regarded by some medical historians as the father of modern surgery. By the time Harry and Maurice were born the family had been settled in England for several generations and had long since dropped the unmistakably Gallic acute accent on the final letter 'e' in their name. Some time towards the latter years of the 19th century Henry William Pare and his wife

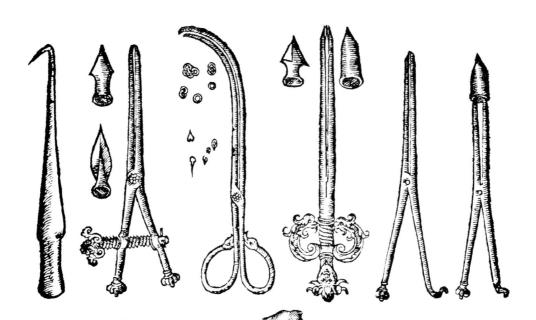

TOP

Clumsy and primitive though they may appear today, these surgical instruments (designed by Ambroise Paré, the famous 16th-century French surgeon and from whom Maurice Pare was descended) were considered extremely advanced in his day.

BOTTOM

An illustration from Paré's famous work, The Practise of Chirugery, *showing 'the fashion of a truss' applied to 'a man burst on both sides'.*

Mary had made their home in Chiswick, a charming and fashionable London suburb reaching down to the River Thames. It was in these elegant surroundings that their children — Lawrence Horton (Mary Pare's son by her first husband), Harry, Maurice and their sister Dorothy — spent their childhood. There had also been twins — a boy and girl — who were both tragically killed in early childhood when they fell out of an upstairs window. Mary Pare was a Roman Catholic (a matter which apparently caused some distress to her staunchly Protestant father-in-law) but her sons attended the famous Church of England school, St Paul's. Founded in 1509, its original home was in the Cathedral precincts, but in the 1880s it moved from the City to Hammersmith, conveniently close to Chiswick. Together, home and school provided a stimulating atmosphere in which to grow up — the brothers' school-fellows included that master of the paradox, poet and author G.K. Chesterton, and the prolific novelist, Compton Mackenzie — and at St Paul's Maurice developed an academic, if quiet, turn of mind.

Another undoubtedly powerful influence in his life — and in Harry's as well — must have been the progressive outlook of their grandfather, William Pare. He had been an ardent supporter of the London Co-operative Society, founded in 1824 and one of the earliest organizations of its kind. At a time when the movement for social reform was at its most active, it was to become one of the largest distributive co-operatives in the British

Empire and a mouthpiece for the tenets for which it stood. William Pare must have been familiar with such members of the Society as John Stuart Mill, the renowned economist and philosopher; critic and artist, John Ruskin; and Charles Kingsley, author, among many other works, of that searing and poignant comment on 19th-century child-abuse, *The Water Babies.* The London Co-operative Society had its original home in rooms at 36 Red Lion Square, where its neighbours included the Co-operative Needlewomen's Association (at Number 31), with which social reformer Olivia Hill was connected, and the firm which William Morris founded to give beauty to industrial art (at Number 8). Morris himself and the painter, Edward Burne Jones, lived for a while at Number 17 — a house formerly occupied by Dante Gabriel Rossetti. In this illustrious company William Pare was no 'also ran'. His own original works include such titles as *The Claims of Capital and Labour* (published in 1854), *Co-operative Agriculture: A Solution of the Land Question . . .* and *A Plan for the Suppression of the Predatory Classes,* this last being a paper read before the third department of the National Association for the Promotion of Social Sciences in 1862. William Pare was a delegate at the co-operative congress of 1869, a great event in the history of the co-operative movement, at which the tripartite resolution of the Christian Socialists became the basis of the Co-operative Union, with E.V. Neale as its secretary. In London's Kensal Green cemetery an obelisk bearing

Pare's name and those of 73 others commemorates 'those men and women associated with the various reform movements in the metropolis in the busy years of the last century'.

Tales of such a grandfather could not fail to have left a profound impression on the young minds of Harry and Maurice Pare, yet their parents remain shadowy characters about whom little is known. According to present-generation members of the family, Henry William Pare was a man of independent means whose literary turn of mind manifested itself in the writing of poetry. One of his poems which has survived was dedicated to Henry Alfred — or Harry — Pare on his first birthday and is an outpouring of the the poet's emotion and delight with his charming little son. What is certain is that both brothers were born in London, Harry on 26 March 1879 and Maurice on 14 May 1883. Once schooldays were over, Maurice settled for a quiet life as a clerk in a London office, but the more adventurous Harry joined the Royal Navy as an engineer. It was this choice of profession that brought him to the Cape on 18 April 1904 when his ship, H.M.S. *Crescent*, flagship of Vice-Admiral Sir John Durnford, docked in Simon's Town. And it was largely because of Harry's influence and the

TOP
H.M.S. Crescent *which brought Maurice Pare's brother, Harry, to Simon's Town in 1904. The friendships he made eventually led the Pare brothers to settle at the Cape.*
BOTTOM
Photography was one of Maurice Pare's life-long interests. Here he sets up his tripod on a desolate beach.

friends that he made during his time in Simon's Town that Maurice eventually settled in South Africa as well.

Soon after the arrival of H.M.S. *Crescent*, the ship's officers discovered that not far away, at the rectory of Holy Trinity Church, Kalk Bay, there lived three lively and uncommonly pretty sisters, Charlotte, Lucy and Helen Brooke, whose charms were such that it was worth braving the frowns of their fierce elderly father in order to secure their company. Harry Pare set his heart on Lucy, but at this stage marriage, from a financial point of view, was quite out of the question. By hook or by crook he would have to make some money before he dared to ask fiery old Archdeacon Brooke for his daughter's hand in marriage.

The solution to his problem provided itself later in that year when H.M.S. *Crescent*, while on one of her regular cruises, visited the islands of the Indian Ocean. At the club in Victoria on Mahé, the largest of the Seychelles, Harry Pare ran into a Frenchman named à Court Bergne, whom he recognized as an old friend of his stepbrother, Lawrence Horton. Bergne, who was living on the island, owned a thriving light engineering works which specialized in ship-building and repairing, but as he intended returning to Europe for the educa-

TOP
*Ninita Pare with her daughter, Elsa,
born on Mahé in the Seychelles in 1914.
A second child, Peter, was born before
the Pares left the islands.*
BOTTOM
Maurice Pare as a young married man.

tion of his three sons, he was looking at that time for a buyer for his business. To Harry Pare, this was a heaven-sent opportunity to enter the business world in his own field. A deal was struck; Harry returned to Simon's Town with his ship, announced his engagement to Lucy Brooke, went on to England and resigned from the Royal Navy. He then took a refresher course at Sir John Thornycroft's famous marine engineering works at Chiswick, where he had originally studied, and in due course sent for Lucy and married her in 1906. After a brief honeymoon in Devonshire, the young couple travelled, via Paris, Marseilles and the Suez Canal, to the Seychelles. The engineering works prospered and after a short time Harry successfully persuaded his brother Maurice, still a bachelor, to leave England and join him in the administration of the business.

Life on the Seychelles was idyllic. The Pares' home, a large colonial-style house named Belair, was situated on the top of Mahé's highest hill and blessed with glorious views on all sides. Living was cheap, the climate was almost perfect and the scenery so beautiful that General Charles 'Chinese' Gordon (of Khartoum), for one, felt sure that the islands must have been the original Garden of Eden. The social life enjoyed by the small English community was pleasant enough, but not sufficient to prevent Lucy Pare from pining for her close-knit family and her friends at the Cape. In 1909 she welcomed the arrival of her younger sister, who had come to help run the house when her second baby was born, and was overjoyed when Helen obligingly fell in love with – and became engaged to – Michael Power, a charming young Irish doctor in the colonial service. Helen returned to the Cape for her wedding, at which one of her bridesmaids was her great friend, Ninita Smith. So enchanted was Ninita by Helen's accounts of life on the islands that she made up her mind to visit her friends there as soon as she could and showed considerable courage (for those days) in travelling to the Seychelles alone. Tiny, slim and golden-haired, Ninita soon attracted the attentive interest of the reserved but kindly Maurice Pare, and when she eventually returned to her home at the Cape, he followed her with heart and mind set on matrimony. Ninita and Maurice were married on 5 November 1913 at Christ Church, Kenilworth; it was a happy and successful marriage, destined to last until Maurice Pare's death 33 years later.

As scanty as are the known facts regarding Maurice Pare's parents, so is there an abundance of information

regarding Ninita's family. Her father, Charles Thomas Smith, born in London in 1823, read for the Bar at the Inner Temple and graduated with a B.A. degree from Caius College, Cambridge in 1847. While tutoring at the University, he distinguished himself as an oarsman and in the 1854 boat race against Oxford was cox for Cambridge – this position possibly being an indication that he was small of stature. After practising at the Bar in England for some years, he sailed for the Cape in 1869 to take up the office of judge of the eastern division of the Colony's Supreme Court in Grahamstown. Here he met Emily Greathead, whom he married three years later, much to the surprise of her friends and family – they had been under the impression that the 49-year-old bachelor was courting her widowed mother, Julia. Emily belonged to an interesting and enterprising family. Her grandfather, James Henry Greathead, a land surveyor, had been leader of a party of Settlers who arrived in Algoa Bay in April 1820 on board the *Kennersley Castle* and eventually settled in Bathurst. They brought with them their first child, the second James Henry, later to become a member of the Legislative Council for Albany, husband of Julia Wright, also of 1820 Settler stock, and father of 12 children. Among them was a third James Henry, born in Grahamstown in

PAGE 74: TOP
The Pare children photographed soon after they left Nederburg in 1924. Left to right: Nancy, Elsa, Timothy, Eileen and Peter.
BOTTOM LEFT
Courting days on the luxuriant Seychelles: Maurice Pare and a coy Ninita Smith.
BOTTOM RIGHT
In pinafore and rompers, Elsa Pare and brother Peter at play on Nederburg's stoep.
PAGE 75
Known to the Pare children as 'Yanu', their nanny had accompanied them from the Seychelles but Maurice had to 'pull strings' to obtain permission for her to remain in South Africa.

1844, who achieved considerable distinction as the engineer who designed London's famous and intricate underground electrified railway, opened in 1890. Emily was his sister.

Charles Thomas and Emily Smith produced five sons and two daughters, the last of whom was Agnes Ninita, born on 5 March 1888. Her unusual second name, by which she was always known, was a Spanish diminutive meaning 'little girl', and had been the nickname of a Mexican-born Greathead great-aunt baptized, somewhat cumbersomely, Maria la Guadeloup Anna Antonia. When Ninita was four years old her father retired from the Bench and the family moved to Rosebank at the Cape, where they lived until Judge Smith's death on 10 February 1901. The widowed Emily then decided to take Ninita and her elder sister, Adeline, to England to complete their education. A suitable school at Folkestone was selected and after they had spent some time there the girls moved on to another school in Paris, where they lived with a Russian family who provided suitably chaperoned accommodation for 'young ladies from good homes'. Living in this household proved a culturally stimulating experience for Ninita, whose association with her hosts aroused a great love of all things Russian which she retained

throughout her life. The French school, too, influenced the girls' development considerably for it was extremely progressive: the curriculum included a study of electricity, at which Ninita excelled – not surprisingly, perhaps, for someone whose uncle had been the creator of London's tube train system. The practical knowledge she acquired in this subject must have stood her in good stead later on – for how many women of her generation knew how to mend a fuse or attach an electric plug?

However, in the Seychelles, to which Ninita came as a bride, these were skills that were not required of her at that moment in the world's history. In what truly seemed the land of afternoon she became mistress of a colonial-style house with plenty of ready and willing servants. On Mahé she joyfully joined her friends, Lucy Pare and Helen Power, now with five toddlers between them, and before the year 1914 was out she, too, was the proud mother of a baby daughter, Elsa Mary. But paradise on earth is merely transitory, it seems. The outbreak of the First World War in August 1914 put paid to the Pares' and Powers' idyll on the Seychelles. Fired with the infectious patriotism of the time, Mick Power decided to abandon the colonial service and join up. With Helen and the children, including Harry and Lucy's elder son, who was ready to go to school, they set sail from Mahé in the S.S. *Palatana*, a rusty old tub that was barely seaworthy. One can imagine with what emo-

TOP LEFT
Maurice Pare seated beside a wine vat outside Nederburg's old cellar. In an attempt to make really good wine, he invested a considerable amount of money in improving both buildings and equipment.
TOP RIGHT
With the Klein Drakenstein mountains as a backdrop, Maurice Pare 'introduces' his wife, Ninita, and children, Peter and Elsa, to one of the many fruit trees that he planted.

tions Lucy and Ninita saw them off as they clambered aboard the insalubrious vessel and waved goodbye for ever to their beautiful island paradise. Once at the Cape, Mick Power joined the South African forces as a medical officer and was later one of the few and fortunate survivors of the horror of Delville Wood in 1916.

Meanwhile at the Cape, relatives of the Pares still in the Seychelles were more than a little uneasy about them, for German surface raiders were known to be skulking about the Indian Ocean and presenting a constant threat to the islands. Eventually, early in 1915, Harry Pare sent Lucy and her two younger children back to the Cape and a hazardous voyage they had to say the least, for they were pursued all the way by the German raider, the *Emden*. Ninita, meanwhile, had remained at Mahé, where the Pare brothers were doomed to frustration in their attempts to go to war. Maurice, who was extremely short-sighted, was rejected on medical grounds, though he did manage to serve with the Seychelles defence force, while Harry, who had tried to re-join the Royal Navy, was firmly told by the admiralty that he would be of greater use to them in the Seychelles making certain that no German battleships were allowed to call at Mahé for refuelling, watering or for repairs.

Eventually, thwarted by bureaucracy and poor communications and apparently unwanted in the active

forces, Maurice and Harry Pare abandoned the Seychelles and returned to the Cape to seek a different means of earning their living. In 1917 Harry bought a farm in the Ceres district, changing its name from Dassieklip to Cascade, while Maurice, who had brought Ninita and her two children back from the Seychelles with him, acquired the adjoining property. He called it Petervale in honour of his small son, Peter Irvine, who had been born in January 1916. Harry worked hard to make a success of his new acquisition, but very soon Maurice realized that his project had little potential for success. Besides, he had heard that Harry Currey had decided to sell his farm at Klein Drakenstein and that, so he decided, was an opportunity not to be missed. He made his offer, paid his money and on 28 May 1918, while the war continued to rage in Europe, became Nederburg's sixth owner.

Maurice Pare, short, stocky, affectionate but somewhat retiring by nature, was 35 years old when he settled in South Africa. He had never had any experience of agriculture when he bought Nederburg, but in those days, before academic qualifications were considered a prerequisite for almost every career, it was believed that determination, hard work and a certain feeling for the soil were all that were necessary to make a good farmer. Maurice Pare certainly had all these qualities and a powerful interest in wine production besides. Yet, as

TOP
Maurice Pare enlists the help of two labourers to spray Nederburg's orchards. In the early 1920s horse-drawn wagons were still commonly used for heavy-duty farm work.

every farmer knows, there are invariably setbacks that no one can anticipate. One of these that was to affect Nederburg within six months of the Pares' arrival was the disastrous epidemic of Spanish influenza that struck the Cape in the 'Black October' of 1918 and, with the grief and tragedy that it brought, clouded the joyful tidings of the war's end on 11 November.

Working at Nederburg at the time was a youth named Bayman Jacobs. His parents, as he says today, 'lived in the bush' and never bothered to send him to school, but this lack of formal education in no way dulled his wits. He was perhaps 16 years old — he does not know when he was born — when the 'flu epidemic reached the Klein Drakenstein area and it was his task to help care for Nederburg's sick. He describes how the *solder* above the stables was converted into a makeshift ward and how he carried the patients' food from the homestead — mostly bowls of steaming soup — covering his mouth and nose first with a clean handkerchief. Bayman's iron constitution — it has enabled him to live past his 90th year — obviously protected him from the disease that killed over 6 000 people in Cape Town and its suburbs alone, but the memory of the *griep* and its horrors remains vividly with him.

It was an anxious time for Maurice Pare, too, for when things were at their worst Ninita, who was not strong, gave birth to Nancy Dorothy, her third child

22/11/8.

Dear Mr Merriman,

I am enclosing a letter from Pretoria which speaks for itself.

Can really nothing be done in this matter? Ninita has just had a baby, & servants are quite impossible to obtain in Paarl.

If Ninita were a strong person it would be different, but she is a long way off being so, & in Seychelles she had excellent servants.

The old nurse they want to send back is the only one we have here, except a "help", who is not a help.

It really does seem carrying the Immigration law to an absurd extreme, when settlers coming here from the East are not allowed to bring at least one old & tried servant. Particularly so, in this case, as she is of pure African blood.

I also mention that the old woman is quite contented here, is much attached to the family, is over the age for having more children, & has no desire to be turned out.

I hope you will kindly forgive my troubling you in this matter, especially after all the trouble you have taken in the first instance, but I should be very grateful for your advice as to whether it is any

LEFT
Nancy Pare's birth at Nederburg towards the end of 1918 led Maurice to write to John X. Merriman asking him to use his influence in obtaining permission for the 'old nurse' to remain with the family.

RIGHT
An advertisement for the annual wine show held by the Western Province Agricultural Society. Maurice Pare's white wine was highly commended.

and the first to be born at Nederburg. At this time the immigration authorities were threatening to deport the faithful nurse who had cared for the Pare children since they were born and had accompanied them from the Seychelles. On 22 November 1918, with the armistice barely signed and the epidemic not yet over, Pare wrote an impassioned personal letter to John X. Merriman mentioning neither of these dramatic events. Instead, he begged the erstwhile Cape prime minister to use his influence with the authorities in Pretoria and obtain permission for the 'old woman' to remain, emphasizing that she was 'much attached to the family [and] . . . over the age for having more children'. It seems his plea was successful for old Yanu, as her charges called her, remained with the Pares and nursed two more children who were later born at Nederburg – Eileen Ninita in 1921 and Timothy Charles Maurice in 1923. Another permanent member of the Pare ménage at Nederburg was Ninita's mother's sister, Rosa Greathead, who occupied one of the front bedrooms and ruled the children with all the traditional severity of a Victorian maiden aunt.

Meanwhile, Maurice Pare set about renovating the cellar: the fittings and equipment were improved, a new floor was laid and nine concrete fermenting tanks were installed. Distilling wine was sent to one of the cooperatives that had sprung up locally over the past 15 years and the bulk of the 'good' wine (as opposed to the wine for distilling) that he pressed was exported. On 28 June 1921 a memorandum was drawn up between

Maurice Pare and the well-known London wine merchants, P. B. Burgoyne & Co., by which it was agreed that each year until 1930, a minimum of ten leaguers of Nederburg's red wines and 40 leaguers of white were to be delivered to them through their Cape Town agents, Charles du P. Chiappini. In the days before it was necessary to build into contracts a clause covering anticipated inflation, the price laid down per leaguer of red wine was £12, while that for a leaguer of white wine was £11. (Wine prices had been quoted in sterling since the mid-19th century.) The merchants, naturally, had to protect themselves against the acceptance of an inferior product, so it was agreed that if, after the fifth vintage, the wine proved to be below standard, Burgoyne's, whose agents had the right to inspect it before shipment, could terminate the contract by giving Maurice Pare six months' notice. An important paragraph in the memorandum ensured that if 'the seller' (Pare, or his executors in the event of his death) should decide to sell Nederburg, the purchaser would take over the contract and carry out all the previous owner's obligations.

This contract was signed in Cape Town even though Maurice Pare made a point of keeping in personal touch with his customers abroad. A story is told of how, while on a marketing visit in Europe, he called on a French farmer, who invited him to join him at a meal. When he commented on the excellence of the wine he had been offered, his host laughingly informed him that it had come from Nederburg. 'That can't be possible!' exclaimed Pare, who knew only too well the taste of his own wine. 'What on earth have you done to it?'

'Merely put it into some very old casks to mature,' answered the farmer, 'and you're sampling the result!'

There were apricot orchards on Nederburg when Maurice Pare took it over. He planted more trees, favouring the 'Royal' cultivar, and there were also numerous guavas, peaches and apples in addition to about 40 000 vines, mostly of the Hermitage (Sémillon) cultivar. A herd of cows provided Nederburg's household with milk and butter; six stables housed the horses and mules used to plough the lands and, to provide their food, fields were planted with various kinds of forage. Bedevilled by the south-easter, Nederburg was planted with a windbreak of 7 000 Pinus insignis, but even this could not prevent the young fruit from being blown off the trees when the prevailing early summer gales were doing their worst.

Maurice Pare was a young man and he worked hard, but despite his serious hopes of producing really good wines and of making a financial success of his farm, Nederburg did not prosper as he had intended. No matter how promising the fruit crops, summer after summer the south-easter returned to wreak havoc on the unprotected orchards, stripping fruit from the trees before it was ripe. He was more successful with his export wines and in the early 1920s signed a contract with a London company in which the fixed price of £11 a leaguer was guaranteed until the year 1931. As regards the poorer-quality distilling wine — inevitably and invariably considerably more plentiful than 'good' wine — alas, this was to prove his financial downfall.

Ironically, bearing in mind the past history of the Pare family, the reason for this lay in the developing co-operative movement in the Cape. The five years following 1918, when the K.W.V. was officially founded, had seen a gratifying improvement in the financial situation of most of those wine farmers who had become members of the organization. Wine producers who had been paid only £2. 10s. per leaguer in 1917, now found themselves the happy recipients of at least £5 for wine used for distilling brandy and spirits and £7 for table wine. Things were not so good after 1921, when the industry again experienced a slump and the perennial bugbear of a wine surplus forced the K.W.V. to intervene and fix a lower minimum price — a mere £3 per leaguer for the greater part of the crop. Various forces combined to depress the wine industry yet further and the future of the K.W.V. appeared bleak indeed until, in 1923, the Union Government promulgated the Wine & Spirit Act of 1924. This Act stipulated that any farmer wishing to sell wine for distilling purposes had first to obtain permission from the K.W.V.; it also made it illegal to buy or sell wine at a price lower than that which had been officially laid down. As a result an increasing number of farmers realized the benefits to be gained from joining the organization, which from this time on went from strength to strength.

In the face of mounting and relentless competition from the K.W.V., the smaller co-operatives that had come into existence earlier in the century found it increasingly difficult to maintain their livelihood. Maurice Pare was among those farmers who had supplied his wine for distilling to one of these less powerful companies, and when it fell, he fell with it. It was the custom to pay the farmers an advance — a voorskot — when the wine was delivered to the co-op and a final and usually a considerably larger sum — the agterskot — at the end of the season. At the beginning of the 1923 harvest, the co-operative company to whom Maurice Pare supplied his wine for distilling paid the voorskot as usual, but by the time the agterskot was due, its coffers were empty and it had gone out of business. Maurice Pare struggled on at Nederburg until the end of 1923, but several months before that he realized that there was no alternative but to put the farm onto the market. Although he had faced up to the reality of his shattered dreams, he must surely have felt a pang to see, spread across two columns of the Cape Argus of Saturday 15 December 1923,

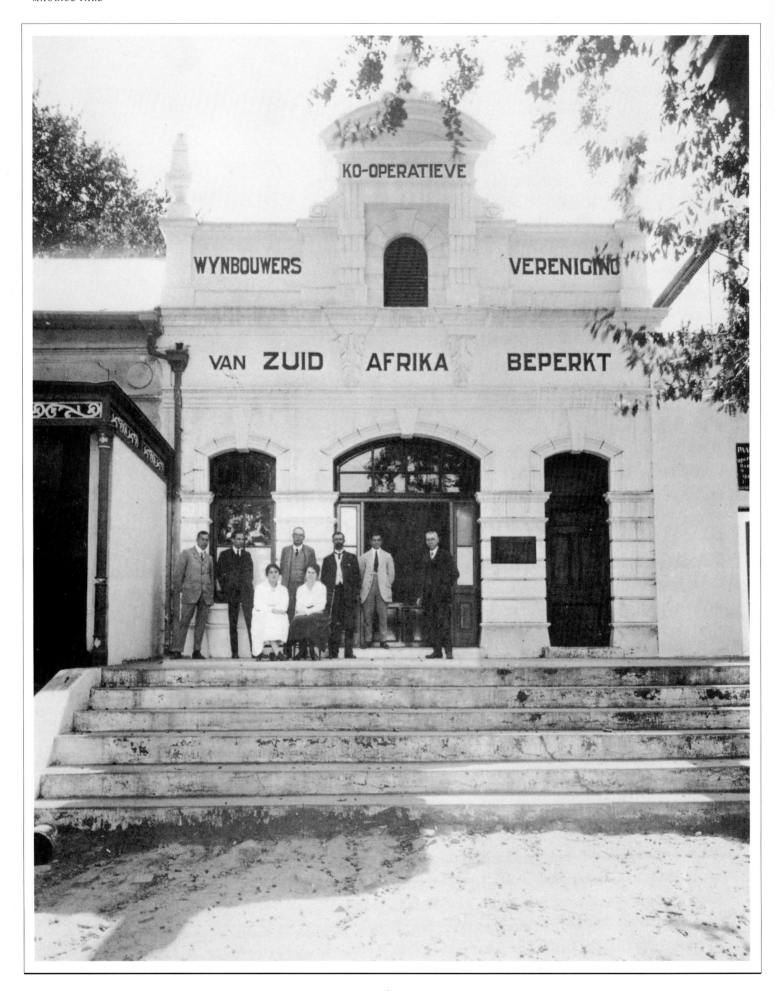

an advertisement for the sale by public auction of 'the famous and historic wine, fruit and tobacco farm, "Nederburg"'. The advertisement gives a detailed — and glowing — description of the house, proudly stating that it was 'one of the finest and best preserved specimens in the country'. At first glance, it is a little difficult to accept the auctioneers' claim that Nederburg contained nine rooms, since the house built by Philippus Bernardus Wolvaart in 1800 had only had five, but at some stage (probably in the days of the fastidious Harry Currey) the two front bedrooms had been divided to give each one its own dressing room. The third bedroom had been turned into two smaller rooms and the back hall had become a breakfast room. Mention is made of the beautiful teak screen (restored by Harry Currey) and the tiled dining hall — once the *agterkamer* — with its magnificent 'Antique Wall Cupboard, in a perfect state of preservation and of great value'. By then a bathroom with piped hot and cold water had been added within one of the courts of the original 'H' plan and the house could boast a 'telephone and all conveniences'. Finally, the advertisement comments on the 'splendid Tiled Stoep' extending right round the whole house, adding the claim that 'this is one of the few remaining Dutch Homesteads with all its original Brass and Antique fittings'.

It sounded attractive enough, especially as the land had been surveyed so that it could be divided into three sections, each to be sold separately. History, it seems, does not record what happened at the sale which the auctioneers, Messrs Faure & Lewis, had set for Tuesday 18 December 1923 at 11 a.m. 'on the spot'. Certainly no reports of the event have been traced in local or Cape Town newspapers, but it appears that none of the bids made on that occasion was considered acceptable. Perhaps the sale failed because the week before Christmas — when the entire south-western Cape abandons itself to total preoccupation with the festivities of the silly season — is hardly a suitable time to sell an important property; or perhaps it was because Maurice Pare had placed too ambitious a reserve price on his farm. Be that as it may, Nederburg remained on the market until the Christmas holidays were over. It was only in mid-February 1924 that it was seen for the first time by the remarkable man who was to become its seventh owner.

Maurice Pare, meanwhile, moved with his family to Cape Town. Here, true to family tradition, he took over the management of the South African Fruit Growers' Co-operative Exchange, a company that still exists under the name of the Co-operative Shipping Service. With his customary diligence, Maurice Pare built it up into a successful business with branches in other South African sea ports. It was on a visit to the Port Elizabeth office that he died suddenly on 21 August 1946, leaving Ninita to outlive him by nearly 20 years. ∎

PAGE 80
An early photograph of the K.W.V. building in Paarl. The co-operative was formed in 1918 and, in the years that followed, was largely responsible for stabilizing the Cape wine industry. Maurice Pare, at Nederburg, was the loser when the small co-operative company to which he sent his wine, went into liquidation.
PAGE 81
In the Cape Argus of 15 December 1923 notice was given of the auction of Nederburg — 'one of the finest estates in the Western Province' — for the following Tuesday. The advertisement gives interesting details of both the homestead and the farm at the time.

PAARL DISTRICT.

One of the Finest Estates in the Western Province in the Market.

A GRAND OPPORTUNITY FOR THE LARGE AND SMALL BUYER.

THE FAMOUS AND HISTORIC
Wine, Fruit and Tobacco Farm,
"NEDERBURG,"
with its Beautiful Old Dutch Homestead,
SITUATED IN THE FERTILE KLEIN DRAKENSTEIN VALLEY,
to be Sold at Public Auction,
On Tuesday, 18th Dec.,
AT 11 A.M., ON THE SPOT.

MESSRS. FAURE & LEWIS, duly instructed by the Owner, MR. M. PARE, who contemplates an extensive absence overseas, will submit to Public Competition his Beautiful Farm, "NEDERBURG," on the above date.

To suit all tastes, the place has been judiciously subdivided into Four Separate Portions, each portion being fully fenced and having an outlet on to the Main Road to Paarl.

The separate portions will first be put up provisionally, and thereafter an opportunity will be given to acquire the whole Farm.

A river forms the boundary, and extends along all four subdivided portions.

PORTION "A."—This is the main portion, in extent 66 morgen, with the historic Dutch Homestead, dated 1800 (surrounded by lovely Oaks), one of the finest and best preserved specimens in the country, containing nine (9) Rooms, including a fine Entrance Lounge, separated by a magnificent Teak Screen from the large Tiled Dining Hall, in which is fitted a beautiful Antique Wall Cupboard, in a perfect state of preservation and of great value. There is a Kitchen, Pantry and Bathroom with hot and cold water laid on, Telephone and all conveniences, whilst a splendid Tiled Stoep extends right round the whole Homestead. This is one of the few remaining Dutch Homesteads, with all its original Brass and Antique Fittings, so often found missing in most houses of a similar character.

The Wine Cellar is up-to-date, with concrete floors and nine concrete fermenting tanks. The present Owner has spent nearly £1,000 alone on the fittings and equipment of this Cellar.

There is a well-built Manager's House of 5 large Rooms and Kitchen, Coachhouse, Stabling for 16 horses, large Cowshed and 3 large Stone Kraals.

The Purchaser will not have to worry about finding a market for his wine, for this has been sold as far ahead as 1931 at £11 per leaguer, and as the wines sent over to London have been most favourably reported on, there is every likelihood of further renewal of present contract.

The lands are planted with about 40,000 vines in deep alluvial soil, and there are about 13,000 fruit trees of best varieties, all in full bearing; also about 7,000 Pinis Insignis trees have been established, whilst there is a large area of land for further development.

The water supply is more than ample. A strong irrigation stream runs all the year, whilst the Palmiet River also runs through the Farm. In addition, the present Owner put down a Borehole, which has been tested out at 40,000 gallons per day.

PORTION "B."—This portion is 22 morgen in extent, and has about 2,000 bearing Apricot trees from four to eight years old, mostly Royals. The whole Orchard is in first-class condition and is cropping heavily. There is a valuable stone-pine wood of beautiful trees, with a magnificent Residential Site adjoining, commanding extensive views in all directions.

There is plenty of scope for further development in the way of export vines, trees and tobacco.

PORTION "C."—20 morgen of land, with 600 Royal Apricot trees, and all the remaining ground most valuable for vines, tobacco and fruit trees, plenty of Timber and an ideal Residential Site.

PORTION "D."—A piece of land 12 morgen in extent, which has been sown in previous years, and very suitable for fruit, tobacco and vines, every part of which can be utilised.

The Divisional Council Hard Road to Huguenot Station forms the boundary of all three portions, "B," "C" and "D."

SITUATION.—The Farm is ideally situated in a most healthy part of the District, within three miles of the Huguenot Railway Station, with a beautiful Hard Road leading right to the door. The close proximity to Railway and Markets renders this an ideal proposition for the export trade. Everything is in tip-top order.

In addition to the Oak and Fir Groves on the Estate, there are numbers of lovely wild olives and willows.

An Estate such as this only comes into the market once in a lifetime

ROBERT ADOLPHUS LYALL:

OFFICER AND GENTLEMAN 1924-1937

Colonel 'Bob' Lyall was 47 years old when he acquired Nederburg, having previously distinguished himself as a soldier in the Indian political service and as a British diplomat. He dreamt of producing superior quality wine but could not overcome the destructive effects on fermentation of Paarl's excessive heat. Eventually the Great Depression forced Lyall to abandon farming and return to England. Nederburg's first recorded prize was won by his wine in 1926.

Colonel Robert Adolphus Lyall, a man of vision, gazes over Nederburg's fields and vineyards towards the lofty Klein Drakenstein mountains

82

industry and character and shown . . . a creditable interest in his work.' On leaving school Robert Adolphus entered the Royal Military College at Sandhurst, where he continued to shine in sport and became heavy-weight boxing champion. To his disappointment he did not achieve a high enough pass for acceptance in the Indian Army but instead obtained a commission in the Gordon Highlanders and in 1897 set sail for Bombay.

In a way the youthful 'Bob' Lyall was going home, for his early childhood had been spent in India and for many years his father's family had been closely associated with the fortunes and administration of that jewel in Queen Victoria's crown. A great-uncle, George Lyall,

army class. Here he gave satisfaction in every way, dis-

tinguishing himself as a sportsman and coming second

in examinations at the end of the 1892 Michaelmas

Half, a few weeks short of his 16th birthday. His house-

master's comment on his school report at this time

reads: 'He has created a very favourable impression as to

had been chairman of the East India Company and his father, Alfred Comyn Lyall, born in 1835, had risen rapidly in the Indian civil service to become foreign secretary to the government of India in 1878 and, three years later, lieutenant-governor of the North-West Provinces and Oudh. Alfred Lyall was, besides, a writer of outstanding ability and achieved distinction both as the author of serious philosophical works and as a poet of imagination and sensitivity. Not surprisingly, it was India — its religions and history, its mystery and the compelling splendour of its landscapes — that often proved the source of his inspiration. Alfred Lyall's achievements in the political sphere did not go unnoticed and his record of honours reads like an intellectual inventory. In 1887 he was made a Knight Commander of the Indian Empire; in 1896 he was promoted to be a Knight Grand Commander of the Indian Empire and on his retirement from the India Office in 1902 he was made a privy councillor. As a philosopher and man of letters, he was honoured by England's two greatest universities: from Oxford he received the degree of D.C.L., while Cambridge granted him an honorary LL. D. and a fellowship of King's College. He was also a fellow of the British Academy and a member of the Academic Committee of the Royal Society of Literature.

With such a record, not to mention the Victorian demand for unquestioning respect from the young, Sir Alfred Lyall must have been regarded with considerable awe by his four children — Robert Adolphus was the younger of the two sons. Yet in his personal writings he

TOP
Much honoured both academically and for his service to the Victorian Empire, Sir Alfred Comyn Lyall chose a South African as his bride in 1862.
BOTTOM
Robert Lyall's mother, born Cornelia Arnoldina Cloete in 1842. It was a search for her home at Great Westerford in Newlands that brought Colonel Lyall to South Africa in 1923.

reveals himself as a man of warmth and considerable humour. And of course, once babyhood was over, the children could have seen little of him for, as was the sad custom of those days, one by one they were packed off to boarding school half a world away in England. One can only guess at the anguish with which their mother must have parted with them: according to her husband's biographer she was not a good correspondent and she apparently kept no diaries. We are, however, left with Sir Alfred's own account of how, early in 1885 as he watched eight-year-old Bob waving forlornly to him from the ship that was to carry him from Bombay to England, he was 'moved to something like tears'.

Alfred Lyall's wife, Cora, was a South African and it was this fact that in the fullness of time brought her son to explore his origins in the Cape — and to buy Nederburg. Born Cornelia Arnoldina Cloete in 1842, the year in which her young father, Pieter Gerhard, died, she belonged to one of the Cape's oldest and best-known families. Jacob Cloete, or Kluten, forefather of all the Cloetes in South Africa, was a Hollander who splashed ashore in 1652 with the Cape's first commander, Jan van Riebeeck, and bequeathed to his country of adoption descendants that, like Abraham's, are as abundant 'as the stars of the heaven and as the sand which is upon the sea shore'. Most famous among them was his great-grandson, Hendrik, born in 1725; it was he who became master of Groot Constantia's broad acres, where he produced what was perhaps the most prized wine ever to be pressed from Cape grapes. The

Cloetes prospered and became wealthy land-owners, one branch of the family acquiring a swathe of the eastern slopes of Table Mountain sweeping up from the point where the wagon road to Wynberg crossed the Liesbeek River. In this area they owned at least two water mills as well as the old estate, Groot Westervoort, which, in accordance with the current fashion, the Cloetes of the mid-19th century Cape Colony, re-named 'Great Westerford'. It was in this house, now sadly demolished in favour of a giant insurance company, that Cora Cloete, great-great granddaughter of Hendrik of Constantia, was born.

Nothing is known of her early childhood, but when she was in her teens she left home for India to visit two of her father's young cousins, sisters named Catharina Dorothea Shuckburgh and Charlotte Smith, who had married English army officers. It was usual, in the days of the British raj, for officers and civil servants on furlough from India to call at Cape Town *en route* for England; unwilling to face the dreariness of a winter in Europe after the sunshine of India, they often preferred to spend their leave at the Cape and it may have been in this way that Captain Shuckburgh and Dr Smith met the Cloete sisters. At all events, they married them and took them back to India with them and it so happened that Cora was their guest when the terror of the Indian Mutiny erupted in May 1857. Cora and her cousins survived; so, unknown to them, did 22-year-old Alfred Lyall — even though at a critical moment he had to escape from his bungalow on horseback while being fired on by rebels. At that stage Alfred was holding his first appointment at Bulandshahr not far from Delhi, but in 1857 neither he nor Cora was aware of the other's existence. Five years were to pass before they met in England, where Alfred was on leave from India, while Cora was probably visiting another family of Cloete cousins who had settled there and become completely anglicized.

Alfred married Cora in Cavendish parish church on 12 November 1862 and proudly took her back to India, where he held the post of assistant magistrate at Agra. Here they lived in a house which had a sweeping view over the Jumna River, on the far side of which stood the Taj Mahal in the shimmering beauty of its glinting domes and minarets. Agra was one of the hottest yet most pleasant stations in the North-West Provinces and during the first months of their marriage Cora, who was lively and abounding in good health, delighted in exhibiting her skills in archery, croquet and horsemanship. Clearly her South African background — a relaxed, informal way of life spent largely in the open air — had prepared her well for what lay in store for her in India. 'She has great nerve,' wrote Alfred, 'and can beat me at riding and at all things

which a man and woman can both do.' In the following December they rejoiced at the birth of their first child, a daughter called Sophia; a son, Alfred, and a second daughter, Evelina, arrived in 1867 and 1868 respectively. And then, after a break of eight years, Robert Adolphus, the afterthought, was born. In giving him the name 'Adolphus' — an unusual one for an Englishman — Alfred Lyall was expressing his admiration for his friend and kinsman, Adolphus de Kantzow, an officer of the Indian Army whom he greatly admired.

From his earliest boyhood Bob Lyall's heart was set on the army and it must have been a proud day when he first put on the romantic uniform of the Gordon Highlanders. Raised in 1787 as the 75th Highland Regiment of Foot, they had seen action on many battlefields and as recently as 1885 had been among the troops that had marched on Khartoum in a brave but futile attempt to relieve the trapped General Charles 'Chinese' Gordon. After leaving the Sudan, the Gordon Highlanders went on to India's North-West Frontier, where they arrived in 1888. The area generally was unsettled at the time, but life passed relatively uneventfully for them until 1895, when they took part in a successful action to rescue the British agent besieged by Pathan rebels in the town of Chitral. It was two years later that young Second Lieutenant R.A. Lyall, fresh from Sandhurst, arrived in India to join the Gordon Highlanders and very soon afterwards found himself in the thick of action.

Since 10 May, when tribesmen had attacked a British political officer travelling through one of the Frontier's remote valleys and killed his escort of 26 officers and soldiers, the situation had been explosive. Matters came to a head on 23 August when the Gordons were attacked by Alfridi tribesmen near the entrance to the Khyber Pass. Some of the British, it seems, enjoyed the fury of battle. 'It was splendid,' wrote an officer, 'to see the way they [the Gordon Highlanders] got the range (3 200 yards) and dropped shell after shell into the enemy's position, while the noise made by the reverberation of the guns in the pass was magnificent.' Unfortunately for the British, despite the accurate fire, the Alfridis succeeded in taking the fort and in so doing secured the Khyber Pass.

Records of this action show that Second Lieutenant Lyall was among the 801 troops involved. Afterwards the Gordon Highlanders withdrew to lick their wounds, remaining inactive at the Fort of Jamrud for almost two months. Then, on 18 and 20 October, they were once more involved in stirring and bloody action at the storming of the Dargai Heights, a battle which, as one chronicler put it, 'abounds in incidents famous in Frontier song and story'. One of these tells of the courage of the young piper, both legs shot through, who continued to pipe on, undaunted by pain or the din and

dust of battle, while sitting on the stony ground. His was one of two Victoria Crosses awarded for valour displayed during this engagement.

Alas for Second Lieutenant Lyall, he was not present to share in the triumph of the Dargai Heights. Shortly before, he had collapsed with a violent attack of fever and had been rushed to hospital at Peshawar. For weeks during the preceding September and October he had endured the discomforts of the overcrowded fort at Jamrud and he was acutely frustrated to have missed the excitement of battle when the time for action arrived at long last. 'Poor Bob!' wrote his father in a letter. 'He writes in greatest distress and disappointment . . . In spite of all the risks I am much troubled at his ill-luck for he will never again have such a chance as he has lost by not being with the Gordon Highlanders in that brilliant action . . .' The day after the storming of the Dargai Heights, when his colleagues were no doubt recovering and rejoicing, Robert Adolphus Lyall celebrated his 21st birthday prostrate in his hospital bed. The malaria that had struck him down was to recur and haunt him for the rest of his life.

PAGE 86: TOP
His long sjambok over his shoulder, the reaper drives his team of mules into Nederburg's fields for the in-gathering of the 1925 harvest.
BOTTOM
Colonel Lyall's threshing machine was the very latest model available when Nederburg's grain harvest was garnered in 1925.
PAGE 87
Early married days at Nederburg. After being separated soon after their London wedding in June 1924, the Lyalls did not meet again until 'Bob' joined Catharine at the Cape in October 1925.

The Gordon Highlanders remained in India for almost a year, sailing from Bombay for England on 7 October 1898. Robert Lyall, now attached to the 32nd Regiment of the Bengal Infantry, stayed on, but when troubles started in China in 1900 took advantage of the leave due to him and volunteered for service with the 34th Pioneers, an Indian infantry battalion attached to the China Expeditionary Force. For a long time trouble had been brewing in and around Peking. Escalating economic impoverishment, a series of natural disasters and rampant foreign aggression give rise to an uprising led by members of a Chinese secret society. Known as the Boxers (their official name, in translation, was The Righteous and Harmonious Fists), they practised certain boxing and calisthenic rites, believing that these gave them supernatural powers and made them impervious to bullets. Their main object was to drive out foreigners and, incensed by the activities of missionaries, to kill all Christians on Chinese soil. The Boxers directed their initial attacks against the ill-equipped foreign legations in Tientsin and Peking and by the end of May 1900 a full-scale bloody conflict had

Note on Water rights

Contract dt 23rd January 1805.
Parties to the contract were —
  J. Cilliers (Dekensvlei)
  J.R. Louw
  Widow de Villiers
  P.B. Wolfard (Nederburg)
  Widow du Toit (Orleans)
Contract takes effect from 1 Oct to 30 April each year.
Cilliers who possesses other water than the Palmiet 48 hours 1st & 2nd Oct. Proviso must allow drinking water to pass. No drinking water for himself as he has other water.
Louw 72 hours Widow de Villiers 72 hours Wolfard 60 hours. Proviso these three must allow drinking water to pass.
Widow du Toit 60 hours. No proviso re drinking water.
After Widow du Toit turns begin again from the top.
—
This agreement was upheld in du Toit vs Malherbe. Menzies Vol II p 317 with the following exception.
Widow de Villiers to have 96 hours instead of 72 hours, while Widow Malherbe (part of Cilliers-Dekensvlei) was allowed drinking water only to be lead back to main stream.
—
Note
The proportions are therefore —

Dekensvlei.	2 days	48 hours
Louw	3 days	72 hours
Widow de Villiers	4 days	96 hours
Nederburg	2½ days	60 hours
Orleans	2½ days	60 hours
Total	14 days	

Nederburg's share should be received every 14 days.

How much of the Nederburg water rights ... was sold ... with the present part of Nederburg held by Widow Malherbe & de Villiers respectively?

Irrigation presents a perennial problem to South African farmers. With his customary meticulousness, Colonel Lyall made this 'note' of Nederburg's water rights which dated back to the days of Philippus Bernardus Wolvaart.

erupted, just at a time when Great Britain was entirely preoccupied with the war in South Africa. Thousands were killed in northern China before international relief forces could reach this remote part of the world, but eventually, on 14 August, a combined military offensive attacked and captured Peking, releasing the foreigners and Christians who had been besieged there for nearly two months. Hostilities — and they were brutal to say the least — did not cease until a protocol was signed in September 1901.

How far Robert Lyall was involved in the action in China is not certain as none of his letters or diaries has survived from this period. However, it is known that he was recalled from leave in mid-July 1900 and soon afterwards sailed from Bombay for Tientsin with the 34th Sikh Pioneers and a large force of Indian troops. By the time they arrived in China, the worst of the battles were over, so it was the task of the Pioneers first to 'mop up' roving bands of Boxers who were causing mayhem in the country between Tientsin and Tu Lieu, 32 miles away, and then to capture some forts at Pei-Tang on the mouth of the Lutai River.

Before 1901 was out Robert Lyall had been promoted to lieutenant and was back in India. He had survived the bloodshed in China, but his elder brother, Alfred, fighting in an equally horrifying war thousands of miles away, had not been so fortunate. It must have grieved the heart of his Cape-born mother to think of him dying, not in the glory of battle but, like so many others, of fever in a makeshift South African hospital. By the time Robert received news of Alfred's death he was attached to another battalion of the Bengal Infantry —

the 32nd Sikh Pioneers. Like the other Pioneer battalions, the 32nd were hewers of wood and drawers of water; they carried heavy equipment and were trained as road-makers and as 'rough railway engineers'. Raised in 1857, when volunteers were needed to quell the Mutiny, the 32nd Sikhs distinguished themselves when, with a convoy of 150 carts and 200 camels, they marched into Delhi and fought their way into the very centre of the city. Their headquarters were in the mountain town of Chitral, but for the next two years Robert Lyall was to be stationed with them some distance to the south at Jhelum, situated on one of the five rivers of the Punjab that drain into the Indus.

Records of 1903 show that in this year Robert Lyall's services were placed at the disposal of the Foreign Department of the Government of India. In other words, he was appointed a political officer and in this capacity held various posts over the following ten years. By the time the First World War broke out in 1914 he held the rank of captain and the responsible position of political agent in the district of Kurram, a beautiful and fertile area that had once been an Afghan stronghold. Immediately, he set about pulling every string he knew to obtain release from the Indian civil service so that he could go to war. He applied to the most senior civil servants he knew for extended leave, or, if they could not grant it, requested them to accept his resignation. He wrote to high-ranking army officers appealing for their support, even offering them his motor car — a rare commodity in those days — boasting that it could do 30 miles an hour on the straight and would undoubtedly be of use on the field of battle. Correspondence piled up and the replies to his letters, though polite and sympathetic, were not encouraging. He was told that specially good men (an inferred compliment to him) were needed in civilian capacities on the Frontier; that leave was out of the question and that his resignation would on no account be accepted. However, at last there did appear a glimmer of hope: he was advised to apply for recall to the Military Department in place of an officer whose recall orders had been issued by the Indian government. Captain Lyall lost no time in setting this particular wheel turning. Backwards and forwards flew the telegrams and the last of them, despatched by the chief commissioner of the North-West Frontier Provinces on 29 October 1914, read: 'Your services will be temporarily placed at the disposal of His Excellency the Commander-in-Chief . . . You may expect to receive orders direct from military authorities.'

Two tedious months later they arrived. Captain Robert Lyall raised a regiment — the 2nd Kashmir Rifles — from local volunteers and with them, early in January 1915, set sail for East Africa to join the British and South African troops bent on driving the Germans

Winter scene at Nederburg.
This unspoilt view of the back of the
house was familiar to the Lyalls; it was lost
when substantial additions were made
in the 1930s.

out of Tanganyika. At first things were quiet and Lyall had time for thinking. 'I often wonder,' he wrote to his sister Sophia on 2 October 1915, 'what England will be like when the war is over . . . We shall be a sobered people and take things seriously, I'm afraid. The Germans have made war a beastly business and I suppose our old sporting outlook in the Napoleonic times is no longer possible.' It was only after the arrival of General Smuts as commander-in-chief in February 1916 that military action began in earnest.

The East African campaign has been well documented in numerous books and in many of them mention is made of Captain — later Major and eventually Lieutenant-Colonel — R.A. Lyall. He was present in almost every major action and became closely associated with General Smuts. In fact, on Christmas Day 1916 he drove to a place called Duthumi by car and celebrated the occasion by lunching with his commander-in-chief. By then he had experienced the worst of a campaign that is remembered not only for desperate battles, but for the appalling conditions in which fighting took place and the high incidence of every sort of fever and tropical disease. Torrential rains, bogged roads, dense bush, multitudinous insect pests and impassable swamps — all these hindered the progress of both sides and frustrated the men beyond endurance. Logistical problems and transport in disarray — the mules sickened and died in their hundreds — meant that the troops were often short of food and resorted to a diet of groundnuts and green guavas. One of the officers whom Robert Lyall remembered with particular admiration was a doctor who worked with unceasing devotion to relieve the miseries of the men. Later he was to move to South Africa and become famous as an author; his name was Francis Brett Young.

For the forces in East Africa, New Year 1917 opened with the sound of battle. The *Pall Mall Gazette* of 4 January reported the action on the Mgeta River in detail, celebrating its successful outcome. For his part in the engagement, General Robert Adolphus Lyall — as he had temporarily become — was awarded the D.S.O.

The war was by no means over. Later in 1917 Lyall took his 2nd Kashmir Rifles first to Egypt and then to Palestine where, under the command of General Allenby, they were to join troops from almost every corner of the British Empire, as well as from Italy and France, in a determined effort to drive the Turks from the Holy Land. After a decisive victory at Gaza in November 1917, Allenby marched on towards Jerusalem, which he captured on 9 December. The following year he continued the campaign into Syria and took Damascus on 19 September, by which stage the Turkish army was practically destroyed. At this battle, which Robert Lyall

considered the most important of his career, the 3rd Kashmir Rifles once more distinguished themselves. Within two months the First World War was over and Lieutenant-Colonel Lyall proudly took his battalion back to Bombay to be reviewed by the governor-general before being disbanded.

By Christmas he was back in England and the church bells at Flitwick in Bedfordshire, where he had spent all his school holidays at the home of his kinswoman, Miss Kate Brooks, pealed in joyous welcome. Then, early in the new year, he began to prepare for a journey round the world; it took him across France, then by sea via Malta through the Suez Canal and then to Karachi, where he landed on Sunday 9 February 1919. He travelled by train (part of the way third class) to Calcutta, Lahore, Delhi and Bombay and then sailed to Madras and Colombo, playing golf — always a favourite pastime — whenever and wherever he could. On 11 June he set sail for Hongkong, Shanghai, Nagasaki and Yokohama and then crossed the wide Pacific to Vancouver, where he arrived on 20 July in time for the peace celebrations. In Canada he visited Banff, Toronto and Montreal; he went south to New York (where he again played golf), and so by sea back to Southampton, which he reached on 4 September, precisely nine months after he had left England.

If Robert Lyall kept any diaries between the end of 1919 and the beginning of 1924, they have disappeared. It is known, however, that he returned to India and climbed sufficiently high on the civil service ladder to be appointed His Britannic Majesty's consul-general in Chinese Turkistan, a post that he was due to take up in the latter half of 1924. But first, long leave was due to him and he decided to return from India via the Cape in order to visit his mother's birthplace and to see for himself the land of his Cloete forebears.

New Year's Day 1924, a Tuesday, found him installed at Coghill's Hotel, a highly respectable hostelry in Wynberg. He celebrated the occasion by visiting Great Westerford and was shocked to find that the gracious gabled old house had been 'Victorianized' 50 years or more earlier, and ruined when its thatch was replaced by a corrugated iron roof. Besides, suburbia was encroaching upon it: altogether, it could not have been at all as his mother had described it. Nevertheless, Cape houses at their best must have captured his imagination and, undaunted by the disappointment of Westerford, he began to seek them out. He went to Somerset West to call first on Sir Lionel and Lady Phillips at Vergelegen and then on his relatives, the Van der Byls, at Morgenster — or 'Morning Star', as he called the adjoining farm — which homestead, so he commented, was 'by far the best'. He visited Alphen and Groot Constantia, magnificent estates both inseparably linked with the

Cloete family, and saw and admired Stellenbosch and the marvellous Franschhoek valley. He took a break to climb Table Mountain and before January was out had had his first view of the burgeoning vineyards of Paarl.

No specific comment in Colonel Lyall's diary points to the precise moment at which he, like so many others, became completely captivated by the magical ambience of the Cape, but by this time there are indications that he had begun to take an interest in wine farms that were up for sale. At first none of them interested him particularly; and then, on Sunday 17 February, Alphen's manager, a man named Van Niekerk, took him to visit Maurice Pare at Nederburg. 'Liked the place very much,' reads that day's entry in his diary. 'Pare asking £9 000 for it.'

Only ten days of his stay in the Cape remained so he had to move quickly. The following Thursday he paid a professional call on his grandmother's second cousin, Philippus Albertus Myburgh Cloete, commonly known as 'Pam' and senior partner in one of Cape Town's best-known legal firms; and negotiations to buy Nederburg were set in motion. On behalf of Robert Adolphus Lyall, an official offer of £8 000 was made to Maurice Pare. It was to remain good until 1 April, but long before that the prospective purchaser had packed his valise and sailed for England in the SS *Usukuma*.

It took Maurice Pare only until 13 March to make up his mind. On that day he wrote to Cloete, Templer & Parker, solicitors, informing them that he had decided to accept Colonel Lyall's offer. Possession would be granted in six weeks' time, but the Pares wished to stay on in the house until the end of May. A cable to this effect was delivered to Robert Lyall when the *Usukuma* docked in Lisbon and a letter in confirmation was directed to his chambers, D3, the Albany in Piccadilly. And so Lieutenant-Colonel Robert Adolphus Lyall, D.S.O., six foot and two inches in height, of commanding presence and military bearing, became Nederburg's next owner. He was balding and 47 years of age. And he was unmarried.

Colonel Lyall did not move into Nederburg until well over a year had passed. Correspondence between the parties concerned with the sale — Cloete, Templer & Parker, Maurice Pare and Robert Lyall — record decisions that were made and progress achieved at Nederburg during that period. Maurice Pare was anxious about the wine that had just been pressed and was maturing in Nederburg's cellars: it belonged to him and he wished to know whether Colonel Lyall was prepared to look after it until October 1925, when it would be ready for despatch to the well-known London wine merchants, P.B. Burgoyne & Co. On the other hand he, Maurice Pare, would be perfectly agreeable if Colonel Lyall would take over the wine for an additional sum of

£500. Unfortunately, documentary evidence as to what was actually agreed upon appears to have been lost, but on 20 May 1924, Percival Rowley Templer, who held Colonel Lyall's power of attorney, signed the deed of sale of Nederburg on his behalf. By then it seems that purchaser and seller had, for some undisclosed reason, agreed to a lower price of £7 250, for this is the sum that appears on the title deed.

Colonel Lyall did, however, take on the contract that Maurice Pare had concluded with Burgoyne's on 28 June 1921 and, as soon as the deed of sale had been signed, met the firm's Mr Cuthbert Burgoyne over luncheon in London so that they could discuss it. Colonel Lyall was apprehensive, to say the least, about the quality of the red wine produced at Nederburg by Maurice Pare. He would rather stand a loss, he told Mr Burgoyne, than supply him with 'inferior stuff', suggesting that in future he should export only white wines. This was a proposal that the wine merchant obviously accepted with considerable relief. Of all the wines sent

to them from the Cape, he told Colonel Lyall, Nederburg's white wine was second only to that produced by John X. Merriman at Schoongezicht; on the other hand, Maurice Pare's 1922 vintage of red wine was so much below standard that it had been rejected.

It is likely that on this occasion Colonel Lyall and Cuthbert Burgoyne discussed the prospects of the K.W.V., for this was the year in which the Wine and Spirit Control Act was passed by the South African Parliament (Act No. 5 of 1924). The K.W.V. now had the power to fix, annually, the minimum price which farmers were to receive for their distilling wine. At the same time the organization began to solve the problem of excess wine by making mature brandy as its main product and also began to make dry table and fortified wines as well as liqueurs.

Clearly Robert Lyall was a more than competent judge of wine. It may be that something of the skills and sensitivity of the connoisseur had been passed down to him from his great-great-great grandfather, Hendrik

1926   **FEBRUARY**

MONDAY 1
Took Miss Cappel to the Station in the morning. Began picking grapes in the afternoon. Test for Sugar gave 19 p.c.

TUESDAY 2
Began pressing. Slight cloud. Must 19½ M - 22¾ Balling. Temperature outside at 7.30 am 75°. Bricks being packed in kiln.

WEDNESDAY 3
Pressing. Fine. Must 20¾ M. Temperature of cellar 74° at 10 a.m. Temperature of yesterdays must 80°. Evening must just over 20 M.

THURSDAY 4 Nederburg
Trouble with pump. Went with Cart to fetch cretan from Paarl 5/-. Acidity 6.15. Van N added 1 lb per leager Tartaric. Sugar just over 20

1926   **FEBRUARY**

FRIDAY 5 Temp of 4: 63° - 85°
New pump arrived costing £27/10. Pressing continued. Sugar just over 19 Mming. Sampled Small Vineyard S. 18½. 60 leagers of Wine from del Vineyard.

SATURDAY 6 Temp of 5: 65° - 94°
Cellar about 80°. Stopped pressing for the day as cellar was full. Carted 43 thousand bricks in Kiln. Large vineyard pressed giving 60 leager approx.

SUNDAY 7
Nederburg. Rained 3 cents during night. Mrs Arbuthnot & her sister in law Mrs Evelyn of Wootton came to luncheon.

MEMORANDA

Cloete, who had perfected the famed Constantia, and certainly the production of high quality wines was among his dreams for Nederburg. 'It is my ambition,' he wrote from London at this time to his legal advisers in Cape Town, 'when the contract with Burgoyne's is ended and I have retired from the Indian Service, to start a brand of Nederburg wines, supervise the making in our (English) winter at the Cape, and market [it] in our (English) summer at home.'

Meanwhile, much had to be done in his absence and he sent specific instructions to his newly-appointed manager, the same Van Niekerk, formerly of Alphen, who had accompanied him on his first visit to Nederburg and was considered an expert wine-maker. He was to be employed at a fixed annual salary of £200 and would be paid, in addition, 3 per cent of the gross profits of the farm. To begin with, he was to live in the 'big house' and was entitled to make use, free of charge, of any of the farm products. He was to see to it, wrote the Colonel firmly, that 'no wine was given to the hands as part of their pay, but there is no objection to giving them wine occasionally as reward for good work'. History does not relate how those 'hands' reacted to such peremptory instructions at a time when the tot or *dop* system was considered the norm on wine farms in the Cape.

Van Niekerk's initial impressions, described in a letter written to Cloete, Templer & Parker on 25 April 1924, were not encouraging. 'I was very disappointed,' he wrote, 'finding the farm Nederburg *very* neglected. The orange and naartjie trees are dying of drought. I told the foreman to have them watered at once.' By the time he moved onto the farm, however, it was early winter, the first rains had fallen and he was able to get to work on weeding and cultivating the lands. With that completed, the fruit trees and vines had to be pruned and the orchards and vineyards fertilized. In accordance with Colonel Lyall's instructions, all the Hermitage vines — bearers of red-wine grapes — were uprooted and white wine grapes (the specific cultivars are unrecorded)

PAGE 92: TOP LEFT
Wine barrels are filled for despatch to Burgoyne's, the London wine merchants.
TOP RIGHT
The last hogshead barrel is hoisted onto the wagon that will take this consignment of wine to Huguenot railway station — the first stage on its journey to London.
BOTTOM
Colonel Lyall does his sums as his first vintage starts off on its long journey across half the world.
PAGE 93
The grape harvest was at its height when Colonel Lyall completed these pages in his diary for 1926. Throughout his years at Nederburg, he kept meticulous records of every detail, from temperature to tree-planting, from rainfall to the births of his sons.

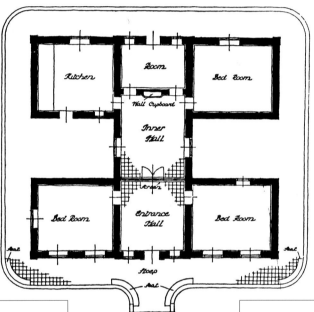

This fine drawing of the front elevation of Nederburg, and the accompanying ground plan, were made in 1928 after a visit to the homestead by Professor Geoffrey Eastcott Pearse (1885-1968) and his architectural students from the University of the Witwatersrand.

planted in their place. Today known as Cinsaut, Hermitage grapes were introduced to the Cape from France in the 1850s and their heavy bearing and high sugar content made the variety popular with local growers. However, bulk wine produced from them by relatively unskilled farmers proved to be thin and light in colour so that it was not surprising that Robert Lyall found it unpalatable. In his opinion, the view from the front of the house could be improved and Van Niekerk was given orders to replace the vines which grew right up to the stoep with a grove of citrus trees. Old and unproductive orchards were planted with 265 new peach trees and 750 apricots, and oats were sown for animal fodder. Tree-planting was always a priority in Colonel Lyall's scheme of things, so an order was placed with the Forestry Department for the first batch of many thousands of *Pinus insignis*, with which Colonel Lyall was eventually to clothe Nederburg's hitherto bare slopes.

While Van Niekerk toiled in the sweet, washed air of the Cape winter when all is green underfoot, Robert Adolphus Lyall, 6 000 miles away in London, had much with which to occupy his time. Letters and diaries indicate that while the demands — and his dreams — of Nederburg preoccupied him to a great extent, there were other equally pressing matters on his mind. Of some urgency were the plans that had to be made for his forthcoming journey to Chinese Turkistan, not to mention the need to familiarize himself with the work he was to undertake there. And then there was something else to be considered — though his diary scarcely hints at it until it was a *fait accompli* on Tuesday 3 June 1924. The brief entry of that day in the diary of Lieutenant-Colonel Robert Adolphus Lyall reads somewhat laconically: 'Cathy and I were married in St James Piccadilly by Dean Inge.' Certainly the name of Catharine Broadwood Rivaz had been mentioned frequently on the pre-

ceding pages of Lyall's diary — they went for drives together, visited the theatre and dined with mutual relatives, for both Bob and Cathy were descended from the famous 18th-century piano-maker, John Broadwood — but never on those pages is there the faintest suggestion of romance. This, of course, is in character with the formality of Robert Lyall's background both as a Victorian (which he was for the first 25 years of his life) and as an army officer. He was, after all, 47 and she was ten years younger. Nevertheless, marry her he did with the blessing of the Very Reverend William Inge and no doubt of the members of their respective families; and, in accordance with the words of the Book of Common Prayer that would have been used on that occasion, they remained thereafter man and wife together until their lives' end.

Catharine Lyall was descended from one John Francis Antoin Rivaz, a Swiss who was born in 1730 and died in 1808. He settled in England and became chairman of Lloyds of London, as did his son, Vincent Francis Rivaz, born in 1765. Catharine's immediate family, like that of her future husband, was much involved with the affairs of India, where she was born in 1887. One uncle, Sir Charles Montgomery Rivaz (1845-1926), was lieutenant-governor of the Punjab from 1902 until 1906. Another, Colonel Vincent Rivaz, born in 1842, saw considerable action on the North-West Frontier and was mentioned in despatches several times. Catharine's father, George Wilmot Rivaz, like his brother Charles, served in the Indian civil service but, unlike him, took the first opportunity to retire and settle peacefully in Canterbury, Kent. Catharine was sent to school at the convent of the Sacré Coeur in France but, like most girls of her class at that time, was also privately educated, with her two sisters, at home.

Early in life Catharine Rivaz showed great personal

concern for the less privileged and, although ladies of her kind were not expected to follow careers in those days, she chose to devote herself to helping the poor of London's East End. The grinding poverty that she came across made a lasting impression on her and throughout her life she never failed to help sufferers whenever she came across them. During the First World War she became a V.A.D. (Voluntary Aid Detachment) nurse and worked in a field hospital stationed on the cliffs outside Boulogne. Conditions were harsh — nurses, patients and operating theatre were all under canvas — and the weather during winter gales was extreme.

Notwithstanding her survival of these experiences, her husband obviously would not consider exposing her to the hardships that were undoubtedly in store for him, not merely in his new post but in the gruelling journey he was obliged to make to reach it. Naturally he was

short of Everest far to the south-east. Parallel ridges, up to 150 miles wide, consist of sheer slopes and craggy crests sometimes cleft by narrow transverse ravines or, towards the summit, smothered by vast glaciers. Dry as a desert in some parts, swept by blizzards in others and beset everywhere by high winds and vastly varying temperatures, these mountains are daunting to the most intrepid of mountaineers. And in 1924, anyone bent on reaching Kashgar from India in the south, had no alternative but to make his way to it in the rarefied air of a series of tortured, cataclysmic mountain passes.

The story of Robert Lyall's journey across the Karakoram mountains reads like an epic. At practically every overnight halt he wrote to his bride and when she eventually received his letters — sometimes many weeks later — she lovingly and painstakingly transcribed into an exercise book all that was not personally

reluctant to leave her behind in England so soon after their marriage so, after a brief honeymoon spent visiting some of the most delightful towns in Sussex, he took her as far as Bombay, which they reached on Friday 27 June. Ten days later they parted, Cathy for Europe by sea and Bob on the first leg of his journey to Kashgar. This ancient oasis city — the Mogul conqueror, Tamerlane, sacked it in the 14th century about halfway through its history — lies in the most westerly corner of China in one of the least accessible spots on the surface of the earth. Between it and what used to be India's North-West Frontier stretches the Karakoram range of the Himalayas, one of the loftiest mountain systems in the world. Along this 300 mile-long barrier — known to the Turks as the 'Black Rock Mountains' — peak after peak claws skywards, the highest being the famous and formidable K2 soaring to 28 250 feet, just 800 feet

LEFT AND RIGHT
Drawn here by Professor Pearse, these beautifully crafted brass escutcheons, probably made by skilled slaves, date back to Nederburg's earliest days.
CENTRE
The plaster urn is one of two which are inseparably linked with Nederburg's front (west-facing) elevation.

addressed to her in order to have a record to show the family. Lyall tells of how he travelled by train to Delhi and then north-east by rail until he reached the nearest point to Srinagar. He spent six days in this most exotic of cities, famed for the romantic Shalimar Gardens and set amid the clear lakes and lofty mountains of the vale of Kashmir. Then he made his way to Badipur, where he engaged 15 porters, bought each one a pony and acquired for himself a seasoned and doughty black horse named Satan. Only then did the journey proper begin, and the little procession wound its way along the road used since ancient days to bring silk from China into India and, in more modern times, haunted by memories of ambush and slaughter. Up steep slopes they struggled, floundering through snow on the Burzil Pass and then gratefully descending to the town of Gilgit set on a tributary of the Indus. Robert Lyall wrote that it was an 'easy march' along the Hunza River; it flows through a secret, enchanted valley which the writer James Hilton was later to make famous as Shangri La in his novel *The Lost Horizon*. On Friday 4 August Robert Lyall dined in ostentatious formality with the wealthy local ruler, the Mir Muhammed Nazim Khan, then in residence at his summer retreat, and afterwards left him to go on, ever deeper and higher into the desolate mountains. Once the party passed the ruins of a village that had been carried away by floods and on another occasion Satan was almost lost when a stone bridge collapsed under him. Sometimes the road was so narrow and the bends so sharp that the horses could progress only by swimming along the foaming river far below. There were swaying, fragile suspension bridges to be crossed; men and horses skidded and slithered over the treacherous surfaces of glaciers, some of them 11 miles

gar. The journey across the roof of the world was over.

It was not a happy appointment for Robert Lyall. Both the office that he held and the area in which he was stationed were lonely, comforts were few and the weather bitterly cold — on some nights up to 35 degrees of frost were registered. Apart from some Swedish missionaries and a handful of Russians, refugees from the revolution seven years earlier, there were no Europeans in the city and certainly no kindred spirits. Most wretched of all was his enforced separation from his wife and the unreliability of communication with her. By using the radio station that the Chinese had in Kashgar he could establish contact with Peshawar, but it took a month or more for a letter to reach Bombay and the weekly mail was often delayed by snowstorms in the mountain passes. He whiled away the time playing tennis and shooting duck; he visited the famous market

wide, and on one occasion, in a blinding snowstorm, Robert Lyall had to abandon Satan temporarily and struggle through a pass on the back of a yak. Not surprisingly, the porters began to complain, threatening to mutiny unless Lyall increased their wages. Somehow he managed to placate them, but the further they were from home, the more ugly was their attitude. At last they reached the northern side of the mountains, but dust storms and weary marches through stony plains were still to follow and there was always the fear that the Chinese escort that had been promised Colonel Lyall would not arrive to protect him from almost certain attack from bandits. However, all fears on this score proved unfounded and at last, seven weeks after leaving Bombay, His Britannic Majesty's newly-appointed consul-general in Turkistan, travel-stained and weary, led his truculent posse of porters into Kash-

TOP
Nederburg's back gable as drawn by Professor Pearse. It is similar to, but simpler than, the one at the front of the homestead.
BOTTOM LEFT
The wall cupboard set in the agterkamer wall where it remained until it was moved in the 1930s.
BOTTOM RIGHT
Nederburg's south side seen by moonlight. These two oil paintings, now in Cornwall in the possession of John Lyall, are the work of Gordon Taylor (1891-1971), a well-known painter of landscapes and animals.

and bought Cathy a mandarin's coat, a diamond brooch and some carpets. At last, six days before Christmas 1924, he sent her a cable telling her that he had declined further promotion and that he intended to resign from the Indian civil service. Perhaps dreams of faraway Nederburg had tempted him: to Robert Adolphus Lyall it was the obvious place for retirement.

Once more Robert Lyall made the incredible journey over the Karakoram mountains and back into India, but it was not until months later that he was able to meet Cathy at the Cape. She had arrived there early in August, followed soon afterwards by some basic items of furniture, household appurtenances and the Lyalls' very considerable library. It was early spring and farm manager Van Niekerk, writing to Cloete, Templer & Parker commented: 'Everything is looking very well on the farm, especially after the last good rains . . .' He was

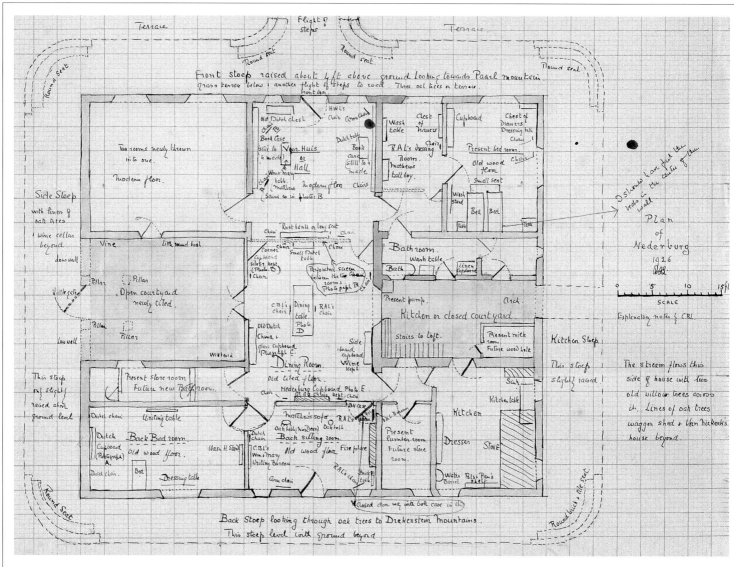

hard at work again in October when Colonel Lyall arrived. The 14 leaguers of wine that had been pressed during the harvest of that year could now be sold and the 5 000 new vines that had been planted along the river were doing well.

Robert Adolphus Lyall had never farmed in his life, yet he brought to the occupation of his retirement the efficiency and discipline that he had learnt in the army. From the beginning he kept meticulous records of the daily duties performed on his farm and of every item bought or sold. Immediately after his arrival he ordered 3 500 more pine trees from Harry Pickstone who had, in 1898, established the Rhodes Fruit Farms and now ran a flourishing nursery at Simondium. This was to become a close and useful relationship. He bought a pig — called Adolphus — and sent his first consignment of fruit to Jones's jam factory in Paarl.

The morning of 1 January 1926 found Bob and Cathy alone together at Nederburg where they made an idyllic start to the new year by breakfasting on ham, two peaches each and strawberries. That month proved an interesting one: Bob attended a course on wine-making at Elsenburg Agricultural College, entertained among others the second Lord de Villiers, son and heir of the jurist and statesman who, in 1910, had been architect of the national constitution of the Union of South Africa; ordered eight different cultivars of table grapes for

PAGE 98: TOP LEFT
The wall cupboard filled with the Lyalls' treasures.
TOP RIGHT
The teak screen, or porte de visite, restored by Harry Currey and still in place during the Lyalls' ownership, divided the voorkamer from the agterkamer.
BOTTOM
A meticulously accurate ground plan of Nederburg drafted by Catharine Lyall.
PAGE 99: TOP
Colonel Lyall relaxes in the morning room — today Nederburg's front hall.
BOTTOM
The stream, now diverted, that flowed along Nederburg's north side.

planting later in the year; sent 114 watermelons to the market in Cape Town; and, finally and most importantly, attended the Paarl Agricultural Show. This was the first recorded occasion on which Nederburg won prizes for its wine — two firsts, one of which was a silver cup presented by Rhodes Fruit Farms for 25 leaguers of unfortified light dry white wine of export quality, and one second. Colonel Lyall was also awarded a first prize for his pears, two firsts for his apples and a second prize for his watermelons. It seems that Van Niekerk must have known his job.

Harvesting of the 1926 vintage began on 1 February and from that day onwards Robert Lyall consistently recorded the maximum and minimum air temperatures at Nederburg as well as the temperature of the fermenting must and its Balling measure, or level of sugar concentration. His diary records that on Sunday 21 February he attended a dinner party in Cape Town that was attended not only by pioneer aviator Alan Cobham, who had just flown out from England in 94 record-breaking hours, but by his friend General Smuts. By Monday 15 March, after days of excessive heat when temperatures outside soared to 102 °F (39 °C) and measured 75 °F (24 °C) in the cellar, the vintage was complete. Now the Lyalls could relax and enjoy themselves shopping for Cape furniture — they bought a *rusbank* for £10 and a table that had once belonged to

Ko-operatieve Wijnbouwers Vereniging van Zuid-Afrika, Bpkt.

Geregistreer onder die Wet op Ko-operatiewe Verenigings, 1922.
Registered under the Co-operative Societies' Act, 1922.

Gereg. REGD. No. *2944*

POSBUS 33,
P.O. BOX

PAARL.

11 . 7 . 1930

M *m. A.J.B. van Niekerk*
Nederburg
P.R.A. Paarl.

Rek./Verkoop No. **A** 3800
A/c Sales

Per bd Lyall.

Verkoop aan
Sold to *Monis Wineries*

(A) Vir Stook en Asynmaak doeleindes.—For Distillation and Vinegar making purposes

VATE. Hhds.	PRODUK Product	GROS GLGS. / LB. Bulk Glns. / lbs.	STERKTE. Strength	GLGS. / LB. Glns./lbs. 20%	PRYS Price	WAARDE—Value £ s. d.
	DRUIWE Grapes					
	STOOKWYN Dist. Wine			846	7½	26 8 9
	STOOKWYN bo 1.4 p.m. Asynsuur Dist. Wine above 1.4 p.m. Volatile Acid (10% bekorting—10% deduction					
	BRANDEWYN Brandy					

Vir Kantoor gebruik alleen. — For Office use only.

GLS. OF / OR LBS. @ 20%.	PRYS. Price.	WAARDE—Value £ s. d.
846 gaels	1/3	52 17 6

MIN BEKORTINGS — LESS DEDUCTIONS.	WAARDE Value		
			52 17 6
Vir Surplus Kontribusie: ¼ per Glg. For Surplus Contribution: ¼ per Gln.	3 2 2		
Vir Kontribusie vir Administrasie en Aandele ¼d For Contribution for Administration and Shares.	2 6 7	26 8 9	
Besonderhede soos bogemeld Particulars as shown above		26 8 9	

(B) Vir ander doeleindes. — For other purposes.

BESONDERHEDE. — PARTICULARS		

TOTAAL — Total £

Kontras deur Koper afgetrek
Contras deducted by Merchant

Balans oorgebring tot u Krediet
Balance carried forward to your Credit   £ 26 8 9

Nagegaan deur
Checked by

Boekhouer — Accountant

Dr Leander Starr Jameson of the ill-fated Raid — and work began on a garage to house their Ford Essex motor car. Distilling wine was sent to the Italian Warehouse, forerunner of Monis' famous wineries in Paarl. Over the next months sweet potatoes, guavas, apples and oranges were despatched to the market; in addition to which, more pine trees, jacarandas and cork oaks were planted, as well as plums and almonds. On Tuesday 12 October there were further successes for Nederburg at the Rosebank Wine Show at which first prizes for export wines were awarded for both the 1925 and 1926 vintages.

In the small hours of Monday 25 October 1926, John Comyn, son of Robert Adolphus and Catharine Lyall, was born at Nederburg, his arrival no doubt marking the high point of the year. The confinement had been long and exhausting for the mother and the baby was so frail that Colonel Lyall, knowing that in an emergency any Christian may perform a baptism, decided to christen the baby himself with the doctor and Van Niekerk's wife as witnesses. This would have been a comfort to Catharine who was, throughout her life, a devout and practising Anglican and never failed to attend church services. Contrary to expectations, how-

While Nederburg's 'good' wine was exported to London, its distilling wine was sold locally, as indicated by this form issued by the K.W.V. in July 1930.

PAGE 101: TOP
Oak vats, wine-filled, dream under the traditional reed ceiling and thatched roof of Nederburg's old cellar in the 1920s.

BOTTOM
Nederburg's original oak-shaded outbuildings, seen here during Colonel Lyall's ownership, were like many others in the south-western Cape at that time.

ever, John throve and some weeks later was taken to Holy Trinity Church in Paarl for a 'proper' christening. This time it was attended by a total of 25 admiring friends and relations.

The moment had come to send the 1925 vintage to London and on 23 November Colonel Lyall saw his first consignment of 32 leaguers — a total of 4 032 gallons — despatched to Burgoyne's in 68 hogsheads. The apricot trees at Nederburg were by now in full bearing and 50 tons at a time were being supplied to the local jam factory. Figs and plums were being harvested; peaches were ripening and the early grapes were looking good — as were the figures reflected in Nederburg's ledger. Between 30 September 1925 and 1 October 1926 the farm's turnover had amounted to £2 659. 2s. 3d.; expenditure over the same period was £2 116. 3s. 4d., resulting in a profit of £542. 18s. 11d. As 1926 drew to a close, Robert and Catharine Lyall had good reason to feel satisfied with their lot.

The following years, from a domestic point of view, passed pleasantly enough. Robert Lyall's diaries, always prefaced by a snapshot pasted onto the endpapers, give the impression of happy family life enjoyed in one of the

loveliest spots on earth. As soon as the 1927 harvest was over the Lyalls took six-month-old John to England and by the time they brought him back to Nederburg in November he was just over a year old and crawling. The farm had been well looked after by Van Niekerk in their absence: 42 leaguers of the 1925 vintage had been despatched to Burgoyne's and the new season's apricot crop looked promising.

It was early in 1928 that, despite fiercely hot weather, Nederburg had an interesting visitor in Professor Geoffrey Eastcott Pearse, who held the first chair of architecture at the University of the Witwatersrand. At that time he was collecting material for his book *Eighteenth Century Architecture in South Africa* and had brought with him a group of students to investigate and measure up the house. The outcome was a magnificent example of draughtsmanship which gives an accurate depiction of the ground-plan of Nederburg as it was originally. Accompanying it are superb drawings of brass escutcheons and other interior details. Later in the year tree-planting continued apace, but it was a severe blow to Colonel Lyall when, in August, Elsenburg tested Nederburg's wine and found it wanting — it

was condemned for being unacceptably high in volatile acids. Wine was sent to the annual show, but did not win any prizes and an examination of the farm's books in September showed a working loss of about £140.

The 1929 grape harvest was at its height when the Lyalls' second son, Francis Valentine, was born in a Cape Town maternity home — his second name being appropriate to his birth date on 14 February, St Valentine's Day. His father continued to plant trees — thousands of them — and added granadillas and pecan nuts to his farm produce. One of his neighbours, Italian-born Ferdinando Costa, who had himself raised over 10 000 olive trees from seeds imported from his homeland, inspired him to transform part of Nederburg by planting olive groves. Another neighbour, D.J. Malan of Salomonsvlei, contracted to supply him with 4 000 new vines every year at an agreed price of £8 per thousand. At this stage prospects looked bright for the wine exports as Britain had recently introduced a preferential tariff for high-strength wines produced in the Commonwealth, but for Robert Lyall they were unrelievedly gloomy. The 'good' wine that year went bad and, following Elsenburg's adverse report in 1928, all the vats in

311 PROGRESSIVE QUARTERLY BALANCE   **312**

Budget for the year 1st October 1934 to 30th Sept 1935

Expenditure

Budget	Head	1st Quarter	2nd Quarter	3rd Quarter	4th Quarter
£ 300	WAGES	79 8 9	134 17 7	180 04 0	
" 60	Working Expenses	4 3 11	12 19 10	20 14 8	
" 80	Live Stock	16 11 9	26 14 7	36 13 10	
" 120	Cultivation	4 6 11	63 19 2	95 5 7	
" 10	Trees & Timber	...	...	1 13 6	
" 60	Wine & Fustage	1 0 0	6 14 2	9 2 2	
" 50	Farm Buildings	12 3 0	13 2 6	14 9 9	
" 10	Manager's Hou	2 0 0	2 0 0	11 11 11	
" 50	maintenance "Nederburg"	5 8 2	5 8 2	5 11 8	
" 120	Manager's Salary	42 0 0	62 0 0	92 0 0	
" 60	Insurance & General	...	21 0 5	50 17 7	
" 50	Unforeseen	2 16 3	5 19 0	28 0 9	
£970	Total £	169 18 9	354 15 5	546 5 5	

Income

Budget	Head	1st Quarter	2nd Quarter	3rd Quarter	4th Quarter
£ 180	Wine x	2 18 6	36 5 11	300 6 0	
- 300	Fruit xx	37 4 7	291 15 87	360 14 93	
- 50	Unforeseen	1 12 0	1 15 0	27 1 3	
£530	Total £	41 15 1	329 16 76	688 1 36	

x 28 leaguers 1933 in stock @ 5 £140
Dutie on Wine etc.   40 / £ 180

xx more plums & peaches in bearing but apricots heavily pruned this year.

Estimated Expenditure £ 970
Estimated Income £ 530
Estimated loss £ 440

R.A. Lyall
1 Oct 1934

Remarks.

Owing to the Lease of the Farm to W. Basson from the 1st June 1935 the estimates for the year were modified as regards expenditure, though practically the whole of the income was realized during the first ¾ of the year. Only the value of the orange, grape-fruit & late guava crop remained to be realized (say £40), so the income from fruit would have been £400 against the £300 estimated. This increase in income from fruit was due to the better price received for dry apricots & increased crop of oranges. The plums were sold advantageously for export. Peaches were a total failure, also almonds. The increase over estimate for wine was due to £24 leaguers of the 1935 vintage being sold to clear cellar before Basson took over.

Expenditure for the first ¾ of the year was about normal and as estimated, but there would have been savings of some £120 under the heads "Wine & Fustage" "Farm Building" & "Maintenance Nederburg".

Had the year ended normally the probable expenditure would have been £850 & probable income £600 – leaving an adverse balance of £250.

Actually the income was £688 and the expenditure £546, showing an actual profit on the ¾ year working of £142.

R.A. Lyall
SS "Ulysses"
crossing the Line F. 1935
June 19, 1935

Nederburg's cellars were standing hollow and empty. Colonel Lyall foresaw an estimated loss in 1930 of £715.

However, in 1930 things improved a little — 300 bottles of sherry were made from wine harvested in 1927 and 40 leaguers of 'good' wine were produced — but in 1931 the vintage was disappointing once more. On his return in August from a three months' visit to England — where Catharine and the children remained behind — Colonel Lyall learnt that of eight vats of wine submitted to the Cape Town agents for export, three had been rejected. As if this were not depressing enough, the analysis he made of the farm's financial situation proved in no uncertain terms that the effects of the Great Depression, combined with a phenomenally bad vintage, were taking their toll on Nederburg. At the end of October 1931 the accounts showed a loss of £727 over the year, largely as a result of a poor vintage and abysmally low prices paid for the apricots and other fruit.

Nevertheless Robert Lyall, alone at Nederburg, bravely soldiered on. His diaries, ledgers, daybooks and correspondence all reveal his unflagging, dedicated hard work and his meticulous attention to detail. He continued planting vines and grafting olives and per-

To everything that he did, Colonel Lyall brought the orderliness of an army-trained mind — as seen in this detailed progressive quarterly balance completed when he had decided that the time had come to give up farming at Nederburg.

sisted with the routine of the farm even though relentless south-east gales blew the fruit off the trees, excessive heat ripened the peaches too quickly and one batch of plums proved unsaleable. On 21 December 1931, while working hard on the apricots, he looked up to see a big aeroplane lumbering overhead in the direction of Cape Town. It was carrying the first airmail from England and among those letters were two from Cathy. Their arrival must have cheered him, especially as he was facing a lonely Christmas at Nederburg, no doubt burdened with the realization that things on his farm — and in the world in general — were showing no signs of improvement. It was, as he expressed it, a period of 'financial stringency' and the first step he took to relieve the situation was to visit his legal advisers — now Cloete, Templer & Parker — in Cape Town on 14 January 1932 and arrange a mortgage of £1 000 on Nederburg. Next, he had the unpleasant task of informing Van Niekerk and his foreman, a man named Willie Basson, that they could either accept reduced salaries or look for work elsewhere. Jobs were not easy to come by and it must have been with more than a little reluctance they both agreed to stay on at the lower wage. Van

Niekerk's was reduced from £16. 13s. 4d. to £10. 13s. 4d. a month and Basson's from £9 to £7. In an attempt to lessen their gloom, Colonel Lyall assured them that he would make good their loss as soon as the farm profits warranted it.

The grape harvest started a few weeks later, but once again fate seemed against Robert Adolphus Lyall. Insufferably hot weather was followed by unseasonably heavy rains which fell continuously for four days and burst open the skins of the ripened grapes. Surprisingly, 35 leaguers of 'good' wine were produced and once the pressing was over Nederburg's master closed the doors of cellar and homestead (not many months earlier he had put up the beautiful brass dolphin knockers still there today) and sailed for England. Soon after his arrival he and Cathy went house-hunting in the south of England. They found nothing that suited them, but clearly Colonel Lyall's dream of making a great wine farm of Nederburg was beginning to fade.

But the time to abandon it had not yet arrived and a fortnight before Christmas 1932 Robert Lyall was back on his wine farm, once more without Cathy and the children. The entry in his diary for Wednesday 28 De-

Nederburg flanked by its old oaks, leafless in winter. In Colonel Lyall's day the homestead was a family home overlooking a rose garden.

cember reads: 'Van Niekerk looked in before breakfast with the news that South Africa was off the gold standard.' It was a critical step to have taken and perhaps the economy of the country would now begin to improve. However, the weather did not encourage any optimism among Cape fruit farmers for the rainfall for that December – 33,38 inches or 848 millimetres – had been abnormally high and could not have done the ripening crops any good. 'The year ends in uncertainty,' Robert Lyall wrote in his diary on New Year's Eve, 'with South Africa off the gold standard and political parties manoeuvring for position . . .'

He was always interested in politics and throughout his diaries there are comments on world affairs – just as there are on weather conditions and temperatures and, at Nederburg, on the daily activities on the farm and in the wine cellar. It was cheering to be awarded first prize on his 'sherry-type wine' at the Paarl Wine Show on 25 January 1933, even though the unfortified light dry white wine that he entered was not successful, but the quality of the grapes harvested the following month was exceedingly disappointing. December's heavy rains had been followed by scorching heat and

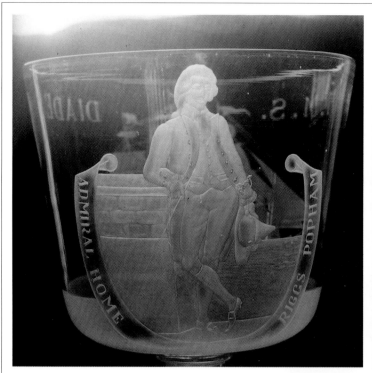

Two crystal goblets, owned by Colonel Lyall, commemorate the Battle of Blaauwberg and the second British occupation (1806). Colonel Lyall sold the goblets to an antique dealer before leaving South Africa in 1935 but today their whereabouts are unknown.

TOP RIGHT AND LEFT
This goblet featured Admiral Sir Home Popham on one side and the vessel from which he directed the fleet of 63 ships on the other.

BOTTOM
The second goblet featured this portrait of Lieutenant-General Sir David Baird, officer commanding the 6 500 invading British troops.

many of the grapes were burnt and overripe. On 5 March Colonel Lyall took stock of the contents of the cellar. It contained 570 bottles of sherry – 370 of the 1927 vintage and the rest three years younger – and four vats each of 1932 and 1933 wine which, combined, made a total of 53 leaguers. The quarterly figures in the farm's books showed that during the first three months of the year, Nederburg had made a profit of £14. 9s. 7d. In comparison with the loss of £113. 5s. 9d. on the three months ending on 31 December 1932 this was an improvement, but the outlook for the second quarter of 1933 was dismal.

There was nothing for it: the now ageing Van Niekerk, who had been on Nederburg for nine years, would have to go. Reluctantly, Colonel Lyall gave him notice to leave at the end of April and Basson, a much younger man, stepped into his shoes at an increased salary of £10 a month. Van Niekerk did not leave without lining his own threadbare pockets – just a little. Colonel Lyall remained impassive and silent as he observed him, through one of Nederburg's windows, driving off first with a lorry-load of firewood and then, for the last time, with another of manure. Three days later Cathy and the boys – now six and four years old – arrived accompanied by their English nanny, a Miss Ledger, who later became – briefly – engaged to Basson. The family was to remain on Nederburg for the following two years.

In June 1933 Colonel Lyall managed to pay off

£500 of the mortgage on the farm and that winter he optimistically planted grapefruit, table grapes, potatoes – and roses. The following year the vintage looked promising, even though during harvest-time the temperature in the shade rose to 104 °F (40 °C), and when the weather was cool enough more and yet more trees were put in – 2 000 bluegums, over 600 olives, Santa Rosa and Satsuma plums. But in that summer of 1934 the deciduous fruit was of very poor quality, not only at Nederburg but throughout the district and soaring temperatures – again over 104 °F (40 °C) – during February 1935 did not bode well for that year's vintage. Colonel Lyall was finding it increasingly difficult to market Nederburg's wine locally: he had tried in vain to sell 'good' wine harvested in 1930 at a shilling a bottle and it proved equally difficult to dispose of the 1934 vintage at £5. 10s. a leaguer for distilling purposes.

During that year, the farm had shown a loss of £472. 18s. 4d. Granted, things had been worse in the past – in 1930, for instance, Nederburg's ledgers had reflected a deficit of £738 – but over the years Colonel Lyall had invested a vast amount in his estate. Enormous numbers of trees of all varieties had been planted; vineyards and orchards had been extended and quantities of farm and cellar equipment had been acquired. Now, in 1934, he took ruthless stock of the situation. Despite his high hopes, the quality of the vintage did not appear to have improved: he had entered his wines at various

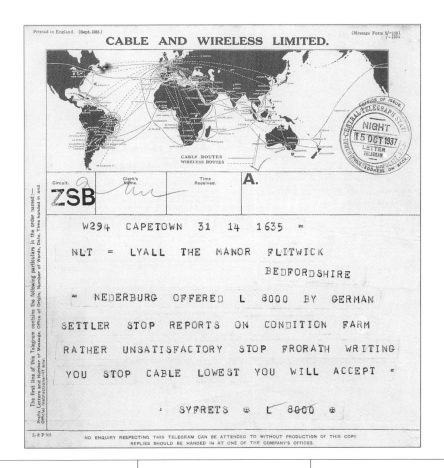

The cable sent by Syfrets Trust Company of Cape Town to Colonel Lyall informing him of the offer for Nederburg made by Johann Georg Graue. Frorath, who farmed nearby, was a German friend of Johann Graue.

shows, but not since his early successes had he gained any awards worth boasting about. In August 1934 Robert Lyall faced the fact that drastic action would have to be taken and he visited both his solicitors and Syfrets Trust Company with a view to selling Nederburg.

Months passed and as no offers worth considering had been made by the following May, he accepted the proposal of his foreman, Willie Basson, and agreed to let the farm to him. Any doubts that he might have had about returning to live in England permanently were dispelled by the news that he had inherited Flitwick Manor in Bedfordshire from Miss Kate Brooks, who had died the previous October. There would be no question of house-hunting, for a gracious, ready-made home, with which he had been familiar since childhood, was awaiting him and his family. Besides, the boys were reaching an age when they would need to go to school and, in keeping with family tradition, Colonel Lyall had Eton in mind for them. Willie Basson knew Nederburg and seemed the obvious tenant; he would continue to farm it until it was sold or either he or Colonel Lyall gave six months' notice. An agreement was drawn up: he would pay an annual rental of £150; and while the Lyalls would retain the homestead for their own use or for that of their guests, Basson would occupy and maintain all the other buildings. He was to cultivate the vineyards at Colonel Lyall's request and expense, but all the wine and other produce would be his to dispose of to his own

advantage. When all was signed and sealed the Lyalls sold their faithful Essex Ford for £75 (it had bumped its way over 27 000 miles of appalling roads during the past ten years) and Robert and Catharine Lyall, John, Francis and Nanny Ledger (unmarried) set sail from Table Bay harbour on Wednesday 12 June 1935.

Colonel Lyall did not return to Nederburg. He turned his attention to his family and the needs of Flitwick Manor; later he became high sheriff of Bedfordshire and, during the Second World War, played an active part in the local Home Guard. He died on 5 September 1948, leaving his widow, Catharine, to outlive him by 21 years.

Willie Basson continued to farm Nederburg — much to his benefit, according to local opinion — for two years after taking it over. He worked hard, but at the back of his mind there must have been the constant awareness that some day it would be sold. So, on a spring day in 1937, when Nederburg and the blue mountains behind it were looking their best, it must have been with a good deal of apprehension that he observed a certain German-speaking visitor inspecting the farm with considerable and critical interest. Had Willie Basson been the owner of a crystal ball he might have gazed into it that day and seen that in the heart and mind — and pocket — of that German-speaking gentleman lay the bright secret of Nederburg's future.

∎

CHAPTER SEVEN

THE NEDERBURG REVOLUTION:

THE GENIUS OF THE GRAUES 1937-1953

The arrival from Germany of Johann Georg Graue heralded a new era
in Nederburg's history. By careful selection of vines and matching cultivars to
location, he implemented his theory that good wine has its origins
in the soil. Aided by the skill of his son, Arnold, he introduced to Nederburg
the process of cold fermentation by which the destructive effects of high
temperatures on wine-making were overcome.

*Seen by every visitor introduced to
Nederburg's cellars, this vat-front, carved
by Karl Wilhelm and his son,
commemorates Johann Georg and Arnold
Graue, to whose genius Nederburg, as
it is known today, owes its origins.*
PAGE 107: TOP TO BOTTOM
*The Graue family, owners of Nederburg
from 1937 until 1959: Johann Georg
Graue, who introduced the revolutionary
system of cold fermentation to Nederburg;
his wife and helpmate, Ilse; their son,
Arnold, who developed and perfected his
father's methods and who died tragically at
the age of 29.*

By the mid-1930s the Great Depression
was virtually over and the Western world seemed set fair
towards economic recovery. Yet, politically, all was not
entirely well and there were those who noticed with apprehension the sinister stirrings of a wind that was to
blow disaster across Europe before the decade was over.
Among those with foresight was one Johann Peter
Koster, a South African immigrant of German birth,
and the measures that he took to protect his family from
that disaster were to prove that invariably every ill wind
does blow somebody some good. For one of Johann
Koster's three daughters was married to a man named
Johann Richard Georg Graue, whose arrival at the
Cape from Germany in 1937 was to herald the beginning of a new and glorious era for Nederburg and ulti-
mately to lead to the transformation of the entire South
African wine industry.

Georg Graue, as he was known to his family and
friends — he ignored the second of his three names entirely — was born in the great industrial city of Bremen,
Germany's second largest port, on 1 November 1892
and baptized in the Protestant cathedral of St Peter on
12 February of the following year. He came from a well-
to-do upper middle-class family and grew up in a home
in which the good things of life were both appreciated
and respected. His forebears had founded the well-

known Haake-Beck brewery, producers of Becks Beer, which is enjoyed all over Europe to this day, and his father, Hermann Heinrich Graue, was one of its directors. Johann Georg Graue was educated at the Bremen Gymnasium and, as a preparation for a career in the brewery, at the Institute for Fermentation Science in Berlin. He then went on to train in viticulture and beer-making at various wine estates and breweries, but it was in the tea trade that he gained his first practical experience of the business world.. On the outbreak of the First World War in 1914 his skill as a horseman — hunting was one of his favourite pastimes — led him to join a cavalry regiment of the German army, the Fourth Hussars, in which he held the rank of lieutenant when the armistice was signed in 1918. On his demobilization, Johann Georg Graue followed in his father's footsteps by joining the staff of the Haake-Beck brewery, later becoming a director and part-owner. Meanwhile, in marrying Ilse Sophie Koster in the early 1920s, he established a link with South Africa which was to remain unbroken for the rest of his life.

Ilse was born in Johannesburg on 9 March 1898. Her father had left his native Germany as a young bachelor some time in the 1870s to seek a better life in South Africa, at that time burgeoning industrially as a result of the discovery of diamonds. He obtained a post in Port Elizabeth, then an important marketing centre for goods from the interior, as a clerk in the well-known mercantile firm of Mosenthal Brothers, where he had every opportunity to meet passing traders and hear their accounts of fortunes grouted from the arid sands of the northern Cape. Lured by their tales, he abandoned the security of Mosenthals' ledgers and climbed aboard a wagon loaded with adventurers heading for the diamond fields. However, it was not in the fabulous blue ground of the Kimberley Mine that Johann Koster was to find his fortune. Alfred Beit, who not long before had come to South Africa from Europe as buyer for a firm of Amsterdam diamond dealers, met Johann Koster in Kimberley and quickly recognized the young Koster's natural business acumen; and when gold was discovered on the Witwatersrand in 1886, he suggested that he should accompany him to the Reef. During the following years, partly as a result of Beit's generosity in giving him small participations in new gold-mining ventures and partly as a result of an inspired hunch that there was still gold to be found in the Boksburg area after the big companies had discontinued operations, Johann Koster built up a very substantial bank balance. Still a bachelor in his late thirties, he returned to Germany for a holiday and while in Bremen was captivated — at a distance — by the charms of a young girl he saw seated on the top of a horse bus. When she alighted he secretly followed her until she reached home and then returned

the following day to present himself to her parents in typical, formal German manner. He discovered that the object of his instant infatuation lived with her foster-parents, Herr and Frau Liebermann, that her name was May Margaret Elizabeth Schernekau and that she was actually of aristocratic Russian birth. Johann Peter Koster must have found favour with the Liebermanns for he and May were married fairly soon afterwards and left Germany to make their home in Johannesburg.

These were troubled times in South Africa and when the South African War broke out in October 1899, Johann Koster, who had taken out Transvaal citizenship some time before, decided to retire from business and return to Germany. Ilse, their first child and 18 months old at the time, was thus to spend her childhood and schooldays in Bremen. But if the Kosters — there were eventually three daughters and two sons — escaped the worst of the South African War, they were destined to be in the thick of it in Germany when the Great War broke out in 1914. Johann's valuable assets in South Africa were confiscated by the Custodian of Enemy Property and it was only in 1920 that he was able to return to fight for their restitution. The sum that he was paid out was a mere fraction of the current market value of his various shares but, undeterred, he made a new home in Cape Town and set about restoring his lost fortune by shrewd speculation on the stock exchange.

And perhaps this shrewdness was Johann Koster's most outstanding quality, for by 1937 he had become certain of the ominous direction in which Nazi Germany was heading and was convinced that a Second World War was inevitable. Understandably, his concern for his two daughters, then living in Bremen, was paramount, for by then Ilse was married to Johann Georg Graue and her youngest sister, Vera, was the wife of Lalo Claussen. With a determination that was yet another of his characteristics, Johann Koster urged both couples to leave Germany for good and settle with their children in South Africa. The third Koster daughter, Noel, was married to Clive Corder, a director of Syfrets Trust Company in Cape Town, and with his aid and the security of £20 000 held on their behalf for investment, arrangements were made for the immigration of the two families. History does not record the conflicting emotions with which the Graues and the Claussens disposed of their homes in Bremen and packed up their possessions, nor how they felt as they stepped ashore from the German liner, the S.S. *Pretoria*, when she docked in Cape Town harbour on 2 September 1937, precisely two years before the outbreak of war; but, according to the memoirs of Clive Corder, neither family ever regretted the move.

Lalo and Vera Claussen had brought with them

their three small children, while Georg and Ilse Graue were accompanied by their only son, Johann Heinrich Arnold, a bright and lively 13-year-old always known by his third given name. It was fortunate that while the two families made up their minds where to settle, the Kosters were able to accommodate them all in their large and comfortable home, Tenterden, in Wellington Avenue, Wynberg. Lalo Claussen eventually bought a farm in Banghoek beyond Stellenbosch while, fortunately for posterity, Johann Georg Graue decided that Nederburg was the place for him.

He had several German friends in the area and, besides that attraction, it is likely that Clive Corder had recommended the purchase for, as a director of Syfrets Trust Company, which managed Colonel Robert Lyall's business affairs at the Cape, he would have known that it was on the market. Unfortunately, by 1937 Nederburg was undoubtedly in a run-down condition. Colonel Lyall had invested a considerable amount of money in the farm's development and had worked with dedication during the 11 years that he lived there, but since 1935 he had been out of touch with it, for it had been leased to his former manager. All the same, Johann Georg Graue saw its potential and was prepared to pay £28 270 for it — £21 020 more than it had cost Colonel Lyall in 1924. Transfer was passed on 30 December and the following day — New Year's Eve and the high point of the Cape's silly season — Graue moved in, temporarily opting for accommodation in one of the outbuildings. The house was due to be extensively renovated and as Paarl at the height of midsummer was no place for a woman and child fresh from the gentler climate of

northern Europe, Ilse and Arnold remained with the Kosters in the relatively cool suburb of Wynberg.

On New Year's Day 1938, when Johann Georg Graue appraised his new domain, he had at his side two important assistants: one was Corrie Coetzee, his newly-appointed and youthful manager, and the other was Hein Schräder, a 'maintenance man' he had brought out from Germany. Together they tramped over Nederburg's 118 morgen and 398 square roods and found that all the land that the previous owners had considered suitable was under vines, then in the lush beauty of full leaf. There was a block of one of the drought- and sunburn-resistant Pedro cultivars, while the remaining vineyards were under the popular Sémillon, or Green Grape, as it was generally known locally. Colonel Lyall had planted extensive olive groves, but since this fruit held little appeal for Johann Georg Graue he soon afterwards gave Corrie Coetzee instructions to pull up the trees and plant apricots instead. There were, in fact, several apricot orchards already in full bearing; most of the crop would be dried before being marketed. Peaches and plums were the other summer fruits then cultivated at Nederburg and orchards of various forms of citrus were flourishing, as well as guavas and almonds. But naturally — since his background lay in the liquor industry — it was the vines that captured Graue's imagination. The harvest was fast approaching and the grapes were swelling and sweetening under a blistering summer sun. Soon it would be time to gather the fruit in bushel baskets, to load it into mule-drawn wagons and bring it into the old thatched wine cellar below the homestead. Then would follow the initial step

in wine production which, in those days, was to tip the ripe grapes into a small hand-turned crusher balanced over a concrete tank into which the juice drained. These tanks were used for storage, though of course a good deal of the must was allowed to ferment in the seven giant oak vats inherited from some unknown past owner long since dead. From dawn to dusk throughout the hottest period of the year the harvest would continue; only in April would the doors of the cellar be closed and the remainder of the wine-making process left to Nature to complete in the dim silence within.

For Johann Georg Graue at this stage, wine-making at Nederburg was little more than a hobby and time and again he had to appeal to the authorities both at the K.W.V. and at Elsenburg Agricultural College for advice. What concerned him most during that vintage of 1938 was that the farm should pay its way; the grand ideal of creating Cape wines of a quality comparable to the finest that Europe could produce was hardly the shadow of a dream.

Meanwhile, all was activity in and about the homestead itself. Perhaps it is not surprising that Nederburg's charms did not entirely captivate Ilse Graue, accustomed as she was to a sophisticated style of living in the city of Bremen. Photographs show the home that she shared there with Georg and Arnold to be a square stolidly-designed three-storey house with a fourth floor, no doubt accommodating servants, in the roof. Rows of windows, identical and unblinking, allowed the pale northern sunshine to illuminate what must have been a capacious interior. In comparison Nederburg, with its simple H-plan and small, shuttered casements, must

PAGE 108: TOP LEFT
Glass in hand, Johann Georg Graue samples one of Nederburg's white wines.
TOP RIGHT
Ilse Graue, now a widow, proudly displays one of the rare bottles of wine produced by the short-lived company, Johann Graue Estates.
BOTTOM
To Arnold, life in all its facets presented a challenge. Here he is seen against the background of the snow-covered Matroosberg where he delighted in skiing.
PAGE 109
Farm manager, Corrie Coetzee, and maintenance man, Hein Schräder, pose to allow 14-year-old Arnold Graue to photograph them.

have seemed hardly more than a cottage. To Ilse Graue's way of thinking, one did not sleep on the ground level, so a double-storeyed wing — later known as 'the flat' — was added. Thatched like the rest of the house, its upper floor contained bedrooms and two bathrooms, while the lower storey consisted of two suites, one for the resident German housekeeper and the other for guests. As there was insufficient space in the house for Ilse's grand piano, the front room on the south side was extended to the edge of the encircling stoep and, to retain at least a semblance of symmetry, a sun porch was added at the opposite end. Because of the roof-structure, these two extensions were considerably lower than the original wing and, since they lacked the fine yellowwood beams of the rest of the house, the whole of the enlarged drawingroom was given a plaster ceiling.

Next, the front windows were doubled in size. Ilse Graue loved light — perhaps a salient characteristic of a person who was open and honest and radiated gentle warmth — and Nederburg's first owners, with Paarl's notoriously hot summers in mind, had done their best to banish sunshine and keep its interior cool and shadowy. The noble *bo-en-onder* front door with its gleaming brass escutcheons and the dolphin knocker added by Colonel Lyall was banished to a more lowly position at the entrance of the flat and supplanted by a new one with clear glass panes. French windows, leading into the courts between the wings, brought winter sunshine into the house, and the interior was opened up by the removal of the carved teak screen between *voor-* and *agterkamer*. By this time the ancient broad yellowwood floorboards probably needed replacement, so they were

SYFRET'S TRUST COMPANY LIMITED.

CHAIRMAN
GERALD EDWARD D'ARCY ORPEN
MANAGING DIRECTORS
CECIL LOUIS SHORT
HENRY ARCHIBALD JESSE
DIRECTORS
KENNETH WILMAN JOHNSTON
WILLIAM KERR GIBSON
CLIVE SINCLAIR CORDER

THE COMPANY UNDERTAKES
THE INVESTMENT OF CAPITAL, EXECUTORSHIPS.
TRUST ESTATE & AGENCY BUSINESS OF EVERY
DESCRIPTION.

TELEGRAPHIC & CABLE ADDRESS
"SYFRETS"

TELEPHONE
Nº2-6162.(5 LINES)

POST OFFICE BOX
Nº 206

CSC/JM

⅚ WALE & BURG STREETS.
CAPE TOWN.

25th August, 19 37.

PLEASE ADDRESS ALL COMMUNICATIONS TO P.O. BOX 206 CAPE TOWN.

Principal Immigration Officer,
Bouquet Street,
CAPE TOWN.

Dear Sir,
      re: Entrance Permits - G. Graue and family
           and G.F. Claussen and family.

        We refer to previous correspondence in connection herewith and, in terms of our conversation with Mr. Thompson over the telephone to-day, confirm that the financial position of both the above-mentioned immigrants is sound and that we ourselves are holding an amount of approximately £20,000. for investment on be--half of both Mr. Graue and Mr. Claussen.   An Affidavit to this effect was forwarded some time ago to the South African Embassy in Berlin.

        Yours faithfully,

        DIRECTOR.

G.P.-S.2769—1937—15,000-100. S.

South African
CONFIDENTIAL.
Police.

Vr.4/1/9/42.

S.A.P. 21.

Suid-Afrikaanse
Polisie.

Office of the District Commandant,
P.O.Box 15, WORCESTER, 31. 10. 1942.

The Magistrate/Control Officer,
C a l e d o n.

      re : Mr J.G. GRAUE OF PAARL.

        Your minute 17/25/35 dated 29th inst refers.
        In view of the fact that Graue is allowed to visit Cape Town where all the shipping activities is going on, I now see no reason why he should not be allowed to visit Hermanus and must therefore recind my previous views.
        The annexure to your minute is herewith returned.

        INSPECTOR.
DISTRICT COMMANDANT,NO.7. DISTRICT...

ripped up and replaced by the then fashionable parquet blocks. And, in a major alteration, the entire orientation of the house was swung about: the west-facing aspect, originally the front, now looked over Mrs Graue's new and glorious rose garden and the east-facing former morningroom, looking towards the Klein Drakenstein mountains, became the new entrance to the house. To give point to this room, the Batavian tiles, dating back to the days of Dutch East India Company rule, were prised off the *agterkamer* floor and re-laid within the entrance and the beautiful stinkwood and yellowwood wall-cupboard was removed from its original niche and set in the wall facing the door where every visitor to the house could see it.

This transformation — or transmogrification — of Nederburg homestead would not have charmed Dorothea Fairbridge, pioneer protagonist of local vernacular architecture, had she lived to see it. In an article that appeared in the periodical, *The State*, in November 1911, she wrote of Nederburg that it was 'a rare experience . . . to find an old Cape homestead upon which the sacrilegious hand of the restorer has been arrested'. Undoubtedly she would have deplored the loss of the original elegant proportions of the house, the disappearance — for ever, it seems — of the *porte-de-visite* screen and the insensitive interruption of the wide sweep of the encircling *stoep* by the new front extensions. Today, 80 years later, her sentiments are echoed by many purists who believe that the Cape's remaining heritage of gabled 'Dutch' houses should be cherished untouched — but such thoughts rarely occurred to people in the 1930s. Ilse Graue's intention was to make Nederburg the sort of home in which she and her family could live in comfort and where she could entertain guests with the hospitality at which she excelled.

When at last the house was complete the time had arrived for six enormous packing cases containing the Graues' possessions to be delivered and unpacked. The farm staff stood by as they were offloaded from the vans that brought them from storage. They watched as officials pronounced that all was well and gave permission for the metal hoops that bound the cases to be ripped off and the wooden sides to be wrenched open. Then out came the heavy German furniture, a long-case clock as old as Nederburg itself, Mrs Graue's beloved Bechstein piano, priceless paintings, silver, porcelain, crystal glass . . . A complete mystery to the workers who unpacked it was the elaborate central-heating system that had been brought out with the Graues from Bremen. When installed at Nederburg it worked perfectly and for years provided comfort in the winter to many a guest who would otherwise have shivered. There was no doubt that the Graues intended to live in the homestead permanently and to farm Nederburg for the rest of their lives.

And all the while, during this first year — and for the rest of his life — Johann Georg Graue observed and took heed of all that happened on the farm. Every morning he saddled his horse and rode all over his estate; he constantly supervised and instructed, making sure that the daily round, the seasonal duties, were performed with the meticulousness one tends to associate with the Teutonic ethos. For advice, he turned to a Polish immigrant, Dr Josef Kukuriewics, who was able to pass on to him his invaluable knowledge of cloning. Before long he developed an almost uncanny ability to assess the quality of each individual vine: he would scrutinize every plant, appraise the state of its health, notice its shape and the amount of fruit it was bearing. Then, he would taste the grapes just before ripening and estimate their sugar-acid ratio for, with his fine palate, he could foretell what quality and character of wine they would produce. The stems of the vines that came up to his high standard were marked with white paint and used the following season for grafting purposes, but those that he did not select were not rejected, for it soon became Johann Georg Graue's principal objective to expand as rapidly as possible and to increase the tonnage of grapes harvested annually. In any case, the life-span of each and every vine was between five and ten years, so they would all have to be uprooted eventually.

Plant selection was undoubtedly one of Johann Georg Graue's strongest points as a viticulturist. Another was his ability to recognize that particular cultivars flourished and produced high-quality grapes on certain soil where others failed — yet in other areas, with a different kind of soil, those 'failures' became 'successes'. Nederburg's soil, as Johann Georg Graue soon discovered, was by no means suitable for every type of grape; therefore, he reasoned, if he wished to make a variety of wines, he would have to buy in a variety of grapes from farms where the specific cultivars were known to do well. So his policy and practice of selection began to develop and as he perfected it he established one of the corner-stones of his success as a viticulturist *par excellence*. Meanwhile, on Nederburg itself he established a nursery and began to replace existing varieties with those, such as Clairette blanche, Steen and Riesling, that were better suited to its soil. All plantings were painstakingly recorded, as was the lineage and performance of every individual vine on the farm and, with experience, Johann Georg Graue began to develop a philosophy as regards wine-making. Good wine, he maintained, is produced by healthy vines, for only a healthy vine will produce good grapes. And, fundamentally, the health of those vines has its origin in the soil.

To produce perfect vines, therefore, he had to provide them with ideal conditions. Here, again, Johann Georg Graue was ahead of his time for he believed firmly in what was then considered an ultra-modern agricultural method, namely, biodynamics. Scarcely heard of in the South Africa of those days, it was inspired by the philosophy of Rudolf Steiner and involved making compost consisting exclusively of organic materials: every leaf dropped from vine or oak tree was collected, all waste matter from wine pressings was saved and added to manure provided by his own farm animals, as well as that acquired from elsewhere. Guano was bought in and tons of Karoo sheep manure was dumped in the compost yard under the oaks. Methodical as ever, Johann Georg Graue would keep a careful check on the temperature generated as the great steaming mass slowly decomposed. Its addition to the farm lands was part and parcel of his conviction that good wine has its origin in healthy soil; indeed, his theories proved so successful that he was invited to give a lecture-demonstration on the subject at Elsenburg Agricultural College.

In time Johann Georg Graue's preoccupation with viticulture superseded all other interests and one by one Nederburg's orchards of deciduous fruit and citrus were uprooted to be replaced by vineyards. With his German background he tended to concentrate mainly on the white-wine cultivars, particularly those of the Moselle and Riesling type, but later he extended his scope and began to experiment with the reds — Cabernet was one of the first that he introduced.

But Nederburg's ultimate success as a producer of superb wines was the result of more than Johann Georg Graue's genius for selection combined with his advanced farming methods, important though they certainly were. That success lay, eventually, in the perfection of a technique known as 'cold fermentation', and it was the mastery of this process at Nederburg that was to raise the quality of its wines above all others at the Cape (see Chapters Eight and Ten). When Georg Graue first learnt about it, the theory was not a new one: experiments which had been conducted at the K.W.V. since the 1920s had involved an attempt to produce wine in conditions simulating as far as possible those of the cellars of Europe. The idea had arisen from an awareness that the inferiority of Cape wines to those of Europe had some connection with the fact that the local harvest occurs when high summer temperatures reach their peak, whereas in countries such as France and Germany the ripe grapes reach the cellars in the cool air of early autumn. Consequently, fermentation at the Cape occurs far more rapidly than it does in Europe and this undoubtedly has a detrimental effect, particularly on white wines. In fact, when fermentation takes place in excessively hot weather the natural process can be speeded up to such an extent that the yeast cells are

PAGE 110: TOP
Clive Corder, brother-in-law of Johann Georg Graue and Lalo Claussens, and a director of Syfrets Trust Company, handled the 'red tape' involved in obtaining the Graues' entrance permits in 1937.
BOTTOM
Although Johann Georg Graue was not interned during the Second World War, certain restrictions were placed on his movements, as this document shows.

paralysed, thus leading to 'stuck' fermentation. At these high temperatures, large quantities of volatile esters and bouquet substances escape and are lost for ever.

With this knowledge — and the benefit of the expertise of their technical adviser, Nino Costa — Nederburg's neighbours, Monis Wineries in Paarl, had begun to experiment with cold fermentation in the 1930s. They had had some startling results, particularly in the production of sparkling wine, but the outbreak of the Second World War put paid to further expansion because of the impossibility of importing essential machinery and jacketed tanks from France. In September 1939 the Graues were on a holiday visit to Europe and a cable dated the 20th of that month, which an agitated Clive Corder sent to them in Zurich, gives some indication of the seriousness of their position. It reads: 'Cannot guarantee you would not be interned but consider this unlikely by reason circumstances under which you settled in South Africa stop we all think it advisable Ilse Arnold return farm whilst you could remain in Lourenço Marques if your position doubtful stop new local exchange restrictions may make further remittance to you impossible stop final decision must rest with you stop meanwhile arranging confirmation immigration visa.' The following day Clive Corder received a brusque telegram from the commissioner of Immigration and Asiatic Affairs in Pretoria stating unequivocally that

TOP
Nederburg homestead shortly after
the Graues had altered and enlarged it.
The additions to the front façade
can be seen, as well as the roof of the
double-storeyed 'flat' (behind, left).
The windows have been doubled in size
and the old bo-en-onder door replaced by
one with clear glass panes.
BOTTOM
The gable-end of the new 'flat'
added in 1938.

the Graues were forbidden permission to re-enter the Union of South Africa. However, the necessary strings must have been pulled, for a letter written to Clive Corder from the same office on 6 October reads: 'I have to inform you that as a result of further representations made to Honourable Minister in regard to the return to the Union of Mr J.A.G. [*sic*] Graue, it has been decided that this man should be allowed to re-enter . . .' As a result the Graues obtained berths in an Italian ship sailing to the Cape via the east coast of Africa and returned to Nederburg in time to find the vines bursting into new spring growth.

The war years were not easy for Johann Georg Graue. Unlike many German subjects, including his brother-in-law, Lalo Claussen, who was married to Ilse's sister Vera, he was not interned — but until he and Arnold were officially granted South African citizenship on 26 March 1944, his movements were considerably restricted. Each time he wished to move beyond a certain distance from Nederburg he had to obtain permission from the magistrate in the relevant district and, once at his destination, report regularly to the local police station. Fortunately Ilse had never given up her South African citizenship and was not affected by the regulations, but Georg discovered that permission was not always granted him without demur, an irritation that must have irked him considerably when the family

wished to take their annual summer holiday in Hermanus. These holidays were always a source of enormous joy to the Graues. They built a fine house named 'Inruh' at Voëlklip; it was at Hermanus that Arnold, now growing up, made some of his closest friends and it was here that he enjoyed the pleasures of sea and sun and the open-air life to the full. Years later, he was to write to his parents from a snow-bound Zurich hotel that he was thinking of them at 'our beloved Hermanus' with its 'happiness, laziness, warmth . . .'

But wartime restrictions must have given Johann Georg Graue time to turn his interests inwards on the farm that was his home and to concentrate on his techniques of wine-making. Sadly, the records of vine-plantings that he kept with such painstaking precision have not survived, so it is not possible to follow the evolution and development of his systems. There is no doubt that wine-making had been taking place at Nederburg since immediately after the Graues' arrival — to begin with most of the annual vintage was sent in bulk to the K.W.V. for distilling purposes — but no one is certain of the precise date or even the year in which Johann Georg Graue began to bottle his own wine. Nevertheless, there are those still living who recall the actual occasion of that original bottling; among them is Corrie Coetzee who, using a somewhat primitive revolving device, laboriously filled over a thousand bottles by hand. Then they were brought into the homestead so that Ilse and Georg could label them — again by hand — and pack them into boxes. Once a dozen or so cases were ready, the Graues loaded them into their motor car and drove off to Cape Town in high good spirits, determined to introduce their first bottled wine to the local market. They aimed high by calling first on the Mount Nelson Hotel, but no one was interested. Then they drove on to the Cecil Hotel in Newlands, then to the well-known Vineyard Hotel nearby and so on to the St James Hotel overlooking False Bay. But, perhaps not surprisingly, no one had ever heard of Nederburg wines and not one of the hoteliers they saw was prepared to take a chance and buy even a single bottle. Undaunted, Georg and Ilse turned their attention to the Atlantic seaboard and, still smiling bravely, offered their unknown product to the manager of the historic and renowned Queen's Hotel, later the President and now destined for replacement by a larger hotel complex. To their delight he agreed, perhaps a little grudgingly or possibly out of pity, to buy a case and, in celebration and gratitude, they reserved a table in the restaurant for dinner that night. Dressed for the occasion, they arrived at the hotel a few hours later and in due course the wine list was presented. Having examined it, Johann Georg Graue confidently ordered a bottle of Nederburg Riesling — much to the perplexity

of the waiter, whose knowledge of wines certainly did not include one of that name. With an air of authority Georg told him to make enquiries from the manager and, sure enough, stashed away under the reception desk, they found the wine the Graues had sold to the hotel that afternoon. Hastily a bottle was unpacked and presented to the guests who had ordered it. Johann Georg Graue nodded approvingly at the label, tasted the wine, pronounced it excellent and then – after having himself grown and pressed the grapes; made, bottled, labelled and sold the wine – drank a toast with it to Nederburg.

This must have happened at some unrecorded moment during the war years. Arnold had matriculated at the end of 1941 and, early in the following year, signed on as a pupil air-gunner in the crash-boat wing of the South African Air Force. Joining up for South Africans during the Second World War was voluntary; so was signing on for combat anywhere in the world – doing so entitled one to have the letter 'V' (for victory) after one's name and number. Yet German-born Arnold, who was not yet a naturalized South African citizen, elected to do both these things, possibly as a gesture of loyalty and gratitude to his country of adoption. Then, too, his friends of Hermanus days, including Denis Taylor and 'Torrie' Gain – both of whom were later to work at Nederburg – had joined up immediately after leaving school. It has been said that Arnold, with his German background, had no choice but to join the crash-boats, since they were non-combatant and served an essentially humanitarian purpose in saving lives at sea. This may be, but enlisting in this wing of the South

African Air Force also gave him an opportunity to master speed in sea and sky – crash-boat personnel were known as 'sailor airmen' since they gained experience in both sailing and flying – as well as to enjoy the pleasures of the outdoors that so much appealed to him. After a spell at Gordon's Bay training centre, Arnold was posted to various crash-boat anchorages along the coast, but his letters, faithfully written to his parents each week, indicate that after a time life on what had become inactive service eventually began to pall.

Meanwhile, Arnold's father was far from idle. Observant visitors to the annual Cape Wine Show held at Paarl on 14 October 1942 might have noticed that several entries had been submitted by Nederburg Farm & Winery, but since they won no prizes they attracted scant attention from Press or public. Even the following year, when one of the five classes of white wine Johann Georg Graue had been bold enough to submit was awarded a prize, it was scarcely considered worthy of comment. Yet this modest beginning was indeed a sign of great things to come, for in 1944, and at every wine show in the years that followed, Nederburg's wines were awarded a steadily increasing number of trophies.

A single farm ledger has survived, bulky and leather-bound, which gives an insight into those years, 1944 to 1948, when Nederburg wines were winning their first prizes. Things might have been changing, but Nederburg was undoubtedly still a working farm: pigs, chickens, calves, sheep and horses were bought and sold; cows were milked, butter was churned and honey was collected from hives in the orchards. In July 1945, 32 cauliflowers brought in £1. 2s. 8d. while 100 lbs. of

potatoes were sold 'to house' for £1. 4s. 8d. Yet, at the same time, more accommodation was required for the increasing quantity of wine that was being made. During the years 1944 and 1945 a new cellar was built (it cost £6 207. 9s. 9d.) as well as a new store (costing £2 033. 14s. 10d.) and a reservoir. Bottles were in short supply and sometimes were obtainable only second-hand, but there are indications that by 1944 Nederburg wine, even in makeshift containers, was being supplied regularly to a number of retailers. At the end of the financial year, 30 June 1944, there was a stock of 1 553 dozen full bottles of wine in Nederburg's cellars and the gross wine-trading account amounted to £7 475. 5s. 1d. A year later the figure had reached £12 716. 0s. 6d.

By this time the war was all but over. Pressure of work had increased to such an extent that early in August 1945, after two atom bombs had dropped conclusively on Japanese cities, Graue began to bombard Arnold's commanding officer with letters urging him to release his son from military duties. His services, he insisted, were urgently required on the farm but, notwithstanding his pleas, over two months were to pass before Arnold was finally demobilized. He returned to Nederburg just in time for the fruit season and was paid a salary of £15 a month. (Corrie Coetzee, after eight years as manager, earned only £5 more, though no doubt with the addition of certain perks.) At this stage there was talk of sending Arnold to the United States to study wine-making, but in the meantime, in March of 1946, before the wine harvest had reached its peak, he registered as a student in the faculty of engineering at the University of Cape Town. During the week he

lived with his grandmother Koster, widowed since 1938, in Claremont and travelled to and from his studies – and to Nederburg over the weekends – by motorbike. To Arnold Graue, speed on land, sea or in the sky, was always a challenge.

But engineering failed to captivate him and before many months had passed his mind was made up – no doubt completely to his father's satisfaction. He would become a master oenologist, and in order to achieve this ambition arrangements were made for him to train in every aspect of the profession at the best schools that Europe had to offer. Travelling in those early post-war days was difficult, but Arnold managed to secure an air-booking to London and from there to Zurich, where he arrived on 21 October 1946. From then on, his meticulous father kept copies of every letter that he wrote to his son – invariably typed and in German – as well as the original of every one – most of them in English – that Arnold wrote home each weekend.

While those letters are a revelation of the devotion between son and parents, they are also an indication of Arnold's total commitment to the training to which he had submitted himself – and to his joy in the glorious outdoors of Switzerland when time allowed him to relax. He went skiing during the weekends at what he described as 'heavenly, healthy, harmonious . . . Arosa', but he enjoyed equally the essential experience of ploughing and planting in the sun. 'Hard manual labour does me good,' he commented on one occasion. His training in viniculture began with the science of wine-making, which he studied at Werdenswiel Wine Research Institute, on Lake Zurich under the famous

Dr Lüthi, writing home with comments on what he was learning and passing on suggestions to his father. Johann Georg Graue, meanwhile, reported on events and progress at Nederburg and sent samples of his wine for Arnold to introduce to his teachers and fellow-students. On 2 May 1947, after he had opened some bottles to share with his colleagues and the cellar-master, he reported that 'although the Riesling was appreciated as a high class, clean and faultless wine equivalent to the best Swiss wines . . . the Cabernet was regarded as even higher in quality and it was more or less admitted that one couldn't find anything to equal it so easily in Switzerland. So you see, Pappi,' he wrote cheerfully, 'we can be quite proud of our product − [we] must only try to keep it like this.' Arnold's intelligent approach and enquiring mind must have impressed his lecturers: in one of his letters he remarks on the attention they were prepared to give him and commends them for their patience, for, he says, 'they must be tired of answering my questions'.

Meanwhile, in 1946 Johann Georg Graue had taken on the services of a young German named Werner Thielscher who was to remain at Nederburg, first as his secretary and later as a director, for ten years. Thielscher was responsible for administration and, later, of sales, while Sarel Rossouw, later wine-maker at Simons-

TOP
An aerial photograph of Nederburg taken in the early 1950s, probably by Arnold Graue. The additions to the house and the enlarged cellars are clearly visible, as are the thatched stables and other farm buildings behind the old manager's house.
BOTTOM
The bottling plant introduced by Johann Georg Graue. One of the secrets of his success was the meticulous cleanliness observed in every stage of wine-making.

vlei Co-operative Wine Cellars, was in charge of the cellars, and a Swiss named Thomann looked after the vineyards. Theirs was a very happy relationship, but even with their help, the staff at Nederburg could not handle all that had to be done and one and all looked forward to Arnold's return. By mid-1947 he had moved on to continue his studies in Lausanne, which he described as 'the greatest place', but clearly he was longing to return home and put his new-found knowledge to the test. He urged his father to improve Nederburg's cellar techniques 'to a very high standard' for he was convinced that 'we should (and can already) produce wine in South Africa that should be at least equal to and [could] even surpass the European wines'. When his father's letters conveyed that he was under considerable pressure at Nederburg, Arnold wrote, 'I do hope the time won't be too distant anymore when I shall be in a position to release you of [sic] some of this strain and stand at your side.' But that moment had still to arrive for Arnold had not yet begun what was possibly the most important period of training at the world-famous viticultural school founded in 1872 at Geisenheim in the Rheingau region of Germany. By the time he returned to Nederburg in 1948, his natural technical abilities had been honed and developed and his skills as an oenologist perfected. His knowledge and abilities in

TOP
*Decanting wine off the lees after fermentation
and transferring to wooden vats.*
BOTTOM
Arnold Graue at the champagne bottle filler.

the wine cellar complemented perfectly those of his father in the vineyard.

Happy in his work, healthy and intensely active, Arnold Graue in his early twenties reveals himself in his letters as a young man brimful of ambition in a world to which peace had returned, bringing promise of prosperity for all. In him lay the fulfilment of all his parents' hopes for the future and all his father's dreams for Nederburg. His training completed, he went on to experience all he could of the winelands of Europe. He visited Bordeaux with the express purpose of learning as much as possible there so as to help achieve his father's ambition of making Cabernet wines of the same high quality as those produced in that famous region.

But life did not stand still in Klein Drakenstein while Arnold absorbed all that was best in Europe. During the war years Johann Georg Graue had been obliged to 'make do' with equipment borrowed from Monis in his cellars and now, at last, restrictions had been lifted and he could order new machinery for the winery from abroad. As early as February 1946 a champagne plant arrived from the Société Casquet in Bordeaux and at about the same time hydraulic wine-presses were acquired for the first time. The following January a cooling machine was bought for £1 012. 2s. 7d. and by September of that year the automatic bottling and

labelling line was in use. Now, at last, he could make use of the most modern plant and machinery to implement and develop the theory of cold fermentation, much of the knowledge of which he had acquired from his friendly association with Monis. The first stage involved making use of the newly-arrived jacketed champagne fermenters in which brine contained in an outer sleeve maintained the low temperature of the white wine must in an internal drum. This marked the beginning of a most important phase in the history of Nederburg: by introducing meticulous temperature control to his wine-making, Johann Georg Graue brought to his cellars the same degree of precision that his practice of selection had given him in his vineyards. It was this combination, developed and refined, that was in time to place Johann Georg Graue in the forefront of South Africa's wine producers.

It was at the 1947 Cape Wine Show – almost in justification of his theories and all the costly expansion that their implementation had involved – that Nederburg, which had been awarded an increasing number of prizes each year, broke its own record by carrying off seven first prizes, including the Frank Myburgh Perpetual Floating Trophy for the most outstanding exhibit of white wine of the hock type. October saw the incorporation of Nederburg Winery (Pty) Limited as a company with Georg and Ilse Graue as directors and Werner Thielscher as secretary. New offices were completed as well as an additional cellar and by the end of the financial year 1947-1948, the farm land and buildings were valued at £33 360 – an increase of almost £13 000 over the figure of four years earlier. The 'bottom line' in Nederburg's record of wine sales during the same period reveals a figure of £20 742. 9s. 7d. – almost three times the turnover of 1944-1945. Johann Georg Graue certainly had every reason to feel satisfied.

When Arnold returned from Europe he immediately set about putting his newly acquired knowledge and ideas into practice, both in the vineyards and in the cellars. First and foremost a technician, he was naturally anxious to refine the newly-introduced cold fermentation process, and he converted the old office into a laboratory where he could conduct experiments and tests. Any challenge to advance the technology of wine-making was eagerly taken up, so it is no surprise to find Arnold boldly introducing to Nederburg the complex process of sterile bottling that he had come across, unperfected, in Germany. In this, the finished, clarified wines are run through filters consisting of 4 millimetre-thick cellulose pads packed with a fairly high proportion of asbestos fibre, the whole thing being so fine that even a single yeast cell will be retained. This method of preserving without recourse to pasteurization or the use of preservatives is so demanding of meticulous vigilance and scrupulous hygiene that it had never been fully accepted in Europe; yet Arnold installed it at Nederburg with a success unparalleled anywhere in the world. He used the same efficient method for the bottling of grape juice, a product that he later abandoned as it proved uneconomical and did not really conform with Nederburg's image as a wine farm.

Despite his single-minded dedication to his work, Arnold did find time for those leisure activities that meant so much to him – swimming, surfing and fishing at Hermanus and gathering his friends together for mountain-climbing expeditions whenever possible. His enthusiasm for flying was no doubt originally inspired by stories told by his daredevil uncle, Hans Koster, whose numerous hair-raising adventures included piloting an amphibian aircraft up and down China's Yangtze River for 18 months. Arnold could handle an aircraft with expertise and Werner Thielscher still has happy memories of flying with him. The heady sense of the liberty of the skies and the challenge of speed that flying presented were all part of Arnold's nature, for there was no holding his free spirit. For £2. 14s. he could hire a Piper light aircraft from Owen Air at Youngsfield for an afternoon's entertainment and on occasions would fly low over Nederburg, dipping a wing in greeting – always to the considerable alarm of his mother.

Nederburg's crest and the initials of Johann Georg and Arnold Graue moulded in plaster on the end wall of the cellar built in 1948. The crest incorporates the crossed anchors featured in the coat of arms of the Haake-Beck Brewery, of which Johann Georg Graue was a director before emigrating from Germany.

Arnold's presence at Nederburg enabled his parents to make regular visits to Europe, confident that all would be cared for in their absence. By 1950 Johann Georg Graue had enough faith in his wines to send several entries to the Empire Wine Exhibition in London and one imagines the excitement at Nederburg when it was learnt that its wines had been awarded four prizes – one first, two seconds and a third. When the Cape Wine Show was held on 29 September of that year Georg and Ilse were in Europe, but the staff at home lost no time in informing them of the results. 'Missing our managing director,' the cable read. 'Celebrating with our own excellent Nederburg champagne outstanding success today's wine show. Received following awards gold medal for most points six cups seven first two second and two third prizes congratulations and sincerest greetings.' At last Nederburg had been awarded the prestigious *Farmer's Weekly* gold medal; it was to win it on many occasions to come.

Naturally, the success of Nederburg's wines stimulated increased public interest in them and it soon became obvious that the demand was rapidly exceeding the supply. In fact, for some time Nederburg was in the unique position of having to ration some of its wines. Unfortunately this situation could not be resolved merely by planting more vines, for in an attempt to eliminate the age-old problem of surplus wines at the Cape, the K.W.V. had, for many years, laid down strict limits of production, allocating a certain quota, and no more, to each farm. Nederburg had reached its limit and the only way to increase it was to buy more farm land on which there was already a wine quota. So, in 1950, when the neighbouring farm 'Highlands', comprising 41,773 morgen of the old Huguenot farms of St Omer and Calais, came on to the market, the Graues bought it for £9 500. For the purpose of ratifying and adopting an agreement of purchase and sale between Highlands' former owner, Gideon Abraham Rousseau Uijs, and Johann Richard Georg Graue, a new company was formed on 28 November 1950. Its name was Nederburg Estates (Pty) Limited and the directors were the Graues, father and son.

An estate, by definition and to the Graues' way of thinking, was a large area of landed property, generally in the country. It conveyed a sense of expansiveness, of dignity, of a civilized lifestyle and, of course, of beauty of buildings and of landscape. In Germany an estate such as Nederburg would be known as a *weingut*: it would comprise a vineyard of substantial size, a cellar where wine-making and bottling took place and a homestead where the owner and his family lived in elegant and gracious style. Both Nederburg and Highlands – or 'Hochheim', as Johann Georg Graue later renamed it – could be accurately described as *weingute* in

IN LOVING MEMORY OF

ARNOLD GRAUE.

WINE EXPERT AND TECHNICAL DIRECTOR OF
NEDERBURG ESTATE.
BORN 23.2.1924 IN BREMEN, GERMANY,
UNDER WHOSE DIRECTION THIS CELLAR WAS ERECTED
DURING 1952/53.
HE WAS TRAGICALLY KILLED IN A FLYING ACCIDENT
AT YOUNGSFIELD AERODROME, CAPE TOWN
ON SEPTEMBER THE 12TH 1953.

every connotation of the word and Nederburg Estates (Pty) Limited was the obvious and appropriate name for the new company.

These were halcyon days for Nederburg and its owners. The wines produced at this time were mainly Riesling or Cabernet types and Johann Georg Graue was also making a certain amount of sherry. Arnold had set up a bachelor establishment in the old house, Hochheim, and from the Riesling grapes that he grew there the new Hochheimer wine was made. Meanwhile, busy in cellar and laboratory, Arnold was making progress on the process of cold fermentation. Prizes continued to be heaped on an increasing variety of wines whose popularity surpassed all expectations. Yet Johann Georg Graue was beginning to feel the effects of advancing age – he celebrated his 60th birthday on 1 November 1952 – and was suffering severely from arthritis. In 1953, he and Ilse decided that it would be wise to visit the renowned German spa of Baden-Baden during their annual European holiday and 'take the waters' in an attempt to relieve the complaint. Arnold, once more, was left in charge of Nederburg.

On the evening of Friday 11 September he wrote to his parents from Hochheim, covering seven pages of ruled, blue 'linen-face' paper with his scrawling handwriting. 'Meine lieben . . .' he starts and continues, in German, to commiserate with his father on the apparent failure of the waters of Baden-Baden to effect a cure. He describes in detail his latest plans for Nederburg,

The plaque erected in memory of Arnold Graue in the entrance to Nederburg's cellars. The brilliant and promising only child of Johann Georg and Ilse Graue was killed in an air collision in September 1953.

including an elaborate but foolproof new irrigation system. He talks of the glorious spring weather that the Cape is enjoying and reports that all is well in vineyard and wine cellar. Then he must have been interrupted; the letter was never completed.

The next day he drove in to Cape Town and lunched with a girlfriend and his uncle, Clive Corder, at the Royal Cape Golf Club in Wynberg. It was perfect weather and as Arnold took leave of his uncle – he was always formal in manner, clicking his heels and bowing in the best Teutonic style – he said that he intended hiring a Piper Cruiser from Owen Air, almost opposite the golf club, and taking a 'flip' over the Peninsula. Clive Corder collected his clubs, waved good-bye to his guests as the girlfriend went her way on her own, and set off to meet the challenge of 18 holes. For both men, the afternoon held pleasing prospects.

Halfway through the afternoon a dull but chilling thud caused Clive Corder to look up in alarm from the golf course. In the blue spring sky above Youngsfield, a South African Air Force Harvard trainer coming in to land was locked in mid-air with a small commercial aircraft. Even as Clive Corder focused his dazed eyes on them, both aeroplanes exploded in a searing sheet of flame and a tangle of molten metal crashed to the ground close to the nearby railway station. In a single devastating instant, Clive Corder, sick with horror, knew that the pilot of one of those aircraft had been Arnold Graue. ∎

CHAPTER EIGHT

FROM GRAUE TO MONIS:

THE YEARS OF EXPANSION 1953-1966

Three years after Arnold's tragic death, Graue handed over
50 per cent of Nederburg's control to Monis Wineries. That year,
Günter Brözel arrived from Germany as cellar assistant and it
was his genius, coupled with the technological expertise of Dr Nino Costa,
that developed and perfected the work begun by the Graues.
When Johann Georg Graue died in 1959 Nederburg had become
South Africa's most renowned wine producer.

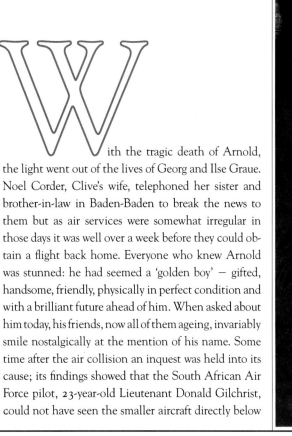ith the tragic death of Arnold, the light went out of the lives of Georg and Ilse Graue. Noel Corder, Clive's wife, telephoned her sister and brother-in-law in Baden-Baden to break the news to them but as air services were somewhat irregular in those days it was well over a week before they could obtain a flight back home. Everyone who knew Arnold was stunned: he had seemed a 'golden boy' — gifted, handsome, friendly, physically in perfect condition and with a brilliant future ahead of him. When asked about him today, his friends, now all of them ageing, invariably smile nostalgically at the mention of his name. Some time after the air collision an inquest was held into its cause; its findings showed that the South African Air Force pilot, 23-year-old Lieutenant Donald Gilchrist, could not have seen the smaller aircraft directly below him as his view of it was obscured by the Harvard's wing situated under the cockpit. For that matter, Arnold had not been able to see Gilchrist's aircraft either for, in the case of the Piper Cruiser, the wing was above the cockpit. But what did it matter, who was to blame when two young men, both full of promise, had died?

The shadow of the tragedy hung heavily over the annual Western Province Wine Show held at Paarl less than a fortnight after the accident. That year, for the first time, Nederburg broke all records by winning 12 first prizes and two thirds as well as the sought-after *Farmer's Weekly* gold medal for the highest number of points awarded and the General Smuts cup for the most outstanding wine on the show. But the man responsible for making those superb wines was not there to receive the trophies and one by one, as the secretary of the

Show read out the results, the prizes were set aside to be unobtrusively collected later by a member of the Nederburg staff. And when it was publicly announced — and to no one's surprise — that Arnold Graue had been selected as 'wine king' of the year, instead of responding with the usual applause, every person in the crowded Paarl Town Hall stood with head bowed in respectful and sorrowful silence.

Arnold was dead, and at first Johann Georg Graue could not come to terms with remaining at Nederburg. He seriously contemplated selling the farm and winery, but when he eventually braced himself to take stock of the situation he realized that if he gave up Nederburg everything that he and Arnold had achieved there would be lost. At that time there was no one working in Nederburg's cellars or vineyards suited or qualified to take his son's place: obviously someone else would have to be found. That would be no easy task, for Arnold, with his rare dedication and even rarer skills, had been unique. A solution seemed to lie in the person and family of Johann Georg Graue's brother-in-law, Clive Corder, a man of undoubted business acumen and considerable experience in the world of finance. Corder's son, Peter, at that time an undergraduate reading law at Cambridge, seemed the person who might inherit Arnold's role at Nederburg, even though at that stage he had had little experience of, and no training in, wine-making. Considerably younger than Arnold, he had admired, even hero-worshipped, his cousin and would be well-disposed towards following in his footsteps. A cable was hurriedly despatched to him; the new academic year — Peter's last at Cambridge — was due to begin in three days and he was given that brief time in which to make up his mind between a future in the legal profession or in farming. It was no easy decision to make but before

the three days were up Nederburg had won the day. Soon afterwards Peter put away his law books and enrolled at Geisenheim, as Arnold had done, to study the skills and science of viticulture and wine-making.

Meanwhile, on Wednesday 31 March 1954, at a joint meeting of the directors of Nederburg Estates (Pty) Limited and of Nederburg Winery (Pty) Limited, Mrs Ilse Graue, who had been on both boards since their inception, gave notice that she wished to retire from participation in the companies. Consequently, following an offer by Johann Georg Graue, a 50 per cent share in the combined business was then assumed by Clive Corder. According to Clive's privately published memoirs, *Coat of Many Colours*, it was understood that Peter would eventually take over his father's half share in the winery and that Clive Corder would have the option to assume the remaining 50 per cent on Georg Graue's death. However, things did not work out according to plan and Clive Corder sold back his 50 per cent share to his brother-in-law without profit. In fact, he handed in his resignation from Nederburg at a meeting on 29 June 1954, less than three months after he had taken on the directorships. Peter continued his training at Geisenheim but when he returned to South Africa it was not to farm at Nederburg.

For over a year Johann Georg Graue, now hampered by severe arthritis, battled on, though there was no doubt that since Arnold's death he had had no heart for wine-making. Horst Saalwächter, who had arrived from Germany in February 1953 as a cellar assistant, had taken over the supervision of the winery, but it was clear that further specialized help was required. Advertisements placed in German wine journals brought almost overwhelming response as many young men, tired of the austerity of post-war Germany, were looking for the proverbial place in the sun. Eventually, towards the end of 1955, Graue decided to send his secretary and fellow director, Werner Thielscher, to Germany to find a suitable young wine-maker and it was through the renowned and respected Ernst Klenk, director of the State Training School for Wine and Fruit Research at Weinsberg, that an appointment was made to interview three promising and recently-qualified graduates, all of whom were interested in coming to South Africa. One of them was a young man named Günter Brözel.

The 21-year-old Brözel, born into a family with a long coopering tradition and at that time employed by a co-operative company in the historic region of Schwaben in south-west Germany, had graduated *cum laude* from Weinsberg the previous year. His training had been a thorough one, beginning with the duties of the humblest labourer and gradually progressing, so that by the time he was actually allowed to open his first wine

Günter Brözel (front, left) shares a bottle of wine and an entertaining story with a group of Nederburg's workers.

cask he was familiar with all the basic requirements of cellar routine and maintenance. Vital in this and every stage of his training was scrupulous attention to cleanliness and rigid discipline – qualities that have stood him in good stead ever since. If Brözel was impressed with Thielscher, whom he describes as 'very dynamic', then Werner Thielscher was even more impressed with Brözel, whom he discovered to be forthright and honest and gifted with what seemed an almost inborn sensitivity to wine. When presented with a number of different wines to savour and comment upon he made no attempt to hide his genuine opinion and criticized them openly where he felt criticism was due. 'I thought,' Günter recalls, 'let's be straight. Maybe if I speak my mind it will decide for me not to go to South Africa or perhaps I'll be hooked and Nederburg will get me after all!' He told Thielscher quite frankly that he recognized the presence of certain foreign flavour components in some of the wines; these, he subsequently learnt, were derived from citric acid, which is commonly added to Cape wines, naturally high in sugar content, to obtain a balanced sugar-acid ratio. Brözel's immediate recogni-

tion of the presence of this unfamiliar component impressed Werner Thielscher, for it was an indication of the extent of his experience and of the finesse of his palate. At all events, Brözel passed the tests with flying colours and Thielscher, to whom Nederburg must be eternally grateful, recommended his appointment. This was duly confirmed and after a voyage on the *Rhodesia Castle*, which he remembers as 'just marvellous and wonderful and unforgettable', he landed in a mist-enshrouded Cape Town on 6 February 1956. By then Werner Thielscher had left Nederburg to enter the hotel industry (and later to be appointed honorary German consul in the East London area), so Brözel was met and, later that afternoon, taken out to Paarl by the office manager, Max Seipel. Tired and bewildered as he was, Nederburg's new employee insisted on visiting his workplace before settling in the accommodation that had been found for him in Paarl. 'I looked round the cellars,' he says today, 'and then I knew that Nederburg was where I wanted to be.' Engaged as a humble cellar assistant, Brözel remained with Nederburg for over 30 years, but many decades will pass before

his name ceases to be associated with all it stands for.

The harvest had just begun and somehow in this hive of activity the youthful Brözel had to find his niche. He spoke a certain amount of English but had never before heard Afrikaans — the lingua franca of labourers and officials alike. The language might have been unfamiliar, but the heat and brilliant light of Paarl in high summer were more so and at first he suffered excruciating agonies from sunburn and eyestrain. Nevertheless, these discomforts did nothing to dampen his enthusiasm for his work and on occasions, in those early days, he would cheerfully mount his 250cc B.S.A. motorcycle before dawn and, with full throttle and dust flying, roar up to Nederburg to keep pace with the demands of the cellar.

Günter Brözel's zealous interest in his work and his meticulous approach to every facet of it did not pass unnoticed by Johann Georg Graue. Nor, for that matter, was Brözel unaware of his employer's high standards and firm Teutonic discipline, characteristics which he as a fellow German fully understood and appreciated. 'At that time,' he recalls, 'Mr Graue would always appear

TOP
For this photograph, taken early in the 20th century, Mrs Bonafede (in the foreground) turned her back on the curious combination of cows and wine barrels outside Bonafede's winery in Paarl.
BOTTOM
An all-purpose horse-drawn cart of the Bonafede era.

with a walking-stick which was a very handy and very useful identification tool as it always warned me of his approach down the passage. Sometimes he would give away his presence by banging hard with the stick to force the door open . . .'

Looking back to his earliest days as a cellar assistant, Günter Brözel tells a story of a confrontation he had with his immediate superior at the time. This arose because he had been instructed to fill a number of 600-litre barrels with Cabernet which was to be exported to London. Brözel, an expert cooper in his own right, took one look at the vats and refused to fill them: in neither quality nor style were they fit, he said, to carry Nederburg's liquid gospel into Great Britain. A heated argument ensued, but the younger man was adamant: he was working for Nederburg and Nederburg's name would not be tarnished by the use of inferior barrels. Only when Johann Georg Graue, looking exceedingly grim, suddenly appeared from round a corner did he realize that the entire argument had been overheard and his employer's fierce 'Get out!' directed at him left him with no doubts as to the impression his intransi-

gence had made. To his surprise, two days later the coopers who had supplied the offending vats arrived to collect them and new, acceptable barrels were delivered in their place. Even more surprisingly, some weeks later Georg Graue sent for his stubborn young cellar assistant and informed him that his immediate superior was leaving forthwith and that he would take over his duties the following day.

These events occurred towards the end of 1956, a year in which – some months earlier – one of the most important milestones in Nederburg's history had been reached. For some time Georg Graue had become increasingly aware of the gap so sadly left by Arnold's death and of his own steadily fading interest in the business. Yet, dispirited as he was, he was not anxious to relinquish the reins completely: the vineyards and the cellars continued to hold some of their old charm for him, but there were certain responsibilities that he felt ready to hand over to someone else. It was round about the time of Günter Brözel's arrival, and some months before he was placed in charge of the cellar, that Johann Georg Graue gave the first indication that things might be about to change at Nederburg. He did this by initiating negotiations between his two companies – Neder-

burg Estates and Nederburg Winery – and Monis Wineries of Paarl.

For many years a close association had existed between the Graues and the well-known Moni brothers, Giacomo, Pietro and Roberto, whose family background lay in generations of wine-making in one of the most beautiful regions of Italy. Born in Tuscany, the Monis had made their home in South Africa early in the century and from modest beginnings in the food trade had built up a successful business that had later spread throughout the country. The difficulty of obtaining chianti during the First World War led the Monis to start marketing South African claret in its place and their successful experience in this field enabled the brothers to expand into the wine industry with the return of peace. While the brothers Giacomo and Pietro remained at their headquarters in Johannesburg, Roberto moved to the Cape in 1921 to found the Italian Warehouse Company, a liquor firm, in Paarl. Here the Monis made a wide variety of wines, both fortified and unfortified: their products included several wines in the medium price range, a number of popular wines and some excellent ports and sherries. By 1928, the Italian Warehouse Company had become Monis Wineries

PAGE 124: TOP
Destined to be absorbed by Monis Wineries later in the century, R. Bonafede & Co. was among the founders of the Italian wine-making tradition in Paarl.
BOTTOM
Nederburg Sylvaner and Nederburg Late Harvest, two wines particularly popular during the 1960s.
PAGE 125: TOP LEFT
Nederburg Cabernet, one of the most sought-after wines ever produced at Nederburg.
CENTRE
Year by year Nederburg's trophies increased in importance and number, as shown by this proud collection.
TOP RIGHT
Nederburg's superb grape juice was completely free of preservatives.

Limited and it was in their cellars, before the Second World War, that Roberto Moni anticipated Johann Georg Graue's later success in wine-making by pioneering the process of cold fermentation. This he achieved by means of a large imported refrigeration plant first put to successful use by a young technical expert named Erminio Natale Costa — known as 'Nino' to one and all. Also of Italian parentage, Nino Costa had grown up on the well-known olive farm, Nervi, which his father had established outside Paarl, and had been familiar with Nederburg and the Graues since his boyhood. It was largely thanks to his outstanding skills as a chemist and technician, and to the co-operation of Monis over the years, that the system of cold fermentation had been so successfully developed at Nederburg, where by 1956 it had become accepted practice. As Johann Georg Graue became increasingly aware of the lack of Arnold's supervision and technical expertise, it was logical that he should see that the solution to his problem lay in handing over that particular sphere of activity to Monis, equipped as they were with laboratories and with the benefit of Nino Costa's specialized knowledge. Besides, Nederburg's wines needed expert marketing, an area in which Monis also excelled. So, after due discus-

sion, an agreement was drawn up which, on Thursday 24 May 1956, was laid on the table at a meeting of Nederburg's directors, Johann Georg Graue and Torrens Gain, at that time secretary and public officer of the two companies and successor on the board to Werner Thielscher. The terms of the agreement included the sale of 50 per cent of Nederburg's shares to Monis, who would then undertake quality control in their laboratories, provide regular technical advice through Nino Costa and be responsible for marketing. Nederburg itself, under director Johann Georg Graue, would continue to maintain the vineyards and cellars and produce the wine. At that historic meeting it was decided to accept the terms of the agreement in full and from then on Nederburg and Monis operated virtually in tandem.

It was a successful merging and led to a decade of enormous expansion. As time passed, the wines steadily improved in variety, subtlety and individuality of character. At the annual wine show held by the Western Province Agricultural Society in the spring of 1958 Nederburg was awarded a half share in the *Farmer's Weekly* gold medal, 17 first prizes, six seconds, one third, and five perpetual floating trophies. For Johann Georg Graue this wine show must have been a particu-

larly happy occasion for, the sorrow of Arnold's death aside, he was seeing the fulfilment of all his dreams for Nederburg. Clearly there were still great things in store for the vineyards and winery that he had developed but, sadly, in their future he was destined to play no part. Six months later, on Sunday 12 April 1959, Johann Richard Georg Graue died in a Cape Town nursing home at the age of 66, having suffered a heart attack a few days before while on holiday at Hermanus. With no children to succeed him, he was the last of his particular line, yet in the upliftment of the quality and character of Nederburg's wines and the influence of his methods on the entire industry, he left a heritage of excellence that will remain as long as vineyards are cultivated and wine continues to be made in the cellars of the Cape.

For Johann Georg Graue, his achievements and his perfectionist standards, Günter Brözel had tremendous admiration, but at the same time he was aware of the enormously important role Mrs Graue had played in her husband's career. It was she, he says, who was the balancing influence in Georg Graue's life — the mother-figure, gentle and supportive, yet also the one who noticed small shortcomings and tactfully pointed out details that could be improved upon. In describing her as 'a great and beautiful lady' Günter is certainly not alone: everyone who knew Ilse Graue admired her for

TOP LEFT
Nederburg's Cuvées, seen here in the 1960s, were produced by a natural process of fermentation, using special cultures from the Champagne district of France.

TOP RIGHT
Nederburg Hochheimer (left) was made from Riesling grapes grown on Arnold Graue's farm, Hochheim. Steen grapes (used to produce fragrant Nederburg Stein) are a local mutation of Sauvignon.

her elegance, her graciousness, her qualities as a hostess and as a woman who was truly warm-hearted. Undoubtedly, she was Georg's strength and stay in every hour of his need. Now that he was dead she had no wish to stay on alone at Nederburg. For many years the family house at Hermanus had been her second home and it was here that she settled after her husband's death. She was to outlive him for 25 years in the seaside town so beloved by her young son. Today her name is not forgotten, for in Hermanus it has been perpetuated in the Ilse Graue Centre, financed by her bequest to the Child and Family Welfare Society.

According to the agreement made when Monis acquired their half share in Nederburg in 1956, they were entitled to buy the balance of the shares on Johann Georg Graue's death, an option they took up soon afterwards. And so the link forged between the Graue family and Nederburg was broken, but the direction that had been set and the methods established by father and son lived on. At the annual wine show held at the Goodwood showgrounds by the Western Province Agricultural Society 18 months after Georg Graue's death, Nederburg once more broke all records. 'Never before . . .' wrote an enthusiastic reporter in the *Paarl Post*, 'has anyone achieved anything like the success of the Nederburg products at the current [1960] show.'

Altogether, Nederburg's wines were awarded two gold medals, 19 first prizes, three seconds, two thirds, seven floating trophies and eight specials in their respective classes. Among these prizes was the coveted General Smuts floating trophy, which had never before been won by a dry table wine. For Max Seipel, Nederburg's manager at the time who received that cup, and for other members of the staff, this triumphant event must have given rise to conflicting emotions. Overwhelming all others, there must have been a feeling of tremendous pride, but there must also have been an awareness of the deep poignancy of the occasion. There were those who undoubtedly thought of Arnold and of the prizes he won the year of his death; but there would have been others in whose minds memories of Johann Richard Georg Graue predominated. Without his dedication and skills Nederburg might never have been more than just another farm.

Until that time, relying heavily on the success attained by Nederburg at the annual Western Province Wine Show, Johann Georg Graue had sold his wines almost entirely by personal contact with all the larger and 'up-market' hotels in South Africa. Now, taking their distribution responsibility seriously, Monis, under the direction of Bruno Mori, Pietro Moni's son-in-law, began to advertise Nederburg's wines more extensively and to market them through wholesale merchants as well as through Monis' own branches in various parts of the country. As a result and undoubtedly because of the steadily improving quality of Nederburg's products and the status they were rapidly acquiring, the demand for them increased to such an extent that the cellars, already extended in the 1940s, had to be enlarged yet further to accommodate a new maturation store and a packing warehouse. Between 1956, when Monis acquired its half share in Nederburg, and 1965, the total quantity of still wines despatched from the cellars almost doubled, increasing from 85 163 gallons to 162 580 in those nine years. Of this latter quantity, 17 850 gallons were exported not only to the United Kingdom, but also to the Far East, Bermuda and New Zealand, while of the 144 730 sold in the Republic and South-West Africa, 31 500 gallons graced the tables of the Cape Peninsula alone. Fashions in wine, as in other commodities, constantly fluctuate: in 1955, 24 430 gallons of Nederburg Riesling were sold, making it top seller that year, whereas a decade later, when the demand for Riesling had increased by only 500 gallons, its sales were completely outshone by those of Nederburg Stein, with a total output of 35 213 gallons. Nederburg rosé, too, had grown enormously in popularity: in 1955, 966 gallons were sold — a mere drop in the ocean when compared with the 23 397 gallons despatched from the cellars ten years later.

Loading up Nederburg's sparkling wine for export: a regular scene in Cape Town's docks during the 1960s.

From the beginning of his association with Nederburg, when those results were as yet undreamt-of, Nino Costa made regular calls to the cellars, always providing advice and ready to discuss new ideas. Since Georg Graue's death, he, the expert technician, and Günter Brözel, the meticulous craftsman, had worked together in synergy, striving to achieve excellence through the perfection of the cold fermentation process and to develop Nederburg into South Africa's leading wine farm. The days of the harsh, almost crude wines of the pre-war years were long since over, but Brözel was still aiming at creating a product that was pressed, matured and filtered to perfection to remain both brilliant in appearance and delicate and lively to the taste. There remained the likelihood that in transferring wine in the process of fermentation they were losing some of its fine aroma and other subtle properties through the release of carbon dioxide. Gradually they began to evolve a method of accurate temperature control by continuously flushing refrigerated water over the tank shells during fermentation. To begin with, the implementation of what became known as the cascade system was fraught with problems and Günter Brözel admits that while he found the challenge tremendously exciting, he was always afraid that something might go wrong. Since the process had been hitherto unknown, no data were available and the whole idea was so novel that there was simply no one who could be referred to for advice. The whole scheme, in fact, was simply an inspired matter of trial and error.

At first the tanks were laid horizontally with their bodies in the cold section of the cellar and their heads exposed in the passage. Then, later, the entire cellar was insulated to maintain a constant low temperature — Günter Brözel well remembers the conglomerate atmosphere of bitumen, compressed cork and polystyrene that prevailed at the time. Nevertheless, he says, despite hitches and hesitations, the cooling system was installed proudly by the staff of Nederburg and Monis Wineries and the thrilling outcome was wine of a delicacy never before known at the Cape. No one was ever allowed to forget that the emphasis was on fastidious cleanliness and precise temperature control during the entire process, and to Günter Brözel and his assistants this became, as he says, 'not only a daily routine but a very holy performance'. So holy was it, in fact, that at the height of the pressing season he often kept solemn vigil in the cellars throughout the night.

Meanwhile the range of wines was being extended, the label on each bottle characterized by Nederburg's heraldic logo — a shield bearing crossed anchors — which had been adapted from the arms of the Haake-Beck Brewery in Bremen where Johann Georg Graue had once been director. A new wine list issued in 1957

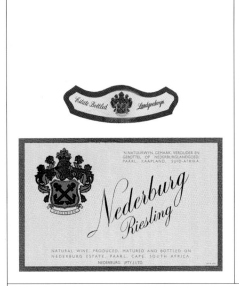

gives all the varieties available and quotes in each case the price of a dozen quart bottles. In that year Nederburg was producing Late Harvest at £6 per dozen as well as the somewhat less costly Rhine-type Nederburg Hochheimer, Nederburg Stein, Nederburg Selected Riesling (£2. 7s. 6d.) and the relatively inexpensive and extremely popular Nederburg Riesling at £2. 1s. 6d. Only two red wines were made at this time – Nederburg's sought-after Selected Cabernet, costing £3. 2s. 0d. for 12 bottles, and Nederburg Cabernet at two guineas per dozen. Also available at two guineas per dozen reputed quarts was Nederburg rosé. In those days Nederburg's cellars produced various sherries – dry, medium, golden oloroso and old brown, their prices ranging between £2. 6s. and £2. 1s. per dozen, while red and white grape juice was available at 13s. 6d. for 12 bottles of 10 oz. each. Made by the natural fermentation method were Nederburg's Champagne-type wines – Riesling Cuvée at £3. 12s. 6d. per dozen reputed quarts, Riesling Cuvée Extra Dry, Riesling Cuvée Medium and, the very latest to be produced, Nederburg's superb Cuvée Cordon Bleu at £3. 9s. 6d. per dozen bottles. To produce, in these sparkling wines, a character and effervescence reminiscent of genuine champagne, special cultures had been imported from

TOP LEFT AND RIGHT
Nederburg Riesling and Nederburg Selected Riesling were both made from petite Riesling thoroughbred grapes – but only wines from prize-winning vats qualified as 'selected'.

TOP CENTRE
After the 1964 Cape Wine Show, Nederburg proudly advertised that its wines had won no fewer than 19 awards.

the district of France where the unique 'singing wine' has its origins.

As Nederburg's popularity grew, it became clear to Dr Nino Costa that new sources of grapes would have to be found, for it was proving impossible to produce sufficient wine from those grown in the farm's own vineyards. The stringencies laid down by K.W.V.'s quota system meant that the planting of new vines on Nederburg's own land was out of the question, for the maximum number permitted to be grown there had long since been reached. Hochheim, bordering on Nederburg and once Arnold's home, was proving a useful neighbour; it had been sold by Johann Georg Graue some years earlier on condition that the grapes it produced would continue to be sold exclusively to him, but even with this extra contribution Nederburg could not meet the demand for its wines. There was no alternative, concluded Nino Costa, but to look beyond the farm's boundaries for suppliers able to provide grapes of sufficiently high quality. An immediate answer to the problem was to extend the already established system of buying in grapes from other selected vineyards, but a more satisfactory long-term solution was the acquisition of additional farms, each with its independent K.W.V. quota. With Georg Graue's philosophy that good wine

TOP

Styles of wine and labels may change but Nederburg's quality remains unaltered.

BOTTOM CENTRE

From time to time the design of the crest changes, but it always incorporates the familiar crossed anchors inspired by Haake-Beck Brewery.

begins in the soil and that particular cultivars succeed in particular areas constantly in mind, Nino Costa selected farms suitable for the cultivation of individual varieties of grapes. He began to look out for suitable properties in the early sixties and in 1963 made his first two purchases. These were Zoekmekaar and Uitkomst, both part of the old farm St Omer which lay on Nederburg's north side and, in a much smaller form, had originally been granted to Huguenot settler, Amant Veron, in 1699. Later, in May 1965, another portion of St Omer was acquired. This was Fonternel, bordering on Hochheim and comprising almost 56 morgen, which was to provide Nederburg with a site for its new dam. Grapes from these farms were brought into Nederburg's cellars for pressing, fermenting and maturing, and every bottle into which the wine eventually found its way bore Nederburg's distinctive label.

Yet, as well as gaining new farms during this period, Nederburg also lost some of its land. These were the days of rigid apartheid when, by law, land was demarcated for the sole use of one or other race group. A township for coloured people was required on the outskirts of the expanding industrial quarter of Paarl and it was for this purpose that the Community Development Board requisitioned an extensive area on Nederburg's south side. The sale was concluded on 8 August 1966 and the price paid was R30 000. Nederburg lost some of its vineyards, but in addition to what was then considered a fair sum of money it also maintained the right to rent some of the land not used for housing.

At this time Nederburg, under Monis' umbrella, was the scene of yet another innovation in wine production at the Cape. It arose from a visit made in the early sixties by Dr Nino Costa to the vineyards of California, where he was so impressed by the method by which noble late harvest wine was being produced there that he decided to experiment with making it at Nederburg. In European vineyards, noble wines are made from ripe grapes attacked by the fungus *Botrytis cinerea*, known as 'noble rot' or *Edelfäule*, which does its work only when conditions of temperature and humidity — warm summers and river or mountain breezes — are suitable. Then, as the fungus develops, the moisture within the grapes evaporates, causing the berries to shrivel while the relative sugar content and flavouring esters increase. Taking advantage of this natural phenomenon, European viniculturists make use of the 'noble rot' to produce rich, sweet wines such as the classic Sauternes, Trockenbeerenauslese and Tokays, but in California, so Dr Costa discovered, the conditions in

NEDERBURG LATE HARVEST — A selected vintage wine in character of the "Spätlese" wines of the Rhine.
Quarts only : **120/-** per dozen.

NEDERBURG HOCHHEIMER — A Rhine wine type selected vintage wine of outstanding character.
Quarts only: **75/-** per dozen.

NEDERBURG STEIN WINE — A light white table wine of the Rhine type, smooth and full-bodied. Selected Vintage.
Quarts: **50/-** per dozen
Pints: **28/9** per dozen

NEDERBURG SELECTED RIESLING — A light dry white table wine of the Moselle type. Selected Vintage.
Quarts: **47/6** per dozen.
Pints: **27/6** per dozen.

NEDERBURG RIESLING — A light dry white table wine of the Moselle type.
Quarts: **41/6** per dozen.
Pints: **24/9** per dozen.

NEDERBURG SELECTED CABERNET — A light dry red selected vintage wine of the Bordeaux type
Quarts only: **62/-** per dozen.

NEDERBURG CABERNET — A light dry red table wine of the Bordeaux type.
Quarts: **42/-** per dozen.
Pints: **24/9** per dozen.

NEDERBURG ROSÉ — A Rosé wine, semi-sweet, light and pleasant.
Quarts xxtx **45/-** per dozen.
Pints : **26/6** per dozen.

SHERRY, dry (Flor type). — Quarts only: **46/-** per dozen.

SHERRY, Medium. — Quarts only: **46/-** per dozen.

SHERRY, Golden Oloroso — Quarts only: **42/-** per dozen.

SHERRY, Old Brown. — Quarts only: **41/-** per dozen.

NEDERBURG GRAPE JUICE
White and Red — A pure natural Grape Juice, non-alcoholic, no preservatives.
13/6 per dozen 10 ounce bottles

NEDERBURG CHAMPAGNE TYPE SPARKLING WINES.
(natural fermentation)

"RIESLING CUVEE" BRUT. — **72/6** per dozen Quarts

"RIESLING CUVEE" EXTRA DRY — **69/6** per dozen Quarts,

"RIESLING CUVEE" MEDIUM — **69/6** per dozen Quarts,

"CUVEE" CORDON BLEU — **69/6** per dozen Quarts.

EMPTIES ARE NOT RETURNABLE.

ALL NEDERBURG WINES ARE PRODUCED, MATURED AND BOTTLED ON NEDERBURG ESTATE.

which the fungus would develop were being artificially created. This was done by placing the ripe grapes on trays, inoculating them with *Botrytis cinerea* and leaving them for several days under a hermetic tarpaulin or plastic sheets in conditions humid enough for the development of the fungus.

When Dr Costa returned to South Africa he discussed the process with Günter Brözel and they decided to set up experiments on precisely the same lines. However, the system did not prove successful — for one thing, the use of trays did not allow sufficiently large quantities of grapes to be inoculated at one time — so eventually Brözel decided to experiment by infecting entire vineyards. This was an extremely time-consuming process, but ultimately proved worth all the trouble it involved. First, it was necessary to select vineyards that had not been infected by any type of fungus and where the grapes were of the correct cultivar, state of health and ripeness. Then followed the actual inoculation, which involved spraying the grapes with a solution

Nederburg's 1957 price list. Some of the wines whose names appear here are no longer made. Hochheimer is one example.
PAGE 131
Nederburg Late Harvest 1959, one of many award-winners.

of the *Botrytis cinerea* fungus, the cultures of which had been scrupulously prepared in Monis' laboratories. With this stage complete, there followed three to four weeks of waiting while the infection developed to the stage when harvesting could begin — provided, of course, that weather conditions were suitable and the grapes had not been affected by rain or any other calamity. But to recognize the precise moment when the berries had reached optimum condition for pressing required constant and meticulous vigilance, a commitment to which only a dedicated viticulturist would pledge himself. Such a man, according to Dr Nino Costa, was Günter Brözel; but it is to the technical skill and innovative ability of Dr Costa that Brözel, in turn, gives credit for the experiment's success. The fact remains that it was the combined efforts of this dedicated pair that enabled the first noble late harvest wines to be produced at Nederburg.

While tests on the noble wines continued, Nederburg went from strength to strength, winning no fewer than 158 first prizes and 104 trophies at the annual Western Province wine shows during the period 1943 to 1963. One of the new wines first mentioned on the wine list of 1961 was Nederburg Sylvaner, a delicate off-dry white table wine which, when it was introduced at the Western Province Wine Show the previous year, was awarded first prize in its class. The cultivar, grown in Germany and Switzerland, had been imported by Johann Georg Graue a few years earlier and the wine subsequently produced from it at Nederburg had been acclaimed by some of Europe's leading authorities. Then, in 1962, Nederburg rosé sec was introduced; in the wine list of that year this was described as 'the delectable result of the Bordeaux thoroughbred Cabernet Sauvignon and French vinification'. From such a variety of superb wines it must have been difficult to make a choice for a special dinner party held in Nederburg homestead on the evening of Monday 22 February 1965. The guests of honour on this occasion were the renowned gourmet and connoisseur, André Simon, founder of the International Wine and Food Society, and Günter Brözel's former mentor, Ernst Klenk, director of the State Training School for Wine and Fruit Research at Weinsberg. A menu which has survived records that they were treated to Nederburg Stein, Nederburg Selected Cabernet of the 1959 vintage and Nederburg Première Cuvée Brut. The four-course meal which these wines enhanced began with *hors d'oeuvre riche* followed by *le filet de sole 'San Remo'* and *riz Créole*. The main course consisted of *le tournedos 'Nederburg'* with *les artichauts du pays*, *le choix des bolets du Cap* and *les pommes dauphines* as accompaniments. Then there was cheese — *fromages du pays* which included Roquefort and Camembert — and the magnificently prepared meal concluded with *le parfait glacé 'Grand Marnier'*.

As the sixties progressed, there were significant signs of increasing activity elsewhere in the liquor industry: the decade had become one of power concentration, during which many small businesses were being absorbed by bigger companies. In view of this, the directors of Monis, led from the head office in Johannesburg by Pietro — or Peter — the youngest Moni brother, came to the conclusion during 1965 that the moment had come to sell their entire organization. As their company could not compete with the four or five most powerful businesses in the liquor industry, the directors felt that it would be wise to give up when they were still in a position to negotiate a good price. If they waited too long they might find their situation weakened by the big players in the field and be forced to sell for whatever they could get.

Of these players, one of the most dominant was the South African Breweries group which, in 1960, had acquired Stellenbosch Farmers' Winery, the large fam-

ily business directed by its founder, the patriarchal William Charles Winshaw. There were those among S.F.W's competitors in the wine industry who suspected that South African Breweries had taken this step because it wished to safeguard the interests of the brewing industry by suppressing wine sales, but this was certainly not the case. In fact, Breweries, in support of the government's efforts at the time to encourage the consumption of good quality, affordable wines rather than of spirits, was doing everything in its power to stimulate the development of the natural wine market. The acquisition of Monis would be in keeping with its policy, so when the company came on to the market, Stellenbosch Farmers' Winery beat its most serious competitor to the draw by making an offer for it. The sum involved was in the region of R4 million.

But this was not the end of the matter. In the 1960s the South African government took the view that power concentration was not in the interests of the liquor industry and for this reason made it obligatory to obtain the permission of the minister of justice (at that time B.J.Vorster, subsequently prime minister) before any takeover or merger could be finalized. The wheels of the government are apt to turn slowly, so while Breweries' application was under consideration, there remained the possibility of intervention by another potential buyer willing to make a higher offer. Something obviously had to be done to forestall this and in a shrewd move, Ted Sceales, managing director of South African Breweries, persuaded Nedbank, whose chairman, Frans Cronje, was also chairman of Breweries, to hold Monis' shares in trust for the time being on the basis of a gentleman's agreement. This arrangement was possible — and legal — because Nedbank, unlike Breweries, was not a liquor house and therefore under no obligation to obtain anyone's permission to buy Monis. The gamble paid off; Vorster required a certain amount of convincing, but eventually he allowed Stellenbosch Farmers' Winery to acquire Monis provided South African Breweries reduced their shareholding in S.F.W. to 34 per cent. To this condition Breweries agreed and relinquished control of S.F.W by selling off shares to the public. So, in a somewhat roundabout manner following protracted negotiations at the highest level, Monis, in 1966, was taken into the fold of Stellenbosch Farmers' Winery, bringing with it its holdings, including Nederburg. Thus it was that the days of the independent wine farm with its almost symbolic homestead, thatched and gabled and surrounded by ancient oaks, were over for ever and Nederburg, while jealously maintaining its individuality within the fold, has since then been part of one of the giants of South African industry.

■

CHAPTER NINE

NEDERBURG SINCE 1966: AN OVERVIEW

Following Johann Georg Graue's death, Monis Wineries held
full control of Nederburg until Stellenbosch Farmers' Winery acquired
ownership in 1966. Günter Brözel continued to make superb products
and win numerous prizes. He retired in 1989 but the new Nederburg team
maintains the established standard of excellence.
The 1972 Law of Origin legislation now precludes Nederburg from
referring to itself as an estate.

*The Regina Perpetual Floating Trophy
– one of the many silver cups awarded
to Nederburg.*

Since 1966 Nederburg has remained under the wing of Stellenbosch Farmers' Winery. The events that have taken place within the company during the past quarter century are too recent to be classed as history; it remains for a future chronicler to record them in detail. Nevertheless, this account of the fortunes of Nederburg and the people involved in it cannot conclude without a general overview of the chances and changes – some more significant than others – that have taken place during that period.

In 1966 Stellenbosch Farmers' Winery, then the largest company of its kind in South Africa, was a full subsidiary of South African Breweries, but its management control was still vested in the family of its founder, William Charles Winshaw. An American medical doctor whose early career had been adventurous, to say the least, Winshaw first arrived at the Cape in 1899 in charge of a consignment of 4 500 mules required by British troops engaged in the South African War. Winshaw remained in this country, joined the army as a medical officer, married an English nurse and, once hostilities were over, settled on a farm just outside Stellenbosch. Here he began to experiment with winemaking and, after some ups and downs in the early stages, his contribution to the South African industry was to become legendary. He strongly disapproved of the accepted custom at the Cape of strengthening natural wines by the addition of wine alcohol. As a medical man, William Charles Winshaw was convinced that natural wines, with their relatively low alcohol content, were healthier than the powerful concoctions commonly drunk by the South African masses and in this thinking was close to that of both Roberto Moni and Johann Georg Graue.

TOP
*Sliding gracefully down the slipway,
the S.A. Nederburg is launched at the
Verolme-Cork dockyard in Ireland
on 24 April 1967. She was destined to
acquit herself honourably for 23 years
before being scrapped.*
BOTTOM
*Nederburg's public relations officer,
'Bags' Bagnall, presents a painting of the
homestead by Terence McCaw to Captain
Johnson, master of the ship bearing
the farm's name.*

At the time the companies that these two men had founded had been acquired by S.F.W., William Charles Winshaw's eldest son, William Joachim — or Bill, one of South Africa's finest wine-makers — was chairman and managing director. His younger brother, Jack, was also in the business and his brother-in-law, Albert W. Mitchell — known as Wally — was S.F.W.'s financial controller and business manager. Wally Mitchell's right-hand man at the time was Lothar Barth, formerly in the employment of Monis and in 1966 executive director of S.F.W. in charge of finances and administration. When the change occurred, Roberto Moni, who had been active in the management of his family's winery since its earliest days, decided to withdraw and was followed not long afterwards by Dr Nino Costa, Monis' technical director, whose counsel and support had been integral to the development of Nederburg for

many years. After seeing the change-over successfully achieved, Costa consigned the control of the vineyards and cellars to Günter Brözel, but during the following 15 years continued to act as adviser whenever he was called upon. The other director of Monis when it was absorbed by Stellenbosch Farmers' Winery was Bruno Mori, chairman of the Cape Distilling Merchants' Association, an expert in marketing and married to Bianca, the daughter of Pietro — or Peter — Moni. He remained on the board until 1971 when he, too, retired.

With the change of ownership, the directors of Stellenbosch Farmers' Winery had to decide on the role Monis and Nederburg were to play in their organization. Lothar Barth's proposals, after he had studied the situation, were that both should be maintained as separate entities as far as the production of their wines was concerned, but that their sales and distribution should

be integrated with those of S.F.W. For example, Stellenbosch Farmers' Winery undertook to incorporate the activities of Monis' large warehouse in Johannesburg with its own operation, in this way implementing its policy of streamlining the operation. Nederburg, on the other hand, was unlike any other liquor producer: unique in history, character and achievements, by the middle sixties it had been recognized as undisputed leader in South Africa's quality wine market. In its entire operation, Nederburg was identified with Georg Graue's philosophy of selection and with his firm belief that a good wine farmer should make his own wine in his own cellars. S.F.W. honoured Graue's ideals and has continued to do so to this day: the wine contained in every bottle bearing Nederburg's label has been produced either from grapes grown within Nederburg's bounds or from those specifically and critically selected from vineyards elsewhere. In addition, every drop of that wine has been pressed, fermented, matured and bottled in Nederburg's own cellars.

At Nederburg itself Günter Brözel continued to transform Johann Georg Graue's philosophy into reality by creating a wide range of top quality wines. This was possible only because he could select his grapes from a variety of cultivars, each one growing in the specific area, climate and particular soil-type to which it was best suited. And as the decade of the sixties progressed, so did Georg Graue's philosophy validate itself as Nederburg achieved one success after another at the annual Western Province Wine Show. On 28 September 1966, only three months after S.F.W. had assumed

TOP
A sweeping view of Plaisir de Merle
in its dramatic setting on the slopes of
the Simonsberg.
BOTTOM
Ripening in the shade of vine leaves,
these grapes will be pressed to make one of
Nederburg's white wines.

ownership, Nederburg won 15 first prizes, six cups and the gold medal for the most points gained on the show of that year, thus bringing its total number of awards in 24 years to 202 first prizes, 136 cups and 12 gold medals. The following year Nederburg again made a clean sweep at the show by winning, among other prizes, the General Smuts trophy for the most outstanding wine on exhibition and two gold medals, one presented by the *Farmer's Weekly* and the other by *Die Landbouweekblad*. Another prize that Günter Brözel accepted on Nederburg's behalf on this occasion was the Arnold Graue silver salver awarded for 50 leaguers of dry white table wine; Nederburg's red wines, which won eight points out of a possible nine, were also outstanding among the prize-winners. This was not all: in 1966 Nederburg's wines had been awarded nine diplomas when they were exhibited at Ljubljana in Yugoslavia, an indication that at last South African wines were being accepted and appreciated in Europe. Nederburg now stood in the forefront of a new era in wine-making and, inspired by its consistent success, many other old-established farmers and producers were bent on emulating its methods.

Nederburg's triumphs may seem to have little to do with the building in 1967 of a merchant vessel in a remote Irish shipyard — but such was the case for, recognizing that Nederburg was the epitome of excellence in its own sphere, the well-known shipping company, Safmarine, gave the name of the farm and its homestead to its new cargo liner, which represented all that was finest in modern marine design and engineering. The

launching of the S.A. *Nederburg* by Mrs J. A. Thomson, wife of her captain, took place on Monday 24 April 1967 at the Verolme-Cork dockyard situated at Rushbrook on the River Lee; at the celebration which followed, a toast was drunk to the new ship and all who served in her in Nederburg dry sparkling wine specially flown to Ireland for the occasion. The S.A. *Nederburg*, with her fine lines and beautiful, almost yacht-like hull, was certainly a credit to the wine farm whose name she bore. She was 192,25 metres in length and 22,86 metres in breadth; had a gross tonnage of 12 751; and could achieve a maximum speed of 22,99 knots. Diesel-powered, with a six-cylinder turbo-charged engine, she was fully air-conditioned and provided accommodation for a complement of 48 officers and ratings.

The S.A. *Nederburg* sailed for Houston, Texas, in June 1967 and on arrival at Cape Town late in September was formally presented with a specially commissioned painting of Nederburg homestead by the well-known artist, Terence McCaw. At a ceremony in the ship's lounge, the picture was formally hung by Nederburg's public relations officer, Mr A. Gordon Bagnall, who then joined the ship as she continued her maiden voyage to Durban and made sure that Nederburg's wines were served at the celebratory banquets held at every port.

The S.A. *Nederburg*'s career was an interesting one. She not only plied between South Africa and the east coast of the United States, but also made many voyages to and from Australia. She became famous after 17 April 1973 when she steamed through mountainous seas and

'Good wine has its origins in the vineyard.' Johann Georg Graue's maxim is borne out by every bunch of grapes grown on Nederburg or its satellite farms.

gale-force winds to rescue 27 members of the crew of the tanker *Silver Ocean* which had broken apart some 260 kilometres north-east of Durban. Some 14 years later, having acquitted herself honourably, the S.A. *Nederburg* was sold to a shipping company in Hong Kong and was finally scrapped in 1990. It seems that the painting of Nederburg which graced her lounge was sadly lost at some point, for all efforts to trace it have failed.

The end of the sixties saw the appearance of that aristocrat of Cape wines, Edelkeur, the creation of which was a milestone in the history of viniculture in South Africa. With the constant technical advice of Dr Nino Costa, as described in Chapter Eight, Günter Brözel, using all his superlative skill, had taken years to develop this first example of South African noble late harvest wine — or were, as he suggests, the weather conditions of the summer of 1968-1969 responsible for its final perfection? Certainly, several more years were to pass before another vintage equal in quality to the first could be produced.

This newcomer (its name is Afrikaans for 'noble choice'), derives its unique character from the action of the fungus, *Botrytis cinerea*, or noble rot, which is known in Germany as *Edelfäule* and in France as *Pourriture Noble*. Its birth was certainly not without pangs, for existing legislation (Act No. 25 of 1957) restricted the residual sugar content of natural wines to 30 grams per litre, a limitation with which Edelkeur, by its very nature as a noble late harvest wine, could not conform. However, in October 1969, largely as a result of the co-operation and assistance of the Oenological and

Viticultural Research Institute at Nietvoorbij outside Stellenbosch, the law was changed and Nederburg was permitted to sell 'not more than 2 000 gallons [approximately 91 hectolitres] of a specific wine . . . produced during 1969'. Needless to say, this approval was subject to certain conditions, most of which required the strictest supervision by the authorities at Nietvoorbij. According to a publication issued at the time, Edelkeur was 'a natural select wine' comparable with the famous late harvests of Sauternes, the Rhine and Tokay. Its colour was 'brilliant, golden straw to topaz yellow', its texture was velvety and the bouquet was described as 'fruity with a taste of almond'. Günter Brözel described it as 'late-late harvest liquid gold'.

Few people in the wine industry had believed that a wine such as Edelkeur could be produced in South Africa; Nederburg had proved them wrong. In Günter Brözel's own words: 'To me it was just perfect,' and his opinion of the wine was justified when, many years

later, the authorities, in their search for a generic term embracing all that noble late harvest wine stood for, were anxious to make use of the name 'Edelkeur'. However, Nederburg, guarding it jealously, refused to share it and to this day it is identified only with the cellars where it was created.

The début of Edelkeur in 1969 marked a triumph for Günter Brözel and the conclusion of another good year for Nederburg. At the Cape Wine Show in August Nederburg had again received top awards and secured a hat trick by winning for the third consecutive year the coveted General Smuts silver floating trophy for the most outstanding wine exhibited. With the beginning of a new decade, the name of Nederburg Estates had become without question the most respected in the wine industry.

Nederburg's successes, naturally, did not go unnoticed, nor were its triumphs unattended by a certain amount of resentment in certain quarters of the wine

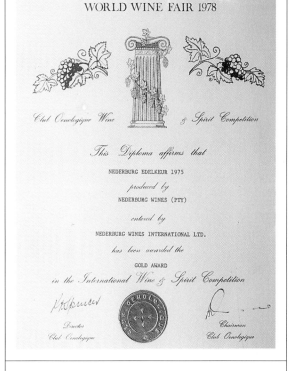

PAGE 136: TOP
Lanquedoc is an important supplier
of grapes to the parent farm, Nederburg.
CENTRE
Left, centre and right: Light and
shade and a gentle spray of water play over
Lanquedoc's burgeoning vineyards.
BOTTOM
Lanquedoc is home to this young mother
and her alert youngster.
PAGE 137
Nederburg is justly proud of the
awards it has won, both locally and
overseas, over the years. This selection is
displayed for the benefit of visitors to
the reception centre.

industry. By the early seventies it had become obvious there were those who queried the term 'wine estate' and the right of any farm to describe itself in this manner. It will be remembered that as early as November 1950 Johann Georg Graue, with his son Arnold as co-director, had formally established the company Nederburg Estates (Pty) Limited. This was because to Graue Nederburg, with its spreading vineyards, its orderly cellars and its gracious homestead — all set in superb natural surroundings — could justly claim to be what in Germany was known as a *weingut* or wine estate. At that stage, and for many years afterwards, the word 'estate' as applied to a farm had no legal standing in South Africa; it simply stood for all that is best and most highly civilized in country living. Yet it was to the term 'wine estate' that there appeared to be serious objections and, to justify these objections, those in authority turned to semantics.

The Wine of Origin Committee, an official body

formed at this time, decided that for a winery to be defined as an estate the grapes must be grown entirely within its own borders and the wine produced in a cellar on the estate. Wheels were set in motion for the framing of legislation to this effect and despite the assiduous efforts of Lothar Barth, then managing director of Stellenbosch Farmers' Winery, to fight the Wine of Origin Committee, it eventually won the day. As a result, in 1972 a new law was introduced and individual wine farms whose operation conformed with the official definition of the term were invited to register as estates. Nederburg, of course, was debarred since the policy its management had inherited from Johann Georg Graue — that of looking beyond Nederburg's own boundaries for the selection of suitable grapes — was in direct conflict with the new legislation. Nederburg responded by announcing that it would separate itself into two entities — Nederburg Wines (Pty) Limited and, using Graue's first name, Johann Graue Estates (Pty) Limited.

1956~1986

Nederburg Wines would obtain grapes from a variety of sources, including Johann Graue Estates, in what had become the established manner, but Johann Graue Estates, with its own separate cellars, would be limited to the production of wine from grapes cultivated on the estate itself. A certain amount of wine was produced by Johann Graue Estates, but the scheme was fraught with problems and bureaucratic stumbling blocks and after three years ceased to operate — leaving those few remaining bottles bearing the label of Johann Graue Estates — and containing superb wine — as collectors' items.

The implementation of Wine of Origin legislation caused widespread and expensive changes in the industry. In addition to granting estate status only to certain farms, it also divided the winelands area of the Cape into official wine-making districts. At the same time, an official Wine of Origin seal was introduced and used by certain producers whose wine qualified for its application. Affixed to capsules covering the cork, it guaranteed the veracity of claims made on the label regarding the origin, vintage and cultivar of the contents. Well aware of the prestige attached to these visible signs, Nederburg's management nevertheless reached the conclusion that none of them was a passport to success; that symbols and seals in themselves do not make good wines but that good wines undoubtedly make good names. According to Lothar Barth, whether Nederburg's wine was called Nederburg Estates Wine or simply Nederburg Wine was of little consequence: it was the quality and the character of the product that was of paramount importance. Johann Georg Graue's belief

TOP
The cover design for the menu at a dinner honouring Günter Brözel's 30 years at Nederburg.
CENTRE
The Stellenrust cup, presented for export quality white wine.
PAGE 139: TOP
The reception centre at Nederburg. The core of this building is believed to be even older than the homestead.
CENTRE
Nederburg's entrance gates overlooked by the snow-capped peaks of the mighty Drakenstein mountains.

that specific grapes should be selected from specific areas had proved its validity over a period of nearly 40 years; it was a heritage on which Nederburg's policy would continue to be built and a tradition that, to Lothar Barth's way of thinking, was firmly upheld by the superb wine-making skills of Günter Brözel.

Far from restricting itself to its own vineyards and those in its immediate vicinity, Nederburg at this time began to seek new sources of grapes, for the demand for its wines continued to exceed the supply. Stellenbosch Wine Farms Limited, a subsidiary of Stellenbosch Farmers' Winery, had for some time been harvesting the vineyards on certain farms it had acquired over the previous decade; now it decided that these would provide grapes almost entirely for the production of Nederburg's wines and to identify itself with this policy changed its name to Nederburg Wine Farms Limited. One of these farms was Groenhof, bought in January 1964. Consisting of 269 hectares spread over the south-western slopes of the Simonsberg near Koelenhof, it was only 75 morgen in size when it was originally granted to a Huguenot named Alexander Blank in 1698. Of a number of buildings that once stood there, only the wine cellar with its elaborate baroque gable remained. The soil at Groenhof is suitable for a wide variety of white-wine cultivars, but Cabernet Sauvignon, Pinot noir and Shiraz are also grown there today.

Not far away from Groenhof lies another farm that, since the seventies, has been devoted to the cultivation of grapes for Nederburg. This is Le Plessis Marlé, whose beautiful vineyards, precise in their geometrical order,

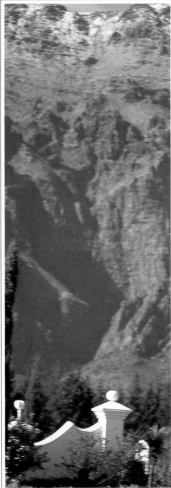

swathe the slopes of the Simonsberg near Simondium. Originally recalling the small town in France from which this farm's first owner, Charles Marais, had fled as a religious refugee, its name has been modified through the three centuries of its existence to Plaisir de Merle — meaning rather charmingly, but quite inappropriately, 'the joy of the blackbird'. Charles Marais settled on its original 60 morgen soon after his arrival at the Cape in 1688, but by the time the land was officially granted to him three years later he had died at the hand of a Khoikhoi labourer whose wrath he had incurred. Nevertheless he left two sons who were to be the forefathers of the innumerable members of the Marais family who people South Africa today. Over the years, and under various owners, Plaisir de Merle spread far beyond its original bounds until, by the time Stellenbosch Farmers' Winery bought it in 1965 for R290 000, it included parts of two neighbouring farms, Wolfe Kloof and Rachelsfontein. Since then, Plaisir de Merle has expanded yet further by the acquisition of additional portions of these two properties and also by the purchase of the farms, La Rochelle and nearby Vrede en Lust, the latter granted in 1694 to that well-to-do and fascinating merchant from the Low Countries, Jacques de Savoye. Today Plaisir de Merle's entire area stretches up the mountainside to a height of 500 metres; it comprises over 974 hectares on which no fewer than 13 different white-wine cultivars and five reds flourish under the care of a highly trained team, consisting of a manager, three assistants, a mechanic and 125 workers. Insepa-

rable from any thought of Plaisir de Merle is the handsome and historic old homestead which was built in 1764 by Jacob Marais, great-grandson of the original owner. Thatched and gabled in the early Cape Dutch style and overlooking a view of incomparable beauty, it is much used for the accommodation and entertainment of Stellenbosch Farmers' Winery's and Nederburg's invited guests.

Close neighbour to Nederburg itself is the farm originally called Languedoc — it was from that former province of south-eastern France, for long a stronghold of Protestantism, that its first owner, Jean Imbert, fled after the revocation of the Edict of Nantes in 1685. Imbert, who suffered blindness later in life, is thought to have arrived at the Cape in April 1688 on board the *Oosterland*, one of the ships that brought Huguenot refugees to these shores. He settled on 50 morgen of land in Klein Drakenstein soon afterwards, but his farm was not officially granted to him until 1694. The gabled old house that — much Victorianized — stands on Languedoc today was built only after Imbert's death, probably by the widow of Jacques Therod (or Theron), owner of the neighbouring farm, Miné, which later became part of Languedoc. Over the years, as has happened frequently at the Cape, the farm's name has been changed to Lanquedoc — a pity, since it has lost its historic association with the part of France that was Imbert's original home. Valued for its vineyards — nine different cultivars, red as well as white, are grown on its west-facing slopes — Lanquedoc is also important as a source of water. Not only does the river on which Nederburg

itself stands flow through it, but in the seventies part of the land recently bought by Nederburg was acquired by the Palmiet River Irrigation Board of the Department of Water Affairs with a view to providing irrigation to farms in the area. On this land, an old dam was extensively enlarged to hold approximately 1 600 million litres, and now water under pressure is supplied from it to Nederburg as well as to a number of neighbouring farms.

In a completely different category is Ernita, consisting of a total area of just over 91 hectares not far to the south-east of Wellington. To Johann Georg Graue, the propagation and cloning of vines from the best available stock was an integral part of his scheme of selection and for this purpose he established a nursery at Nederburg. However, in time the extent and nature of the work expanded beyond the limited area available and in 1974 Ernita was acquired to take over this important function. Today modern research and equipment at Ernita's laboratories, under the management of Tossie Louw, have led to technological advances far beyond Graue's wildest dreams and to the development of the most advanced and hygienic methods of grafting and plant improvement. As a result of experiments and developments during the past 17 years, Ernita's nursery now not only provides the vineyards of Nederburg and its associated farms with plant material of the highest

quality and of every required cultivar, but it supplies young vines to farmers throughout the wine-growing regions of South Africa.

The decade of the seventies was an extremely active one for Nederburg. Not only were many new wines being made, but they — as well as the established classic lines — were winning an increasing number of international certificates and awards, notwithstanding South Africa's escalating political unpopularity at this time. One of the annual European shows to which Nederburg began to submit its wines during the seventies was the famous Monde Sélection which is administered from Belgium but held in a different country each year. In 1971, when the show was held in Brussels, Nederburg received ten Sélection certificates, while 14 were awarded to it the following year when the Monde Sélection took place in Geneva. This was not Nederburg's sole European success in 1972: Mondial in Budapest, Hungary, presented Nederburg's wines — including the famous 1969 Edelkeur — with 13 diplomas, while further successes were achieved at the Monde Sélection shows in 1973 and 1974.

In the annals of Nederburg, 1975 will always be remembered as the year in which the Wine Auction — now internationally one of the top five — was introduced to South Africa and the world. All the details of

its somewhat shaky start, its dramatic development, its eventual matchless success — and the extraordinary efficiency of its organization — are so important to the chronicles of Nederburg that an entire chapter in this book has been devoted to it. Today the name of Neder-burg has become almost synonymous with the term 'wine auction', and the annual event in early autumn is acknowledged as one of the most exciting in South Africa's social and commercial calendar. Besides, and perhaps most important, it was the Nederburg Auction that was largely responsible for maintaining the good image of Cape wines in an unfriendly world during the austere years of sanctions.

But the Auction has certainly not entirely eclipsed the other events that have taken place since the first one was held in 1975. All the while Nederburg has steadily continued to improve its reputation and en-hance its image abroad — and not only by means of its unofficial ambassadors who carry the good news home with them after attending the Auction year after year. At the International Wine and Spirit Competitions of 1976, 1977 and 1978 Nederburg was awarded a total of 23 certificates, of which 13 were gold seals. In 1979 as many as ten certificates of the Monde Sélection were awarded to Nederburg's wines in Paris and in October 1980 it won no fewer than ten medals at the Interna-

PAGE 140: TOP LEFT
The silver trophy awarded annually for the best-kept labourer's cottage at Ernita.
TOP RIGHT
Exterior view of the best-kept cottage at Ernita.
CENTRE LEFT AND RIGHT
Interior of the prize-winning cottage on Ernita.
BOTTOM
Pallets stand stacked, waiting to transport Nederburg's wines to their many destinations.
PAGE 141
Staff welfare is of great concern to Nederburg which has a full-time social worker to care for farm employees' needs. Here children play happily at Ernita's crèche while their parents are at work.

tional Wine and Spirit Competition organized by the Club Oenologique in London. These comprised six gold medals, two silver and two bronze which, together, achieved for Nederburg the distinction of winning the highest number of medals ever awarded to a single range of South African wines. They also brought the total of awards won by Nederburg in local and overseas shows until then to over 650. All the wines submitted by Nederburg — Gewürztraminer, Edelkeur and Buket-traube — to the International Wine and Spirit Compe-titions held during the years 1983 and 1984 won gold awards and in 1985, when 950 wines from all over the world were entered, Günter Brözel was granted the sig-nal honour of being elected International Wine-maker of the Year, an accolade that was formally bestowed upon him at a gala banquet in the British House of Commons. Back home in the same year, the South African branch of the Diners' Club International awarded him the title of Wine-maker of the Year for his Gewürztraminer. In 1986 — the year in which Neder-burg's new red wine, Gamay, was released after only 29 days in the making — Nederburg's world-renowned Edelkeur scored 93,2 points out of a possible 100 at the International Wine and Spirit Competition, the high-est score awarded by that year's panel of judges.

In the years since then, Nederburg has continued

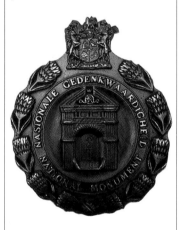

TOP
*Seen against brilliant herbaceous
borders and blue sky, the Johann Graue
Centre is the venue of the annual
Nederburg Auction — one of the five most
important annual events of its kind
in the world.*
BOTTOM
*The bronze plaque of the National
Monuments Council presented to Nederburg
in 1990 when it became the first
farm in South Africa to be declared a
national monument.*

to gather prizes and win acclaim for itself. The list of awards and trophies is seemingly endless and would, no doubt, have amazed the earlier owners of the simple wine farm who dreamed of making really good wine but never succeeded. In fact, to them Nederburg — in appearance, organization, sophistication and reputation — would be barely recognizable and they would have difficulty in finding their way to their old home, for the original entrance on the south side of the farm, and the drive leading from it to the homestead, have been swept away. Instead, splendid new gates open from the north side of the property onto a road taking the visitor through the vineyards, past the security kiosk and the Johann Graue Centre and so to the reception offices. This is a building that has changed enormously, for it was once the farm manager's house — believed by some people to be even older than the homestead itself. Substantial alterations in the 1980s have converted it into public relations and reception offices and it provides special facilities for members of the media attending the auction.

But changes in buildings and policies and people are inevitable, for without them there can be no growth. In 1989, some 33 years after the youthful Günter Brözel first stepped into Nederburg's cellars as the humblest of assistants, he decided that the time had come to move on. Over his three decades as cellar-master *par excellence*, and many years as director, his name had become synonymous with Nederburg itself;

nevertheless, he had reached an age when he could accept early retirement while still being physically and mentally active and leave those whom he had groomed in his skills and his high standards to take over. Indeed, numbers of the Cape's most successful wine-makers have served their apprenticeship in Nederburg's cellars, many of them under the watchful eye of Günter Brözel, who inspired them with his dedication and skill and charmed them with his mellifluous turn of phrase. A doyen among Nederburg's protégés is Joseph Huskisson of Perdeberg Co-operative, who received his initial training under Arnold Graue; of even earlier 'vintage' is Sarel Rossouw, for almost 40 years wine-maker at Simonsvlei Co-operative Wine Cellars and later its administrator. Pieter Daniel du Toit of Groot Constantia spent several years at Nederburg after qualifying at Stellenbosch University; another Nederburg 'graduate' is much-travelled Ross Gower, who has been instrumental in winning acclaim — and trophies — for the wines he has made at the marvellously revived estate of Klein Constantia. Herman du Preez of Bottelary Co-operative Winery also trained at Nederburg; so did Hein Hesebeck, now of Neethlingshof. At Nederburg itself the maintenance of its standards is in the care of its present cellar-master, Newald Marais who, like so many experts, acquired his skills under master wine-maker Günter Brözel and, following in his footsteps, studied further at the West German State Training School for Wine and Fruit Research at Weinsberg. If his ability to continue

Nederburg's traditions has required proof, it was provided by the nine double gold awards won by Nederburg at the 1991 South African National Wine Show. At this event six panels, each consisting of seven judges, tasted a variety of the best wines the Cape had to offer before deciding on the winners — and of them all Nederburg was easily the most successful. In addition to the double golds, Nederburg was awarded eight gold, 14 silver and 15 bronze awards. In the same year Nederburg excelled in the annual judging of Cape wines for inclusion in the South African Airways wine list when its Nederburg Rhine Riesling 1990 and Nederburg Cuvée Brut were among the nine wines finally selected from 75 entrants. The S.A.A. wine list, which serves all domestic flights and Silver Class on international routes, is regarded as a showcase, for it offers local wines to the exclusion of all others. Nor is this all: eight international airlines now calling at South Africa's airports offer Nederburg's wines to passengers travelling all over the world.

Awards and trophies, Nederburg's wine accompanying leading businesspeople and politicians to the four corners of the earth — these are the outward and visible signs of the hard work, dedication and loyalty of the personnel employed on the five farms — Ernita, Lanquedoc, Plaisir de Merle, Groenhof and Nederburg itself. A happy community is a productive community and happy and productive communities make for a happy and productive nation. Aware of this, Nederburg, at the beginning of 1991, devised a development programme for its farm personnel and appointed a dedicated social worker in Albertus Vos to implement it. The first step was for Nederburg to become affiliated with the Rural Foundation, whose headquarters are in Stellenbosch, and the next was to implement its guidelines. The Foundation's aim is to promote a community life that is both physically and spiritually healthy by involving people in self-care, and to achieve justice and a peaceful way of life for all rural people. Through its community development scheme Nederburg aims to help its people, not by hand-outs, but by showing them how to help themselves.

In this they have been helped by voluntary assistants from the Boland College of Education. Each farm is visited twice a week by students who teach literacy skills and handcrafts to adults at a ratio of one instructor to three pupils. As a result of this intimate contact, the pupils not only learn to read and write, but they have the opportunity to discuss their personal problems. Other visitors to the farms include professional social workers who give instructive talks on such topics as health care and family planning. Sport is encouraged to stimulate physical well-being, discipline and pleasure and *jukskei* in particular has become extremely popular. There are householders' competitions in which prizes

Vivid green in the spring sunshine, Plaisir de Merle's vineyards stretch towards the opalescent blue of the distant mountains.

are awarded for the most attractive garden and the best-kept interior, and sewing and handwork exhibitions and contests are organized both within the Nederburg community and nationwide. All this adds up to inculcating in the communities a sense of personal dignity and self-worth.

But Nederburg's children are its first social concern and to stimulate their development during their pre-school years and, at the same time, to relieve their parents of anxiety concerning them during their working hours, crèches have been established on all five farms. Supervisors chosen from among Nederburg's personnel are carefully screened and trained by the Rural Foundation; two meals are provided each day and children from three months old to school-going age play and learn together. At the same time a careful watch is kept on their health.

In 1990 Nederburg made history when it became the first farm in South Africa to be declared a conservation area by the National Monuments Council, while the homestead itself became a national monument. As is customary, the Council's bronze plaque was duly erected and, at a special ceremony on 10 April of that year, unveiled by Mr Eugene Louw, at that time Minister of Home Affairs and National Education. And so, official blessing has been given to the preservation of Nederburg and its buildings, its existing vineyards and its land as yet uncultivated. Townships may crowd in upon it; developers may cast a greedy eye in its direction as Paarl's peripheral industries nudge closer to its borders; but all will be to no avail, for now it is protected. Without specific consent from the National Monuments Council, no one may encroach upon or exploit its territory; no one may use it for any purpose other than wine farming and no one may alter or demolish the buildings.

In the 1790s Philippus Bernardus Wolvaart had a dream of flourishing vineyards and fine wines as he and his horse ranged the wilderness of fynbos that was to become Nederburg. A century and a half later Johann Richard Georg Graue, born 101 years to the day after the land was first granted, fulfilled that dream by making wines of quality and character never before known in South Africa. His legacy, and that of Arnold, his ill-starred son, passed to Günter Brözel, whose meticulous thoroughness and innovative genius developed the wines yet further. Today the Nederburg tradition is maintained by Newald Marais and his team, under the leadership of managing director, Ernst le Roux. Together they look towards Nederburg's third century with confidence, intent on maintaining long established ideals of wine-making and on providing the people of the exciting South Africa of the future with the very best its vineyards and cellars have to offer. ■

CHAPTER TEN

WINE AND WINE-MAKING AT NEDERBURG

Graue's system of selection and cold fermentation, developed
and honed by technological advances, is still practised. At the nursery farm,
Ernita, the best plant material is propagated by cloning and young
vines are grown in areas best suited to each cultivar. Nederburg's range of
wines today comprises the standard 14 wines distributed by retailers,
those produced specifically for export and the special Nederburg Auction
wines and limited vintages.

*Pride in craftsmanship is revealed in this
brass pressure guage, once used by Arnold
Graue in his laboratory at Nederburg.*

The acquisition of Nederburg by Johann Georg Graue in 1937 heralded a new era not only for the farm but for the entire South African wine industry. His motto was simple: good wine, he believed, has its origins in the vineyards, a philosophy maintained by Nederburg to this day. In addition, he was adamant that 'good wine' could be achieved only by meticulous selection of vines and with this in mind he began keeping the fullest possible records of all plantings made on the farm and of the lineage and performance of every one of them. Because of his commitment to quality, Graue set himself the highest standards and, while closely studying the cultivars themselves and the areas in which they grew best, made a number of important discoveries. One of these concerned the varying characteristics of certain varieties, depending on where they were grown.

Nederburg lies on the lower west-facing slopes of the Klein Drakenstein mountains overlooking the fertile Paarl valley. Watered by Hugosrivier and the perennially flowing Palmiet River, its soil is basically of Cape granite origin similar in structure to that of Paarl Mountain. Along the watercourses the ground is apt to be loose and stony with underlying clay layers, while higher up the hillsides it is deeper and more friable and there are fewer stones. Sandy and stony soils lack water-holding capacity and vineyards planted on them need supplementary irrigation during the heat of summer. The deeper soils, on the other hand, naturally hold moisture more effectively and require less intensive watering. Winter rains can usually be relied upon to saturate the soil: according to data compiled by the Agricultural Meteorological Section at Bien Donné Experimental Farm, Nederburg can expect a monthly rainfall of between 120 millimetres and 138 millimetres from May to August. The effect of temperature and

TOP
Trellised vines glory in the spring sunshine.
BOTTOM
*Bearing the scars of long service,
this copper jug was once used for topping
up the vats.*

wind velocity is significant and for this reason water-evaporation is constantly monitored.

By the time Johann Georg Graue took possession of the farm, its lands, consisting at the time of 93 hectares, had been cultivated for 146 years. In addition to orchards in which a variety of fruit trees were growing, there were extensive vineyards which, he discovered, contained a range of cultivars, mainly Steen (today known as Chenin blanc), Cape Riesling, Cinsaut and Cabernet Sauvignon. With his experience in viticulture and his inborn German thoroughness, Graue set about observing and analysing the behaviour and development of these disparate varieties and, as a result, he established that the Cape Riesling, Cinsaut and particularly the Chenin blanc cultivars varied appreciably from one part of the farm to another. The Chenin blanc, in his opinion, was a superior variety and he therefore initiated a selection and development process

in which he used this cultivar as the basis for a high quality white wine. In establishing his system of selection, Johann Georg Graue laid a foundation not only for the future of Nederburg's vineyards, but also for South Africa's entire wine industry, at the same time firmly establishing himself as one of the country's viticultural pioneers.

Today, after many years of experience and experimentation, Nederburg grows specific vines in specific areas, each of which has proved to be suitable for that particular cultivar. For instance, Nederburg's west-facing slopes are exposed to long hours of sunlight which create a meso-climate where grapes with a high sugar content flourish; it is here that vineyards are planted with cultivars from which special late harvest, noble late harvest and full-bodied red wines are made. But since other cultivars require a cooler climate and different types of soil, over the past two decades the

company, Nederburg Wines Limited, has acquired a number of production farms in various parts of the Stellenbosch and Paarl areas. In addition to Nederburg (204 hectares), there is Lanquedoc (162 hectares) in Klein Drakenstein, Groenhof (269 hectares) in the Koelenhof area near Stellenbosch, Plaisir de Merle (974 hectares) near Simondium, between Paarl and Franschhoek, and the nursery and plant propagation farm, Ernita (91 hectares) near Wellington.

The range of varieties grown on these farms is extensive: Nederburg has 97 hectares under vines which stretch over a rolling landscape with Chenin blanc, Muscadel Ottonel, White Muscadel, Sauvignon blanc, Cape Riesling, Weisser Riesling and Cabernet Sauvignon being grown there. Lanquedoc's vineyards are situated against the western foothills of the Du Toitskloof mountains and extend over 87 hectares. Here

TOP LEFT
Twisted like grotesque dancers, bare vines bow before a grey wintry sky.
TOP RIGHT
Winter time is pruning time. Skilled hands know exactly where to cut.
BOTTOM LEFT
In the brilliance of early spring, youthful shoots are trained along the trellises.
BOTTOM RIGHT
High summer at last and the rich harvest is ready for gathering in.
PAGE 147: TOP
Early morning in the Nederburg vineyards.
BOTTOM
Counting grafted vines.

Chardonnay, Chenin blanc, Colombar, Cape Riesling, Weisser Riesling, Cabernet Sauvignon, Ruby Cabernet and Shiraz are grown. Groenhof, with its 107 hectares of vineyard, is situated on the south-western slopes of Simonsberg and produces Chardonnay, Chenin blanc, Gewürztraminer, Sauvignon blanc, S.A. Riesling, Weisser Riesling, Cabernet Sauvignon, Pinot noir and Shiraz. By far the biggest of the wine farms is Plaisir de Merle against the south-eastern slopes of Simonsberg. It has 374 hectares under vineyards and produces Chardonnay, Chenin blanc, Colombar, Gewürztraminer, Morio Muscat, Muscadel Ottonel, White Muscadel, Pinot blanc, Sauvignon blanc, Cape Riesling, Weisser Riesling, Cabernet Sauvignon, Merlot, Pinot noir, Ruby Cabernet and Shiraz.

During an average year, Nederburg's farms provide its cellars with approximately half its total intake of

grapes, the other half being bought from outside grape growers on a contract basis, a policy that has been in operation for more than three and a half decades. For the 1991 vintage, for instance, Nederburg bought grapes from growers in the wine regions of Durbanville, Elgin, Paarl, Stellenbosch and Wellington. Nederburg and its associated farms are not in grape production to compete with these grape growers, but to produce grapes at certain stages of ripeness for specific styles of wine. High-risk grape production — for instance, that which involves leaving grapes on the vine for infection by the fungus *Botrytis cinerea* or noble rot (see Chapter Eight) — is undertaken on Nederburg's own farms. The same rule of home-growing applies to the cultivation of shy-bearing cultivars like Gewürztraminer and Pinot noir as well as to experimentation with new clones and techniques. Once the results of these experiments are

known, they are conveyed to the growers who produce grapes for Nederburg.

Over the years, the Graue philosophy of selection, implemented many years ago, has been developed and sophisticated and is today regarded as the first stage in plant improvement. This process is carried out at Nederburg's vine nursery at Ernita, the former olive farm bought in 1974 to produce grafted vines. In 1976 nursery manager Tossie Louw and his team, under the guidance of Ernst le Roux, at that time Nederburg's chief viticulturist, initiated a scheme involving comprehensive and sophisticated programmes of plant propagation and care, as well as grafting and plant improvement, so providing Nederburg, its satellite farms and other suppliers of grapes with the best quality grafted vines. The nursery clones the best possible plant material through *in vitro* propagation, applies virus

elimination, tests plant material for virus infection and conducts applied research in these areas.

Of the approximately 91 hectares Ernita occupies, 22 are utilized for the nursery itself, 35 for mother blocks (9 hectares of rootstock and 26 hectares of scion material) and 2,2 for plant improvement. Although the creation of quality Nederburg wines is the result of very close co-operation between the viticultural team and the cellar-master and his helpers, the quality of the grapes used — and eventually that of the wine itself — is to a large extent the result of the highly specialized plant improvement programme conducted at Ernita.

This begins with the selection of clones in existing vineyards, where promising plants are marked and observed for three years. In this period each is assessed in terms of vigour, size, shape and compactness of bunches, colour intensity, bearing capacity and resistance to rot, disease, climatic damage and virus infection.

In the second phase of selection, known as interplanting, the best material of a specific cultivar is gathered and grafted separately onto single rootstock clones. These combinations are planted next to each other in commercial vineyards and closely observed for their viticultural and oenological qualities. At this stage, the most promising clones are cleaned to eliminate all harmful viruses. This entails the removal of a small meristemic portion of the plant which is then cultured *in vitro*. When the plant is strong enough, it undergoes heat therapy at about 38°C in a controlled, carbon dioxide-enriched atmosphere. Between 100 and 120 days later, a small part of the apical meristem is again cultured *in vitro* until it is strong enough to be transplanted into a 20-litre container. This now becomes a mother plant and is kept in an insect-proof growing-house to protect it from possible re-infection by flying vectors. All future propagation of a specific clone starts from its single mother plant.

Plants are indexed for viruses by one of three methods. The most commonly used involves field indexing in which a bud of the plant to be tested is grafted onto a virus indicator variety. Another method is the serum test known as the Elisa technique. Although this method is less time-consuming than the first, it cannot detect all viruses. The third method, a new and very fast indexing technique, entails the use of electron microscopes to detect virus particles. This is a costly procedure, however, and requires the employment of highly-trained technical staff.

Once a clone has been cleaned of harmful viruses, further propagation takes place through the use of mist-beds. Cuttings, each consisting of a healthy leaf with a bud and internode, are planted in well-drained steri-lized soil and kept moist with a mist-spray. Only after root growth has been established is the overhead spraying phased out and the plant allowed to acclimatize. In the third phase, the most promising clones intended for commercial plantings are established in mother blocks in which the soil has been deep-ploughed, fumigated to eliminate nematodes and in which a permanent irriga-tion system has been installed.

All scion and rootstock material used for commer-cial grafting at Ernita is obtained from certified mother blocks. Two methods of grafting are used, one being bench grafting and the other field grafting. In the first method, scions are grafted onto rootstocks by means of grafting machines, after which graft unions are allowed to grow together to form a callus under controlled and optimal environmental conditions. These are subse-quently planted out in the field nursery and left to grow for a year before being uprooted and quality tested, after which the young vines are ready to be planted in pro-duction vineyards.

PAGE 148: TOP LEFT
Meristem abscission.
TOP CENTRE
In vitro *propagation of heat-treated vines.*
TOP RIGHT
Conducting the Elisa virus test.
BOTTOM
Cutting scion material from the mother plantation.
PAGE 149
Early summer and it is time to prepare the soil for next season's nursery plantings.

Root cuttings which are too thin to be bench graft-ed are planted directly into the nursery. After a year's growth they are chip-budded *in situ* and then left for a second year before being uprooted. From this stage on-wards they are handled in the same manner as their bench-grafted counterparts.

People who enjoy the pleasures of civilized drinking are often unaware of the effort and expertise involved in the production of a good bottle of wine. Nederburg's cellars invariably seem immense to visitors taken on a conducted tour and often give them some idea of what wine-making entails and of why they are obliged to pay the prices the retailer charges them. However, if they were to visit Ernita — of whose existence most visitors may well be ignorant — they would probably be aston-ished to discover the lengths to which producers go to ensure the excellence of every individual bottle of wine. Even though Ernita was established to safeguard the quality of Nederburg's own products, there is no doubt that the project has benefited the various grape suppli-ers to Nederburg and that its development has had a major influence on the wine industry as a whole.

Johann Georg Graue was aware that the high sum-mer temperatures in the Cape, which reach their peak

during harvest time, have a detrimental effect on fermenting wines, particularly the whites. Sometimes, in fact, the natural process can speed up to such an extent that fermentation ceases altogether, resulting in a wine that is thin in quality and unpalatable to the taste. Cold-fermented white wines, on the other hand, show a freshness and fruitiness of flavour, and have a low volatile acidity. Graue, whose experience as a brewer in Germany had familiarized him with certain cold fermentation techniques, aimed at producing wine of this kind, but to do so he had to obtain a precision of control in his cellars comparable with that he had achieved in his vineyards. A really good white wine, he realized, could be achieved only if he could control temperatures during fermentation. During the years following the end of the Second World War, experiments were conducted in Nederburg's cellars, both by Arnold Graue, who had acquired considerable technical expertise while studying at some of Europe's most renowned vini- and viticultural institutions, and, after his tragic death, by Dr Nino Costa of Monis Wineries in Paarl. Later the process was further developed and refined by Nederburg's outstanding Günter Brözel, and eventually the outcome of the innovations of these three skilful vini-

culturists was a successful system of cold fermentation resulting in the retention of important aromatic constituents in the wine. The process of cold fermentation which was born and perfected at Nederburg subsequently had a major influence on the whole South African wine industry. (See Chapters Seven and Eight.)

Nederburg is, of course, entirely dependent on its wine-makers for upholding the vinicultural tradition established by Johann Georg Graue. It was fortuitous — one is tempted to believe *foreordained* — that Arnold Graue's genius in the cellar should have been succeeded, in 1956, by that of Günter Brözel. Over the years his creative quest has led him to open up new areas for the development of his skills, whether these have lain in experimenting with the potential of new cultivars and wine types, or in pioneering wine-making techniques. For example, at an international wine-making exhibition in France he noticed a rotating fermentation tank for red wines which immediately interested him. He imported one of these vessels for experimental purposes and when, during its first year, it came up to his expectations, he arranged for similar tanks to be made locally.

Günter Brözel has often likened his role to that of the charioteer of old who harnessed the strength of his

PAGE 150: TOP
Holes are punched into plastic mulching in preparation for bench grafted cuttings — a method of rearing young vines practised only by Nederburg.
CENTRE LEFT
Scion material is produced from these vines for grafting into rootstock in the mother plantation.
CENTRE RIGHT
Waxed, grafted cuttings begin to bud after two weeks in the callus rooms.
BOTTOM LEFT
Their incubation period over, the budding cuttings are removed from the callus boxes.
BOTTOM RIGHT
Early spring and the young bench grafted vines are planted out on the plastic mulching.
PAGE 151
Preparing thousands of grafted cuttings for spring planting is a labour intensive operation.

steeds without destroying their character. In the cellar he largely allowed the wines to make themselves, first by creating optimum conditions under which this could happen and then by controlling every aspect of those conditions. Those who know him also know that during the pressing season he virtually lives in the cellar, attending like a midwife to each new wine. His own description of the role of a wine-maker is very apt: 'In making wine you don't work with recipes. You must grow your wines and remain in attendance on them fulltime to lift the veil of uncertainties that envelops them, all the while making decisions that will help you not only express a wine's varietal characteristics, but also its history in terms of soil and climate.'

He also claims that as a wine-maker he has been fortunate in that Nature has been kind to the viticulturists of the Cape. 'We have the right soils,' he says, 'on which to grow excellent grapes, and our long, warm summers in a good year will concentrate in these grapes all the goodness we could possibly want. Our geographical position at 34 degrees south of the Equator ensures a relatively stable climate and early ripening of some cultivars.

'We are blessed by being between two oceans, for breezes from both caress our vineyards with cool air while the nightly dew which occurs even during the dry months refreshes the vines. And the much-maligned "Cape Doctor", when it comes blustering down the

TOP LEFT
Ernst le Roux, Nederburg's managing director, at work in his office.
TOP RIGHT
Nederburg's cellarmaster, Newald Marais.
PAGE 153: TOP
The Nederburg viticulture team.
Left to right: Freddie le Roux, Philip Hugo, Bertie Faure, Jan Prins, Hannes van Rensburg and Dirkie Loubser.
BOTTOM
Left to right: wine-makers Niel Bester, Wilhelm Arnold and Newald Marais apply the taste test.

mountains, cleanses the vineyards which thus require the minimum of pesticide attention.'

During 1989 Günter Brözel decided to take early retirement after 33 years at the helm of a winery which had achieved an unprecedented international reputation. He had always believed that Nederburg should satisfy the whole of the taste spectrum and to this end created a range of natural wines which in scope and variety has no equal in this country. This, in essence, is his true legacy to the wine industry of this region at Africa's southernmost point.

With the retirement of Brözel an important era at Nederburg came to an end and there were those who wondered whether his successors would be a little uncertain of their ability to maintain the high standards set by him. However, they remembered that in accepting the medal of honour of the wine industry in 1986 Brözel expressly stated that his tutor at Nederburg had impressed on him that the end product in a bottle of wine was not the result of one man's labour, but that of many, and added: 'My gratitude therefore [goes] to the Nederburg team, to those men in the vineyards and in the cellars who year after year help to make the miracle of the harvest a reality.'

Günter Brözel himself would be the first to admit that Nederburg's successes in the past had never been a 'one-man show'. Soon after his departure it became clear that although Nederburg had certainly lost a great

character, the infrastructure and the continuing expertise, as well as the long-standing and underlying Nederburg philosophy of optional selection of grapes, were more than sufficient to ensure the maintenance of the highest standards of quality in its wines. And then, interestingly enough, almost all the members of the 'new' team at Nederburg had had a very close association with it at some stage in the past, hence their self-confidence and enthusiasm — not forgetting their combined knowledge and expertise — when they took over the bridge of this stately liner.

When Günter Brözel left, Ernst le Roux, possibly one of South Africa's foremost viticulturists, was appointed managing director in his place. He already knew Nederburg intimately as earlier he had worked in its vineyards for a number of years before taking over as manager of Klein Constantia. After being back in harness at Nederburg for three years, he makes no secret of the fact that 'we are very particular in the people whom we appoint. Only a perfectionist can survive here.' In addition, he emphasizes that Nederburg adheres to a policy in which the most modern technology is combined with a wine-making philosophy that allows Nature, as far as is practically possible, to make the wine itself.

According to Ernst le Roux, the real reason for Nederburg's success is the continued tradition of Johann Georg Graue's practice of optional selection. 'Our wines are intended for the upper sector of the quality market,' he says, 'and to achieve our aim we must begin in the vineyard. Our various satellite farms and the widespread area from which we purchase our grapes make it possible to select the best varietals in the most suitable climate and regions.'

The process begins with the propagation of plant material at the Ernita nursery and is followed by the right plantings in the right places. Le Roux points out that this intensive preparation is not limited to Nederburg's own farms: it is extended to those growers who deliver their grapes to Nederburg for pressing. These growers, he says, are part of the family and a very close liaison is maintained with them. Nederburg is involved from the start and assists with the planning as well as with the planting of new vines.

As managing director of Nederburg, Ernst le Roux primarily plays the role of co-ordinator between viticulturist, wine-maker and marketer. To support him he has the Nederburg team backed, as a whole, by years of experience, though each individual member is a specialist in his own right. Together, they look forward to the nineties as an extremely exciting decade in which the accent will be placed increasingly on the quality of South Africa's premier wines, which have already shown impressive improvements in recent times. Nederburg will not only be involved in new developments, but will take a leadership role on the quality front. The new team, aware of the creative environment of the wine world, of its challenges and the constant call for innovation, will continue its quest for new styles of wine and, to this end, will seek out new clones for use in new experiments in the cellar.

The cellar-master who leads Nederburg's team and must meet the challenges as they arise is Newald Marais. Very much at home in Nederburg's cellars, he was tutored by Günter Brözel, for whom he worked for 12 years from 1976. In 1988 he was moved to Stellenbosch Farmers' Winery to take responsibility for the white wine production, but at the beginning of 1989, when Brözel gave the first indication that he planned to retire, Marais returned to take over the reins.

During his period with S.F.W., Marais, who had spent years in cellars where only 'estate style' wines were made, found himself exposed to a wide variety of commercial products for the first time. This experience broadened his perspective on wine-making and once he returned to Nederburg, several changes were inevitable.

He has certainly not meddled with the winning formu-
lae for Nederburg's range of standard wines, but has his
own and very definite ideas when it comes to the making of the limited editions and the auction wines.

An expression of Marais's individuality is his method of wood-ageing by using smaller oak casks for certain
wines. These he uses mainly for the preparation of reds,
but also for some white wines. In seeking out the right
wood for each wine he has not confined his search to
France alone, as is the case with some wine-makers.

Newald Marais has fine-tuned the principle established by Johann Georg Graue in the 1930s. Electronics
nowadays make it possible to control the temperature of
fermentation in the various tanks so that no room is left
for human error. Like Graue, Newald believes in the
maxim that good wine begins in the vineyard and, by

TOP
*The ageing cellar, where oak vats
slowly and secretly impart their character
to Nederburg's great red wines.*
PAGE 154: BOTTOM
The brass opening of a vat.

maintaining a constant liaison with Nederburg's viticulturists, makes use of every possible opportunity provided by nature.

A third member of the team is Hannes van Rensburg, the viticultural manager of Nederburg and its
satellite farms. The challenge he has to meet in the
vineyard lies in organizing those cultivation practices
which can be controlled and have an influence on
grape and wine quality, and blending these with the un-
controllables of a specific *terroir*. (The concept of *terroir*
– French for 'soil' – deals with the particular environment in which a vineyard has been planted; among the
most important elements of a *terroir* are the climate, soil
and location.) For choice of cultivar, soil preparation,
trellising and pruning systems, fertilizer programmes,
irrigation scheduling and canopy management, the

viticulturist has to rely on his technical knowledge, experience and, to a degree, intuition.

To Nederburg's management team it is clearly an overstatement to claim that wines are made in the vineyard or the cellar alone. Through experience, its various members have learnt that these two facets are inseparable and that wine production, as Johann Georg Graue so firmly believed, begins in the vineyard and is completed in the cellar. According to Van Rensburg, his part of the operation requires the implementation of theoretically correct methods on a practical scale and in an economical manner so as to produce top quality grapes for the making of premium quality wines. He also emphasises that 'while the concept that quality wines are produced in the vineyards is certainly true, bad wine-making techniques can result in a bad product even though good quality grapes were delivered'. It is also contended that the South African wine industry has arrived at a situation where the two disciplines, viticulture and oenology, have been separated to a large

TOP
The design of Nederburg's pedimented administration offices complements the Cape vernacular style of the homestead.
BOTTOM LEFT
Another harvest, another vintage. Grapes arrive at the crusher.
BOTTOM RIGHT
Stainless steel fermentation tanks for white wines.

extent, resulting in a lack of cross-pollination between the two. With these factors in mind, Nederburg's management fully subscribes to a policy of firm teamwork and throughout the year, but particularly during the harvest season, Newald Marais and Hannes van Rensburg spend considerable time working together in both cellar and vineyards.

But it is not only the highly-qualified and experienced members of Nederburg's staff who contribute to the quality of the end-product. Since mid-1991, everyone on the premises who plays any part, no matter how small, in Nederburg's wine production has begun each day by attending a meeting in what is known as 'the green area' of the cellars. Here reports are made on events of the previous day, problems are discussed and achievements commended. Then a programme is mapped out for the day itself for, since wine farming and making are dependent on such vagaries as weather and supply of grapes, a timetable cannot be planned long in advance. According to Newald Marais, these daily

gatherings have served to weld the Nederburg personnel together, to awaken the awareness that every individual is a vital link in the production chain and to stimulate a sense of identity with a proud institution. Part of a scheme to aspire towards excellence in quality, it has improved communication among the staff, from the man who sweeps the cellar floors to those with the highest academic qualifications and, at the same time, has motivated one and all with a desire to succeed.

There can therefore be no doubt in anybody's mind that the future of Nederburg is firmly held in the competent hands of the 'new' old team with its unremitting quest for the best in wine production combined with the established tradition of creativity and innovation. As somebody remarked, dispelling any anxieties regarding the team's ability to carry Nederburg to heights even loftier than those reached in former years: 'I think the Nederburgers can sleep quite peacefully at night.'

Perhaps the latest remarkable achievement and another 'first' for Nederburg is the growing of grapes and

TOP LEFT
Nederburg's red wine cellar with its drowsing oak vats, some of them intricately carved.
TOP RIGHT
The bottle filling hall.
BOTTOM LEFT
Regimented rows of bottles emerge from the bottle washing equipment.
BOTTOM RIGHT
Before labelling, filled bottles are subjected to a second quality control inspection.

the production of wines of origin in the Elgin-Grabouw area. This region is renowned for its deciduous fruit production, particularly that of apples, which over the years has proved so immensely lucrative that the farming community has never considered any alternative. Yet for some time the merits of this area and its potential for the growing of quality grapes have been given considerable attention. In the early seventies post-graduate research conducted by Nederburg's present managing director, Ernst le Roux, indisputably proved that the unique and distinctive characteristics of this particular region make it particularly suitable for the production of quality wine grapes. However, at the time no K.W.V. quota was available and because of the profitability of apple farming nothing positive materialized. However, in the middle eighties, several interested persons, including Ronnie Melck, Günter Brözel, the late Albert Rust and Advocate Hennie Beukes, met at Nederburg and had a searching discussion on the subject of wine farming at Elgin. As a result Ernst le Roux

*The present Nederburg range of wines covers a
broad taste spectrum from dry to semi-sweet, to the 'nectar' taste
of Nederburg Late Harvest and Noble Late Harvest.*

Nederburg wines fall into three main categories:
the standard range sold by retail outlets, those produced specifically for export,
and the special Nederburg Auction and limited vintage wines.

Wines bearing these labels command high prices at the
Nederburg Auction.

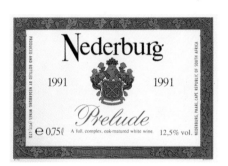

Nederburg wine labels are associated with quality,
tradition and heritage.

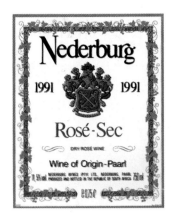

was instructed to investigate a variety of possibilities and submit suitable recommendations for further action. Comparative studies undertaken for Le Roux's post-graduate research work had already shown important similarities between the Elgin area and the French wine-growing region of Burgundy, the traditional home of Pinot noir and Chardonnay. His findings clearly indicated that Elgin had one of the coolest climates in the western Cape and therefore was particularly well-suited to the growing of such cultivars as Pinot noir, Chardonnay, Riesling, Sauvignon blanc and Gewürztraminer.

Le Roux's continued investigation eventually led him to the Cluver family farm, De Rust. The temperatures on this farm are relatively low, especially so against the higher slopes of the surrounding mountains. Because of De Rust's size and the variation in slopes and altitudes, there also exists a diversity of micro-climates which facilitates the choice of blocks for specific cultivars. All this led to an agreement between Nederburg and Dr Paul Cluver, owner of De Rust, eventuating in 1986 in the acquisition of a production quota and the establishment of vineyards on approximately 30 hectares. For the new plantings of the classical European varieties only the best plant material from the Ernita nursery was used. In 1990 the first grapes from De Rust were transported to Nederburg and a pressing of experimental wines was made. The first Elgin wines, tasted in 1990, showed gratifying promise and remarkable potential. Nederburg cellar-master Newald Marais is convinced that when they are released, the wines from Elgin will be recognized as being among the best ever to be made in South Africa.

Important though these wines will be, they will not eclipse those already on the market. The present range covers a broad taste spectrum. It includes sparkling wines such as Nederburg Cuvée Brut, made in the conventional manner with secondary fermentation taking place in tanks, and Nederburg Kap Sekt, initially developed for the European — particularly the German — market and, in compliance with E.E.C. regulations, matured in tanks for nine months. There are dry to semi-sweet white wines including Elégance; Stein (perhaps the best-known semi-sweet in South Africa); Premier Grand Cru; Prelude (a blend of the classic French varietals, Sauvignon blanc and Chardonnay, which give it a distinct French, if not specifically Burgundy, character); the well-known Paarl Riesling; Rhine Riesling; Chardonnay; and Gewürztraminer. Wine drinkers who prefer the 'nectar' taste can choose between Nederburg Special Late Harvest and Nederburg Noble Late Harvest; there are rosé wines including Nederburg rosé, Rosé Sec and Cabernet blanc de noir. The red wine range comprises the famous Paarl Cabernet Sauvignon, Edelrood, Baronne and Pinot noir. To coincide with the celebration of Nederburg's second century, its cellar-masters proudly announced the arrival of Nederburg Blanquette — a new *Méthode Champenoise* sparkling wine. In honour of this special occasion, only 5 000 bottles of the first vintage were produced to be served in the celebration year. Only when the next vintage is produced will Nederburg Blanquette be available commercially. It is a matter of pride that almost all Nederburg's products have been granted the Superior Wine of Origin certification since the introduction of this concept in 1972.

Broadly, Nederburg's wines fall into three categories. First, there is the standard range consisting of the

14 wines distributed by the retail trade; then there are those wines produced for export; and thirdly, there is the range of special Nederburg Auction wines and limited vintages. These include the various Private Bin wines which are special blends, either of whites or reds, produced in restricted quantities and of outstanding quality. Private Bin wines are the pride of the cellar-master who created them and, like the sought-after Edelkeur, fetch high prices at the Auction.

Edelkeur is the nectar-like natural wine whose praises have been sung here and abroad since it was introduced in 1969. After years of experimentation, a special dispensation had to be granted for its production as the residual sugars were far higher than the law allowed. Made with the utmost care from grapes affected by *Botrytis cinerea* (noble rot), it is in the style of the great Tokay wines of Hungary, the Sauternes of France and the Trockenbeerenauslese wines of Germany. In 1972 Nederburg entered the 1969 Edelkeur in an international wine competition in Budapest, Hungary. Against stiff competition it was judged the best wine on exhibition. At the Auction of Rare Cape Wines held at Nederburg, the small available quantities of Edelkeur are regularly snapped up by overseas buyers at prices that reflect the wine's international reputation. Edelkeur has since spawned a number of similar wines in South Africa, but it continues to retain the mystique of being the first of its kind. If Günter Brözel is to be remembered by posterity for any one thing, it will not necessarily be for his work with new cultivars or his innovations in the cellar, important though these are, but for the creation of his incomparable Edelkeur.

But times and fashions change and over the years several wines that once had famous names and were

PAGES 162 AND 163: TOP
Label design is an important aspect of wine packaging
PAGE 162: BOTTOM
Bark of a cork-oak tree planted at Nederburg in the 1920s by Colonel R. A. Lyall. Tests carried out on these trees indicate that the cork is definitely not suitable for use in wine bottles.
PAGE 163: BOTTOM
This piece of equipment was once used to determine the percentage of alcohol in fortified wines.

savoured with delight have disappeared from the market. They include Nederburg Sylvaner, Edeltropfen, Fonternel, Duette, Gamay and the wine that recalls the farm where the young Arnold Graue once had his home, Hochheimer.

Fundamental as quality and character are to the success of any wine, marketing also plays a vital part in the fortunes of every wine company. Advertisements for Nederburg's products have appeared in journals and magazines for many years but, according to marketing manager, Schalk Burger, the first campaign to have a major impact was launched in the early seventies. Full-colour advertisements were placed in South Africa's 'up-market' magazines and, in one series, famous personalities — such as winemaster Günter Brözel — were featured to introduce specific varietals. Since then, various campaigns in the printed and electronic media have created brand awareness among certain identified target groups, always aiming at reinforcing the message of quality combined with tradition and heritage. It is generally accepted that Nederburg has been the market leader in the high-priced market during the past two decades and that it has the reputation of being South Africa's most prestigious wine farm. Since the days when Johann Georg Graue first put his philosophy and theories into practice, Nederburg has excelled as pioneer and innovator in both viti- and viniculture. What is more, it has succeeded in placing South African wines squarely on the map nationally as well as internationally. The dynamic third management generation in vineyard, cellar and administrative office, is intent on keeping it that way.

■

CHAPTER ELEVEN

THE NEDERBURG AUCTION

An auction at Nederburg was conceived as a means
of promoting South Africa's rare wines and stimulating the
local industry. First held in 1975, the annual
Nederburg Auction is now attended by over 1 600 guests
and participants, both South African and foreign,
and with sales passing the R2 million mark, the gala occasion
is now one of the five world leaders in its field.

‘Waters of the world keep us apart, but wines of the world bring us together.’ So wrote American wine writer, Dee Stone, when she returned home to Atlanta, Georgia, after attending the Nederburg Auction in 1985. Many people who have attended this most exciting annual event would readily support her sentiments, for it is on this single day that Nederburg becomes a microcosm of the entire wine world. From all corners of the earth guests gather at this, one of its most lovely spots, all of them, irrespective of race or language, bonded by a shared appreciation of one of the most ancient and respected symbols of civilized living.

*Flags flutter outside the Johann Graue
Centre, welcoming guests from all over the
world to Nederburg's annual auction
of rare wines.*
PAGE 165
*Unquestionably, the Nederburg Auction
is one of the most colourful events in the
South African calendar.*

For many years before its inception in 1975, the idea of holding an auction at Nederburg had been in the mind of Lothar Barth, managing director of Stellenbosch Farmers' Winery. The concept was inspired by his visits to the winelands of Germany, where he had attended — and been impressed by — events of this kind, particularly that held at Kloster Eberbach in Eltville. At home, Lothar Barth found a ready disciple in S.F.W.'s marketing director, Jurgen Burmeister, who was already familiar with the wine auctions of his native Germany and naturally enthusiastic about establishing one at the Cape. A visit to Europe at this time with the express purpose of studying the organization of wine auctions convinced him that the situation, facilities and wines of Nederburg lent themselves particularly well to such an event. From then on, the idea of an auction began to take a definite form in the minds of both Barth and Burmeister. They saw it as providing an opportunity to convince the world that high quality wines were being made in South Africa in general and at Nederburg in particular; it would be a showcase for various rare wines of which only small quantities were available and would make them accessible to a discriminating public; it would also test the current likes and dislikes of consumers and so reflect the changing fashions in wine. Besides, an auction would create the avenue by which Edelkeur, the unique noble wine first produced at Nederburg in 1969, would become more widely known.

The concept was an ambitious one and, while Lothar Barth and Jurgen Burmeister had complete faith in it, the fact remained that the directors of Stellenbosch Farmers' Winery, which was still under the control of South African Breweries, were nervous. They were aware that the entire venture was an enormous risk for not only would it be extremely costly to mount, but failure would seriously damage Nederburg's image. However, despite initial misgivings, Nederburg's plans for its first auction went ahead and the date, 8 March 1975, was selected.

Nederburg itself was the obvious venue, both because of its superb surroundings and amenities and also because it would benefit from the maximum publicity. As a model the Kloster Eberbach auction was chosen although, naturally, changes had to be made to suit local conditions. It was, for example, impossible to emulate Kloster Eberbach in determining a base price for new vintage wines at the auction, as in South Africa this was one of the K.W.V.'s responsibilities. On the other hand, there was nothing to prevent the Nederburg Wine Auction from following Kloster Eberbach's example in establishing premium prices or providing a market for scarce or special wines — aims which it certainly set out to achieve. One of the first decisions was that participants outside Stellenbosch Farmers' Winery and Nederburg would be invited and that any South African wines of the required high standard would be eligible for sale to licensed retailers, but not to the public. The intention was that this would inspire Cape viticulturists to experiment with new cultivars and so stimulate the work undertaken by the Oenological and Viticultural Research Institute at Nietvoorbij. Local retailers would be encouraged to increase their role in wine-marketing and buyers from abroad would be invited to attend, as would luminaries representing various sectors of the local and foreign communities. Finally, and most important, it was agreed that an auctioneer of

world stature would be appointed to conduct the sale and that a high-ranking and well-known personage would be invited to open the proceedings.

Of course, the organizers of every facet of the event had a very great deal to learn but from the beginning the Auction was not a project confined to Nederburg alone, but a company undertaking where co-operation was the watchword. Despite this, it was no easy task to motivate the staff to help: there were those loyal to certain executives who opposed the whole idea while others simply had no interest in volunteering for extra (unpaid) work. In the event, it was Jurgen Burmeister's marketing section at S.F.W. that took on the 'front of house' organization while tents, tarpaulins and toilets became the responsibility of the winery manager, Dave Hughes — a motivating spirit behind the Auction for many years. Jeff Wedgwood, S.F.W.'s chief wine buyer, had the task, then as now, of encouraging outside winemakers to submit their products for sale. On that first occasion only six, including Nederburg and S.F.W., were represented and of the other four, Delheim and Groot Constantia have remained faithful participants in every subsequent Auction. Meanwhile, some 800 people, of whom 300 were licensees (licensed liquor dealers or their agents), had accepted invitations.

Nederburg's first Auction proved an occasion that no one — no matter how tenuously involved — will ever forget, though there was no hint at the time of the sophisticated gala occasion into which it would ultimately develop. Early March had been chosen because at that time of year at the Cape rain is unlikely to fall and put a dampener — literally — on the proceedings. A good enough reason, indeed, but it filled with dismay all those responsible for gathering in the harvest and pressing Nederburg's wine. Not only is this the hottest and most uncomfortable time of the year, but for those in the cellar it is always the most frenetic. For weeks before the first Auction they had been so busy by day and by night that they hardly slept — yet now they had to put all their technical duties aside and devote themselves to the requirements of the Auction. Nevertheless, the event went ahead and was opened by Hendrik Schoeman, then minister of agriculture, with the actual sale of wine being conducted by Patrick Grubb, distinguished auctioneer and director of the wine department of the famous British firm of Sotheby's.

As the Johann Graue Centre, today the pulsing heart of the Auction, was not even a dream in those days, the actual sale of wine took place in an enormous marquee erected on the front lawn, while the lunch was held *al fresco* wherever there was shade enough to give protection from the blistering sun. And blistering it certainly was on that March Saturday in 1975, as Ansie Kemp, Nederburg's public relations officer at the time,

remembers only too vividly. She tells of how caterers in Cape Town had been engaged to provide a meal of cordon bleu standards — and the organizers of the Auction had stipulated that the main course should be hot. Nederburg's homestead has a very fine kitchen, but neither it nor its staff was able to produce — without a hitch — 800 hot meals, especially when the temperature outside was soaring towards the forties. Then the dessert course had to be cold — really cold — and, despite refrigerated equipment, the ice-cream melted and the chocolate liquefied in the short time it took to move the plates from chilled truck to table. Overcome by intolerable heat and intense strain, the young woman in charge of the catering collapsed in a dead faint and had to be carried off to a cool spot — if one could be found — at the very climax of the proceedings.

Nevertheless, the Auction of 1975 broke new ground and provided — in the words of a modern cliché — 'a learning experience'. The total income amounted to R237 000, for which 12 400 cases of wine had been sold, but individual prices in many instances were disappointing. Edelkeur, to the intense chagrin of Günter Brözel, who had produced it with such skill, was sold for no more than the price of Lieberstein, the local popular wine, which made nonsense of the decision that no reserve price should be placed on any Nederburg product. The Auction's critics proved outspoken: some said

An air of tense expectancy fills the carefully prepared Johann Graue Centre on the morning of the Auction.

that the time was not yet ripe for an auction in South Africa; others thought that the prices were too high and that the public was not yet 'adequately wine sophisticated', and warned that growers would not respond to the challenge. Then, too, judging from the small number of participants, there appeared to have been some resistance from outside wine-makers. Many people, however, were positive in their response and, though the directors of Stellenbosch Farmers' Winery remained cautious and reluctant to invest in facilities specifically erected for future auctions, they nevertheless agreed to allow the Auction to continue.

But there was no stopping the ideas and ambitions of cellar-master Günter Brözel. Bearing in mind that one of the main purposes of the Auction was to make rare wines available and that another was to test the tastes and fashions of consumers, he decided at the Auction of 1977 to use the occasion as a platform for the new styles of wine he was creating. Some might be high in sugar, others low; some would be deep in colour, some robust in character; they might be smooth, wood-matured or blended . . . The problem was how to name these new and varied innovations, for the company's registered trademarks were inadequate for the considerable number of new wines being produced. Eventually it was decided to give a certain range of numbers — 100 to 200 — to red wines, with the added prefix of the

initial letter 'R' (for red); dry white wines would be numbered 201 to 300, prefixed by the letter 'D' (for dry); and the romantic late harvests and semi-sweets would be allocated the range from 301 to 400, prefixed by 'S', which stood for either 'sweet' or 'soet'. This numbering system is still in use today. And all the wines were given an added exclusivity by the label 'Private Bin'. Highly sought-after at that Auction and at the subsequent ones, these wines are — in the delightful and characteristic words of Brözel himself — 'small in measure — but, oho, the quality!'

Teething troubles aside, the annual event continued to improve steadily. Year by year the number of participants increased, so that by 1979 no fewer than 17 were offering 55 wines, totalling 7 038 cases, for sale. That year 453 V.I.P. guests had been invited; 1 400 licensees were there to buy and a record number of 220 members of the media came to report on proceedings. It was only too clear that the Nederburg Auction was now a *fait accompli* and that no time should be lost in providing it with a home and facilities in keeping with its prestige. After discussion, it was announced that Stellenbosch Farmers' Winery, backed by South African Breweries, had approved the erection of a permanent building in which all future sales would be conducted. Named in honour of the man who had been the first to place Nederburg's wines on the international

Among the V.I.P.s at the 1991 Nederburg Wine Auction are:
TOP LEFT
Left to right: guest speaker and chairman of the Joseph Drouhin Wine Company, Robert Drouhin; executive chairman of Stellenbosch Farmers' Winery, David Marlow, and Nederburg managing director Ernst le Roux.
TOP RIGHT
Advocate Vuka Tshabalala, liquor store owner and president of Ukhamba, with companion.
BOTTOM LEFT
Lothar Barth, founder of the Auction, and Günter Brözel, Nederburg's cellarmaster for 33 years, relax together over a glass of wine.
BOTTOM RIGHT
Minister of Home Affairs Eugene Louw and his wife, Hantie, with Anna Marlow, wife of David Marlow.

map, largely through his implementation of the cold fermentation process, it was to be called the Johann Graue Centre and would be completed in time for the sixth Nederburg Auction in 1980.

When that day came on Saturday 8 March, the proceedings were introduced by Lothar Barth as director of Nederburg Wines International and opened by Dr Anton Rupert, chairman of the Rembrandt Group. On this special occasion, Günter Brözel had the honour of unveiling a bust of his mentor, Johann Georg Graue, sculpted by Sandy Hendrikz, S.F.W.'s training and development manager. From her home in Hermanus, Graue's widow Ilse, then 82 years old, sent her special greetings. The new auction centre, said Lothar Barth in his speech, was the final confirmation of Stellenbosch Farmers' Winery's belief that the Nederburg Auction would remain a permanent feature of the endeavours of the South African wine industry; that it would stimulate the production of those wines that reflect the unique quality and variety that this country has to offer in terms of cultivar, origin and wine-making expertise; that it would encourage local retailers and consumers to buy these wines; and lastly, that it would promote the export of South African wines in the full knowledge that the relationship between price and quality is unique in the world. To that epoch-making Auction, 15 participants submitted 7 800 cases, representing a total

of 65 wines. The income they brought in amounted to approximately R420 000, of which R231 685 was paid for white wines and R188 659 for reds. The average price of R57,44 per case was a far cry from the mere R19,12 which had been paid at the 1975 Auction.

The erection of the Johann Graue Centre means that at last the organizers of the Auction need no longer look quite so apprehensively towards the skies as the most important day in their calendar draws near. True, some divine agency seems to have arranged the elements so that year after year — despite some bad frights beforehand — the weather has smiled (sometimes rather too warmly) on the Auction — and it has continued to do so unfailingly and miraculously ever since. But the fear of what would happen if some day the Auction turned out to be — literally — a wash-out was dispelled in 1980 when the 2 359 visitors who attended the function that year found everything — winetasting, auction, luncheon — under cover. The centre itself, erected on the site of the old farmyard, was the first of its kind to be built in South Africa's winelands and was designed with the various needs of the Nederburg Auction and of its participants in mind. A sum of R320 000 was set aside for the scheme designed by architect Ernest Ford with the aid of the firm of Botes and Brink, quantity surveyors, and the contractors

Patrick Grubb on the podium in characteristic pose. Winemaster, director of the wine department of Sotheby's of London, and renowned wine auctioneer, he has presided over Nederburg's Auction every year since its inauguration in 1975.
PAGE 169: TOP
Monsieur Robert Drouhin, chairman of the Joseph Drouhin Wine Company and guest of honour, makes the inaugural speech at the 1991 Auction.
CENTRE
Bennie Howard, Stellenbosch Farmers' Winery group public relations manager, who has been responsible for organizing the Auction since 1990. This complex and exacting task occupies a full year.

moved onto the site in August 1979. Today guests attending the Auction gather in a lofty hall suffused with light which filters through clear fibreglass sheeting in the roof, while the most important guests are entertained to lunch in a canopy-covered brick-paved courtyard opening from it. The entire ambience of the complex, like the wines themselves, is one of quality and good taste. Very much part of the 20th century, the Johann Graue Centre, with its whitewashed walls and clean lines, nevertheless blends harmoniously with its historic Cape surroundings while, fluttering mast-high on gala occasions, a cluster of festive flags reminds visitors of the many countries around the world in which Nederburg has friends.

Few of the people who come to buy wines at the Auction, or simply to enjoy its incomparable atmosphere of festivity, are aware of the intricate planning that the event involves or of the way its organization has developed over the years. The names of Jurgen Burmeister, Barry Whitfield, Johann Deale, Christine Rudman, Dave Hughes, Dave Johnson, Sue Wardrop, Astrid Jackson and Bennie Howard will always be associated with the Auction. To all these people, wine-expert Dave Hughes, who has had years of experience with them all, gives credit for fine-tuning the Auction into what it has become today. It is Sue Wardrop, he

says, who deserves to be singled out not only for her astonishing efficiency but for engendering loyalty among all the 'workers' and for developing excellent relations with the wine trade. After the third Auction Dave, by then in charge of wine market development at S.F.W., took over as ground manager, and he has a wealth of anecdotes to tell. The first two events, with their milling crowds, gaudy canvas and lively music (military and naval brass and pipe bands have long been an early morning feature), had reminded him vividly of a circus, so to sort out the problem of erecting and dismantling the tents he called in the assistance of a retired ringmaster. To this veteran, who had spent 30 years moving circuses about the country with speed and efficiency, the logistics of a one-day event — where no account need be taken of performing lions or trapeze artists — was child's play and he and Dave between them worked out a plan of action which is still used.

Since 1990 the complex task of organizing the Auction has been in the hands of group public relations manager, Bennie Howard. Well aware of the importance of early planning, he starts working on each Auction two weeks after the previous one has taken place, though by then he will already have given serious thought to a number of essential strategies for the year after next.

Bennie makes decisions and gives directions, but their implementation is carried out by Arlene Johnston, whom he describes as both his right hand and his left, and an active committee consisting of both Nederburg and S.F.W. staff. It is this committee that, in fact, 'puts the Auction together', as Bennie says. All its members are in full-time employment, but their extra work for the Auction throughout the year is entirely voluntary. Meetings are held regularly and decisions are made on the basis of consensus. Each committee member has an allotted task and each, in turn, delegates responsibility to a variety of people, each vital in his or her own sphere. 'And the beauty of it all,' says Bennie Howard, 'is that most of the people on the Auction committee have served on it for ten years or more.'

Since the sixth Auction, Arlene Johnston has been responsible for administration. She is in charge of a multitude of duties, only one of them being the despatch of some 2 000 invitations and the checking of replies. Buyers make up the majority of guests and tickets are issued on a regional basis. There is also a very extensive V.I.P. list. This includes not only participants who are selling their wines, but senior government officials, foreign ambassadors and diplomats as well as the owners of wine estates and co-operatives, the grape suppliers to Nederburg, the wine suppliers to S.F.W. and a number

of other people in one way or another connected with the wine industry.

In addition to these invited quests, there is the 'international connection' – Nederburg's agents from all over the world who, each year since the inception of the Auction, have been brought to South Africa. The contingent includes business associates, liquor store owners, hoteliers and media representatives. On their arrival, about ten days beforehand, they are taken to some area of spectacular natural beauty – the Drakensberg or the Lowveld, for instance – after which they come to the Cape to learn about Nederburg and S.F.W. and to buy wine at the Auction. They will leave the Cape with a greater knowledge of its wines, particularly those of Nederburg, and act as its ambassadors in their home countries. This, in itself, is an incentive to the local wine industry: participants, knowing that their products may be bought at the Auction and taken to foreign lands, strive to present to the visitors wines that are of outstanding quality.

The number of foreign visitors increased steadily until there were 68 in 1980 and despite sanctions this total

A hundred chefs are required to prepare the luncheon. Here some of them take a well earned break to sample Nederburg's famous wines.

has never fallen below 36. The percentage of sales to foreign buyers over the years rose from 2 per cent in 1978 to 14,81 per cent in 1991. With the recent withdrawal of sanctions, the 25 per cent mark was reached in 1992 with the Taiwanese contingent making history as the single biggest buyer overall on the day of the Auction.

During the months before these overseas visitors arrive, Bennie Howard is in daily contact with professional public relations specialist, Jenny McQueen, now running her own company but involved in the Auction since its third year. One of her tasks is to compile and meticulously check the detailed Auction catalogue; another is to keep the media informed by means of press releases, a result of which has been the burgeoning of an excellent relationship between Nederburg, Jenny McQueen and Associates and the media. On auction day itself local and overseas journalists, reporters and cameramen descend on Nederburg, where they are provided with facilities said to be comparable with those at the United Nations headquarters. To accommodate them, what was once a simple manager's cottage has been converted into modern reception offices

housing a media centre. There they have at their disposal typewriters and the most advanced electronic computers, fax and telex machines and telephones while photographers provide an on-site service to the media. Throughout the course of the Auction, information is constantly passed on to the media centre by the computer-linked terminal in the auction hall and a sound system relays every word of guest speaker and auctioneer to the media centre. Continuous contact between key staff members and personnel from the security department is maintained by two-way radios.

By the end of August of the preceding year, the wines submitted for the following Auction will have been stringently assessed by a selection panel. Apart from those that are very old, all the Nederburg wines are specifically made for the Auction and are labelled accordingly. Most 'outside' participants present mature wines earmarked specifically for the Auction and these bear an extra label giving the date of the particular Auction at which they will be sold. Every single case submitted is opened to check the number of bottles and the level of the wine they contain. Pre-auction tasting

The luncheon on Auction day is one of South Africa's culinary events of the year. No detail is overlooked in its preparation.
TOP CENTRE
Haute couture and haute cuisine are both much in evidence on Auction day. Here Lothar Barth, former chairman and managing director of Stellenbosch Farmers' Winery, is seen with two glamorous models.
TOP RIGHT
Nearly 5 000 plates have to be lined up in preparation for the three-course meal — each plate as attractively presented as the next.

of these wines by potential buyers is also an absolute essential if the buyers are to know what they are bidding for. In the early days the tasting was held at Nederburg itself on the day of the Auction. In 1976 the organizers realized that the only space large enough to accommodate the guests was the large store next to Nederburg's bottling line. Usually thousands of cartons of wine are stacked in this warehouse, but that year everything had to be cleared in advance and Nederburg's entire stock borne away by lorry for storage under lock and key elsewhere. After 1980 — the year of the inauguration of the Johann Graue Centre — the arrangements changed. On that occasion just under 2 400 guests assembled for the tasting — which thus qualified for entry in *The Guinness Book of Records*! It was then decided that future tastings of Auction wines would be held in advance at various different centres. Today the first is held in London just after Christmas, when a full range of Auction wines is presented to Patrick Grubb and a group of potential buyers, many of whom are members of the Institute of Masters of Wine. Then, from January into February, eight tastings are held at various cities

171

in South Africa, the invited guests being the previous Auction's largest buyers. In addition, separate tastings are held for the wine writers.

At Nederburg itself, preparation for the Auction gets under way at least two weeks before the chosen day. Since the beginning, 'Fires' van Vuuren, in charge of security, has proved an Auction stalwart, seeming to have eyes and ears everywhere. When the threat of bombs became only too real it was Fires who arranged for sniffer dogs to be 'on duty' early on the Auction morning to ensure the safety of both guests and staff. Fires knows, too, that gatecrashers have tried every imaginable way of sneaking in, from hiding in the boots of cars to wandering through the vineyards. Special security precautions have to be taken for the wine itself for, from eight o' clock until the last guest leaves, bottles are being opened at various points and glasses filled. Someone is always appointed to organize this operation for, apart from what is to be auctioned, wine for use during the day has to be stored in a 10-ton cooltruck.

Maintenance, of which guests are often unaware because it functions so smoothly, is an immense liability. For years Hannes Marais ran this department with

Under the expert control of Patrick Grubb, the Auction proceeds with never a hitch — even though the atmosphere is charged with excitement throughout.
PAGE 173
Luncheon tables, colour-coded, are laid with meticulous taste and artistry. Anyone fortunate enough to be invited to this magnificent meal will never forget it.

unassuming but punctilious efficiency. He installed extra electrical systems, connected pipes, averted disasters and generally saw to it that all systems worked — and all the while had half his mind on the continued functioning of the equipment inside Nederburg's cellars. Since his retirement his high standards have been maintained by his successor, Johan Steyn who, like everyone else involved in the physical preparation of the Auction, starts every day early and ends late. There are those who prepare the Johann Graue Centre for the Auction and those who erect tents — a giant ampliform is now in use for the early morning tasting — while others check hired glasses, crockery and cutlery. A team has the task of setting up the ramp and dressing-rooms for the fashion show, while preparations have to be made for the tea stall and first-aid personnel. Toilets must be in order, luncheon tables laid (and protected against dust and the weather), flowers arranged and fire-protection checked. Someone blows up balloons and last-minute instructions are given to voluntary helpers — for today there is no shortage of S.F.W. and Nederburg personnel only too willing to offer their voluntary aid in greeting guests and making them feel at home. And meanwhile,

of course, as the energy sparked by teamwork intensifies, the excitement grows apace and anticipation builds up to a climax as the day of the Auction draws closer.

At last it arrives and early in the morning, under the bluest of blue skies, guests and participants begin to arrive at Nederburg's gates, white against the green and gold of autumn vineyards. There are important visitors from abroad, cabinet ministers, foreign diplomats and South Africa's 'beautiful people' — the rich and the famous and the elegant — as well as scores of representatives of the South African wine industry, from bottle-store owners from dusty dorps to noted cellar-masters to township liquor dealers. Flags flutter; balloons — the colours change with each Auction — bob over green lawns laced with gaudy herbaceous borders and striped with canvas-canopied tents. Hostesses hand out cool glasses of buck's fizz and a rising polyglot of voices seems to strain the vast and magnificent ampliform at its moorings. At half past nine the guests, all in their finery, drift into the Johann Graue Centre, where Patrick Grubb, unruffled and urbane, sets the Auction in motion once again.

For 18 consecutive years this leading member of the exclusive Institute of Masters of Wine — aged 25, he was the youngest person ever to be admitted — has conducted the Nederburg Auction single-handed. This may well be a world record. Buyers, participants and guests admire and enjoy his expertise, the clear and well-modulated voice with which he conducts the proceedings, the wit that he brings to the serious business of wine-selling and his manifest confidence and efficiency — not to mention his unique choice of words in appraising the wines. If Nederburg has become synonymous with the term 'wine auction' in South Africa, no less has Patrick Grubb become identified with both.

Welcoming speeches by the senior executives of both S.F.W. and Nederburg set the Auction in motion; next follows an address by a distinguished guest speaker. Over the years some of the most famous personalities in the wine world have graced Nederburg's podium in this capacity and taken back with them memories not only of the Cape's finest wines, but of what is said to be the most efficiently organized wine auction anywhere. Speeches over, there comes up for sale the opening item — always a single lot of old Pinotage, South Africa's own wine variety and its pride. Excitement is in this way

generated at the start, for buyers eagerly outbid one another in an attempt to claim the first offering. Sales continue throughout the morning, with some surprises in store and records invariably broken. Then, at noon, guests in the Johann Graue Centre begin to stir and make their way back to the ampliform, for the Nederburg fashion show is the next item on the programme.

People may wonder what connection exists between high fashion and rare wine. The answer is simple: both represent superb quality in their own fields; both are closely linked with sensuous delight, with skill and creativity and with all that is pleasurable in civilized living. Introduced in 1979 and sponsored in 1981 by the Afrikaans magazine *Sarie* and the South African Wool Board, the fashion show gives the country's top designers an opportunity to display their latest creations to a discriminating audience from all over the world. The Nederburg fashion show is *haute couture* at its most sophisticated: models groomed to the last eyelash step it out with slick confidence, stirring admiration in all and wonder and envy in those not so well shaped — or heeled. When, in 1992, the fashion show

Models take the stage in the giant ampliform. South African designers regard the fashion show on Nederburg's Auction day as one of the most important annual events of its kind.

again featured garments made from local wool, it honoured not only the link between two of South Africa's most important natural products, but also the fact that both Nederburg and the wool industry, founded in 1791, were celebrating their bicentenaries.

Following the fashion show is yet another 'happening' that has made the Nederburg Auction famous. This is the marvellous meal made in heaven, it seems, and fit for Bacchus himself as well as all the other gods. Since 1976, when Southern Sun Hotels took over, the catering has been superb and the luncheon has become an almost legendary culinary triumph. Until 1989 a buffet meal was served; however, today guests are presented with a five-star gourmet meal served at allotted tables in canopied shade, where Nederburg wine flows and sparkles like a mountain stream. Months of preparation go into devising it. From August onwards meetings are held at which every detail is discussed and tastings are conducted; every year something new, something surprising, delicious and delightful is presented. But there is little at this most elegant feast to reveal the frenetic activity that has taken place behind the scenes to

prepare it. Since before dawn temporary kitchens set up days before have been a hive of activity. Presiding over them are up to 100 chefs — as well as 200 staff members — brought to Nederburg from Southern Sun hotels all over the country to contribute their expertise and to ensure that all runs smoothly. Convoys of refrigerated trucks have delivered 2 000 crayfish tails and what seems a ton of meat. Hundreds of lettuces and crates of tomatoes are being converted into crisp salads; gallons of cream must be whipped; a touch of decoration here and there is added to 5 000 plates. At precisely the right moment all must be ready and perfect, borne from kitchen to table and served to 1 650 chattering guests within one hour and 40 minutes. Imaginative in conception and flawless in execution, the Auction luncheon, to those fortunate to have enjoyed it, is a never-to-be-forgotten experience.

Now the guests return to the Johann Graue Centre and the Auction continues. The final item is another single lot of Pinotage and again bidders, by now somewhat euphoric, clamour for the distinction of possessing it. In 1988, for instance, one of them was prepared

Models await their turn to display the latest in designer creations at what has become an exciting feature of Auction day.

to pay R10 500 for a case of Lanzerac Pinotage 1969. But it is the charity auction, held after the sale of rare wines is completed, that often breaks records at the Nederburg Auction, while at the same time raising impressive and much-needed sums for deserving causes. On offer are specially donated wines, usually extremely rare and often very old, that are sold in aid of a nominated charity. In 1982 it was the South African National Council of the Aged that benefited from a stunning bid of R16 000 paid by Transvaal wine merchant, Mr Benny Goldberg, for a bottle of 1811 Cognac. Three years later the Community Chests were the fortunate recipients of the R20 000 that he paid for a bottle of 1940 vintage Chateau Libertas. When he equalled his record in 1987 with a successful bid for a half bottle of that most exquisite of all Cape wines — Constantia made in 1790, the year before Nederburg came into existence — it was to the advantage of the National Cancer Association of South Africa. In 1992 donated wines included a magnum of Californian Napa Valley Cabernet Sauvignon 1979 from the cellars of the guest speaker, Robert Mondavi. For this, a world record price of

R230 000 was paid by Mr Graham Beck of Bellingham and Madeba farms after a fierce bidding battle with Hans Schreiber, owner of Neethlingshof, himself a successful bidder for another item on the same charity auction and a staunch supporter of previous auctions at Nederburg.

The famed auction at the Hospice de Beaune in Burgundy may be regarded as an entirely 'charity event' since the hospice supports itself by auctioning the wine produced from its own vineyards. The auction at Kloster Eberbach, on the other hand, is wholly commercial, while all the money raised at the two held at Napa Valley and Sonoma in California is donated to deserving causes. It is only at Nederburg that a commercial event of this magnitude is combined with a charity function.

When the buying and the selling are over, the 100 and more representatives of the media who have attended the Auction gather for a Press conference. All the facts and figures of the day's sales are already awaiting them. Reporters and journalists can see at once the highest and the lowest prices, the averages paid for red wines and for whites, the percentage breakdowns

V.I.P. guests relax in the homestead's sun-filled voorkamer. In this quiet atmosphere, they can enjoy pleasant company and refreshements throughout Auction day. Left to right: Marion le Roux, Hantie Louw, Anna Marlow, Eugene Louw, Lothar Barth and hostess Magdel Horral.

according to areas, both local and foreign; the numbers of licensees, V.I.P. guests, public and media who have passed through the gates and the total income raised by the end of the day. Orders for photographs which have been on display throughout the day are processed so that by the time they leave each reporter has everything necessary for the story that will appear in the next edition of the newspaper. Telephones, of course, have made the final facts of the Auction available for that evening's newscasts on radio and television.

Since 1975 the Nederburg Auction has progressed enormously and relatively smoothly, though every year there are surprises. On at least one occasion guests overcome by heat — and other things — have leapt into the swimming pool. At one Auction Patrick Grubb, deprived by theft in America of his favourite ivory gavel, knocked down his sales with a smooth river stone provided by Dave Hughes in its stead, while on another occasion a power failure almost silenced the chairman of S.F.W. in mid-speech. Ansie Kemp tells of how, in dead of night preceding the 1978 Auction, she woke up in her quarters at the homestead to hear the unfamiliar sound of spraying water. Snatching the first garment that came to hand – appropriately a rain coat – she dashed outside to discover that somehow the garden sprinkler system had been switched on and that all the luncheon tables, meticulously laid in the open the evening before, were being deluged. Fortunately, with the pressing season in full swing, the cellar staff was on round-the-clock duty and maintenance man Hannes Marais was able to stem the tide with the flick of a switch. Cellar 'hands', from the humblest labourer to the master himself, abandoned presses and vats and turned-to in re-laying the tables and in drying and polishing some 800 glasses before the first guests arrived. Ten years later another potential disaster was averted when a mighty black south-easter blew up on the Sunday before the Auction and ripped off the 12 canopies covering the area outside the auction hall. A second ampliform tent, instantly summoned from Natal, arrived in the nick of time and was hastily erected for the accommodation of luncheon guests. Then there was that memorable moment during the 1990 fashion show when photographers literally leapt at the opportunity to take pictures of a beautiful model as she swept by, her black designer evening gown steadily slipping off her shoulders to reveal her all but topless. 'Unfazed,' wrote a newspaper reporter afterwards, 'she finished her walk with a bounce.'

It was largely as the result of pressure from the cellar personnel that the date of the Auction was moved from March to April. This happened after 1983, when the Auction was arranged for what turned out to be the hottest day of the year. March is not only a hectic time for those involved in the harvest, but wretched for guests and for models, all in 1981 clad in pure new wool. In 1984 the date was moved to 14 April and, with the exception of 1990 it has been held in April ever since. The dates of public holidays and religious festivals, of course, also have to be borne in mind. And just in case there is rain, organizer Bennie Howard has seen to it that there will be room under cover for every one of the guests.

And so the years go by – 1989, when at last the total income reached the magical figure of R2 million and indeed passed it; 1991, when the beneficial effects of President F.W. de Klerk's 'new South Africa' were felt as new doors overseas opened for Cape wines and for the first time foreign clients, as a group, bought more than individual local buyers; 1992, when Nederburg celebrated its bicentenary and, fortuitously, the results of the referendum of 17 March reflected positively on the sales on 4 April and the R2 million mark was passed again. Over the years, its organizers have honed and developed the Auction and reached a fine balance between its commercial and its social functions. What started out as a one-day event has become a year-round marketing and public relations tool that keeps

Max Nederburgh and his wife, Nettie, special guests at the 1992 Auction, travelled to the Cape from Holland for the occasion. Max Nederburgh is a direct descendant of Commissioner Sebastiaan Nederburgh whose name is perpetuated in South Africa's most sought-after wine and in that of the farm where it originated.

Nederburg in the minds and eyes of the people of South Africa and the world. Nederburg's 200th year completed, the Auction has become the largest and probably the most efficiently organized commercial venture of its kind anywhere, and one that during the harsh years of sanctions kept the image of South African wines alive all over the world.

But everyone who comes to Nederburg's auction, set in the autumnal beauty of vineyards overlooked by the shimmering blue of mountains, is exhilarated by the experience. Year by year, overseas visitors and South Africans alike – buyers, sellers, whoever the guests may be, as well as those hundreds of helpers who 'make it all happen' – are entranced by the festive atmosphere of the Nederburg Auction. Captivated by the spirit of the vine, they find the occasion a splendid combination of serious business and fun, an amalgam of sober commerce and frivolous clothes, of brass bands and balloons and buck's fizz, not to mention the most superb food set off by the best wine the Cape has to offer. In this year, 1992, the international world was once more at Nederburg, brought together across the oceans and bonded by a respect and admiration for, and a true appreciation of wine. ∎

AUCTION OF RARE WINES AT NEDERBURG 1975–1992

DATE	8 MARCH 1975	14 FEB. 1976	26 MARCH 1977	4 MARCH 1978	3 MARCH 1979	8 MARCH 1980	7 MARCH 1981	6 MARCH 1982	12 MARCH 1983
SPEAKER	HENDRIK SCHOEMAN	HENDRIK SCHOEMAN	HENDRIK SCHOEMAN	HENDRIK SCHOEMAN	J. KRUGER	ANTON RUPERT	D. J. DE VILLIERS	PROF. M. AMERINE	SIR DE VILLIERS GRAAFF
ATTENDANCE									
LICENSEES	300	450	700	1 200	1 400	1 495	987	1 110	982
V.I.P.'s	100	250	275	420	453	616	595	549	530
FOREIGN GUESTS					67	68	69	71	70
PUBLIC	300	350	380	280	—	—	—	—	—
MEDIA	100	150	100	170	220	180	110	120	117
	800	1 200	1 455	2 070	2 140	2 359	1 761	1 850	1 699
WINES ENTERED	15 WINES	41 WINES	31 WINES	62 WINES	55 WINES	65 WINES	71 WINES	68 WINES	71 WINES
	6 PARTICIPANTS	9 PARTICIPANTS	11 PARTICIPANTS	14 PARTICIPANTS	17 PARTICIPANTS	15 PARTICIPANTS	17 PARTICIPANTS	15 PARTICIPANTS	21 PARTICIPANTS
TOTAL CASES	12 400 CASES	6 689 CASES	5 061 CASES	6 539 CASES	7 038 CASES	7 317 CASES	5 279 CASES	4 568 CASES	5 624 CASES
AVERAGE PRICE (PER CASE)	R19,12 OVERALL AVERAGE PER CASE	R51,56 (RED) R20,43 (WHITE) R26,12 (OVERALL)	R63,00 (RED) R35,00 (WHITE) R45,51 (OVERALL)	R68,59 (RED) R50,80 (WHITE) R56,41 (OVERALL)	R86,82 (RED) R64,99 (WHITE) R73,28 (OVERALL)	R83,21 (RED) R45,87 (WHITE) R57,44 (OVERALL)	R129,28 (RED) R96,29 (WHITE) R106,18 (OVERALL)	R237,42 (RED) R125,71 (WHITE) R161,13 (OVERALL)	R187,33 (RED) R73,82 (WHITE) R119,15 (OVERALL)
AVERAGE PRICE (PER 9 LITRE CASE)									
TOP PRICES									
WHITE	R121 NEDERBURG JOHANN GRAUE EDELKEUR 1873	R41 JOHANN GRAUE EDELKEUR 1873	R68 NEDERBURG EDELKEUR 1974	R145 NEDERBURG EDELKEUR '73 & '74	R410 NEDERBURG EDELKEUR 1973	R215 NEDERBURG EDELKEUR 1976	R360 NEDERBURG EDELKEUR 1976	R480 NEDERBURG BUKETTRAUBE EDELKEUR 1979	R350 NEDERBURG WEISSER RIESLING 1978
RED	R150 NEDERBURG JOHANN GRAUE ESTATE CABERNET SAUVIGNON 1970	R400 ZONNEBLOEM CABERNET 1965	R430 CHATEAU LIBERTAS 1940	R510 NEDERBURG SELECTED CABERNET 1962	R420 NEDERBURG SELECTED CABERNET 1963	R410 ZONNEBLOEM CABERNET 1965	R2 800 NEDERBURG SELECTED CABERNET 1962	R6 150 ZONNEBLOEM CABERNET 1965	R4 000 ZONNEBLOEM CABERNET 1965
TOTAL INCOME	R237 000	R174 780	R230 374	R368 905	R515 815	R420 344	R560 576	R719 930	670 127
BREAKDOWN BY % OF SALES									
WESTERN CAPE	—	—	—	33,2	6,1	10	14	7,09	11,15
ORANGE FREE STATE	—	—	—	0,1	0,1	1	3	3,98	0,60
EASTERN CAPE	—	—	—	0,32	1,0	2	4	3,30	4,06
NATAL	—	—	—	2,2	8,6	5	6	3,24	7,11
TRANSVAAL	—	—	—	59,6	69,6	72	67	77,94	63,75
NAMIBIA	—	—	—	2,5	1,9	3	3	0,79	1,72
FOREIGN	—	—	—	2,0	12,7	7	3	3,66	11,63

14 APRIL 1984	20 APRIL 1985	12 APRIL 1986	4 APRIL 1987	14 APRIL 1988	15 APRIL 1989	31 MARCH 1990	13 APRIL 1991	4 APRIL 1992
TERTIUS MYBURGH	EUGENE LOUW	DR HANS AMBROSI	PAUL BOUCHARD	JEAN HUGEL	MARIMAR TORRES	PAUL PONTALLIER	ROBERT DROUHIN	ROBERT MONDAVI
816	1 038	861	874	966	934	924	844	837
660	547	660	614	613	498	506	557	559
36	65	71	62	47	46	44	76	75
—	—	—	—	—	—	—	—	—
100	110	119	125	126	128	128	128	136
1 612	1 760	1 711	1 675	1 752	1 606	1 602	1 605	1 607
64 WINES	65 WINES	66 WINES	67 WINES	84 WINES	101 WINES	91 WINES	93 WINES	121 WINES
18 PARTICIPANTS	17 PARTICIPANTS	21 PARTICIPANTS	22 PARTICIPANTS	32 PARTICIPANTS	26 PARTICIPANTS	32 PARTICIPANTS	33 PARTICIPANTS	
6 819 CASES	9 373 CASES	9 517 CASES	9 704 CASES	10 216 CASES	11 189 CASES	7 889 CASES	8 152 CASES	10 489 CASES
R181,54 (RED) R79,65 (WHITE) R121,01 (OVERALL)	R159,66 (RED) R57,08 (WHITE) R95,13 (OVERALL)	R149,94 (RED) R77,32 (WHITE) R95,13 (OVERALL)	R209,97 (RED) R99,09 (WHITE) R147,09 (OVERALL)	R269,39 (RED) R125,57 (WHITE) R191,41 (OVERALL)	R323,52 (RED) R127,83 (WHITE) R204,35 (OVERALL)	R341,33 (RED) R158,75 (WHITE) R236,00 (OVERALL)	R344,80 (RED) R183,86 (WHITE) R244,17 (OVERALL)	R300,36 (RED) R124,57 (WHITE) R201,17 (OVERALL)
						R364,48 (RED) R229,65 (WHITE) R296,85 (OVERALL)	R376,19 (RED) R230,33 (WHITE) R292,20 (OVERALL)	R322,40 (RED) R181,89 (WHITE) R255,48 (OVERALL)
R260 NEDERBURG RIESLING EDELKEUR '79 & '81	R410 NEDERBURG EMINENCE 1983	R340 NEDERBURG EMINENCE 1984	R282 NEDERBURG CHARDONNAY 1984 (6 x 750 ml)	R265 NEDERBURG CHARDONNAY 1985 (6 x 750 ml)	R610 OVERGAAUW CHARDONNAY 1987 (6 x 750 ml)	R880 HAMILTON RUSSELL CHARDONNAY 1987 WO	R820 HAMILTON RUSSELL CHARDONNAY 1986 WO	R570 HAMILTON RUSSELL CHARDONNAY 1988 WO
R4 000 ZONNEBLOEM CABERNET 1966	R8 250 ZONNEBLOEM CABERNET 1965	R3 400 ZONNEBLOEM CABERNET 1966	R1 100 LANZERAC PINOTAGE 1968	R10 500 LANZERAC PINOTAGE 1969	R4 300 LANZERAC PINOTAGE 1969	R7 100 RUSTENBERG 1974 WOS	R8 000 LANZERAC PINOTAGE 1969	R3 500 LANZERAC PINOTAGE 1967
R825 201	R891 725	R1 065 647	R1 431 307	R1 955 482	R2 286 477	R1 861 836	R1 990 465	R2 111 300
18,71	22,35	17,92	13,45	27,27	18,87	35,12	36,49	23,38
2,53	2,10	0,19	1,03	1,04	0,80	0,48	1,12	5,84
7,24	4,02	6,98	3,44	2,75	1,83	2,60	4,24	3,43
4,56	13,39	11,19	5,28	9,48	4,69	5,46	10,30	10,76
56,85	44,92	52,31	71,45	46,64	55,70	41,20	30,45	29,65
2,22	1,99	2,18	3,21	3,22	1,63	3,88	2,55	23,55
7,89	11,23	9,23	2,14	9,60	16,48	11,26	14,81	3,35

CHAPTER TWELVE

NEDERBURG AND THE ARTS

For centuries, wine and the cultivation of the vine
have been closely associated with the arts, particularly music
and drama. To affirm this bond, chamber music concerts
are regularly performed at Nederburg during the
winter months and, since 1972, Nederburg has awarded
prizes annually for opera and ballet in the four
South African provinces.

*Andrew Marais, initiator of the
Nederburg Opera and Ballet Awards,
presents the 1984 ballet award to
CAPAB dancer Carol Kinsey.*

Half a world separates Nederburg's orderly green slopes from the terraced vineyards of Greece. Both, it is obvious, exist for the cultivation of the grape, but the link between them is more than merely material or agricultural: it is symbolic of the very origins of Western culture.

Thousands of years ago, not far from the shores of the blue Mediterranean, popular festivals were held in honour of the Greek god, Dionysus, or Bacchus, as the Romans named him. He was held in awe as the deity of wine and of fertility and his worship took the form of poetry and dance, accompanied by music and much flowing of wine. Improvised at first in a spirit of religious ecstasy, the festivals were eventually formalized into drama — both tragedy and comedy — much as it is known today. To the Ancient Greeks, then, the performing arts became as inseparable from the adulation of Dionysus as the trailing vines that traditionally garlanded his form or the wine drunk by all in his honour.

But the civilization and culture of the West is also associated with the visible arts, of which architecture is not the least. Symmetry, proportion, materials of the highest quality — all these, combined and transformed

Guests at one of Nederburg's Sunday evening chamber concerts sip wine and enjoy conversation during the interval.

by the designer's skill, provide men and women with structures in which they can live and work together in harmony and in which a creative imagination can be best expressed.

As in the Mediterranean countries in ancient times, so in the winelands of the Cape today, a powerful spiritual and aesthetic link exists between music — both vocal and instrumental — and drama on one side, and the cultivation of the vine on the other. Conscious of this, Stellenbosch Farmers' Winery, owners of Nederburg, sees itself as a patron of the performing arts in South Africa and it has become its policy to make use

of its resources, both financial and otherwise, to stimulate their development and expression. More than that, it has selected Nederburg homestead, originally one of the finest examples of what is known as Cape Dutch or Cape vernacular architecture, as a setting that is both beautiful and appropriate for the presentation of chamber concerts. On Sunday evenings during the winter months they are presented before an audience in one of Nederburg's front rooms, converted some 50 years ago by Ilse Graue, herself a pianist, into what is now known as the music room. Sometimes well-known and established singers and instrumentalists perform; on other

occasions promising young musicians are given an opportunity to share their skills and talents with a discriminating audience. And afterwards, a light meal is provided, accompanied by the best of Nederburg's wines, so that performers and guests may round off the evening by enjoying the sort of hospitality with which the name of Nederburg has become synonymous throughout its second century.

The list of those who have appeared 'on stage' in Nederburg's music room is an impressive one. First to perform – the date was Sunday 8 September 1974 – were pianist Neville Dove and 'cellist Yehuda Kanar, who played both as duo and as soloists. Among those who followed were Marc Raubenheimer and Steven de Groote, two of the most gifted pianists South Africa has ever produced and both, tragically, now dead. Marc Raubenheimer, aged 31, was killed when the aircraft in which he was travelling across Spain was in collision with another on 7 December 1983. Steven de Groote

Accompanied by Heinrich van der Mescht, soprano Hanna van Niekerk entertains guests in Nederburg's music room.

was 36 when he died in Johannesburg on 22 May 1989; he had been severely injured in an air accident in America some months earlier. Another member of the talented De Groote family, clarinettist Oliver, has played at Nederburg; so have academics and pianists from the University of Cape Town, Peter Klatzow and Lamar Crowson, while a frequent guest from the University of Stellenbosch, both as soloist and in chamber groups, has been flautist Eva Tamassy. From Stellenbosch, too, came well-known composer, Hubert du Plessis, while celebrated Russian-born violinist, Nina Beilina, who performed at Nederburg in 1984, had travelled halfway across the world from her home in the United States. From time to time South Africans who have moved abroad return to entertain an audience at Nederburg; they include Professor Yonty Solomon and pianist Tessa Uys, both London-based. Among these voluntary expatriates are Uliano Marchio, guitarist, and his wife, Marisa, soprano, both former Capetonians now

living in Italy. Memorable voices have also been heard at Nederburg: they include those of world-famous Deon van der Walt, Sasolburg-born and now living and performing in Austria, as well as doyenne soprano Nellie du Toit, Hanneli Rupert, DeWet van Rooyen, Virginia Oosthuizen and Manuel Escorcio — all familiar in Cape musical circles — while opera singer Lawrence Folley, his daughter Roxane and her husband John Treleaven made a happy family group when they sang together.

But there are other occasions besides these winter Sundays when concerts are presented at Nederburg. There was, for instance, the evening of Saturday 24 July 1976, when the cellars echoed with the sound of music. At this event the junior S.A.B.C. orchestra, 90 strong, performed a full concert programme under the baton of Walter Moni while the audience, glasses in hand, perched among wine cases stacked to the ceiling. The players varied in experience and age — though, of course, all were young — and, according to a newspaper

Nederburg's managing director, Ernst le Roux (facing the camera), is host to guests at a Nederburg winter concert.

critique that has survived, the 'jolly programme' devised by the conductor was enhanced by the youthful exuberance of the group. While commending the enthusiasm of the young members of the orchestra the critic did, however, have some derogatory remarks to make about the acoustics, which apparently did nothing to swell the sound — in fact, the winter elements battering the cellar roof made a brave attempt to compete with it. Nevertheless, the originality of the backdrop and the liveliness of the evening undoubtedly compensated for somewhat muted trumpets and violins that failed to soar to a full crescendo — and, after all, what architect ever designed a wine cellar with a full-scale orchestral concert in mind?

On another memorable occasion Nederburg supported the performing arts by arranging a three-day festival of music, mime and drama as part of Paarl's tercentenary celebrations in February 1987. The first event took the form of a gala concert presented by

the orchestra and some of the finest soloists of the Cape Performing Arts Board (CAPAB) in Nederburg's Johann Graue Hall, a venue more familiar with the ringing tones of a wine auctioneer than with the vocal acrobatics of a coloratura soprano.

But without doubt Nederburg's most important contribution to fostering the performing arts in South Africa has been the establishment of prizes awarded annually since 1971 for opera and, since 1972, for ballet. The idea of recognizing artists for their excellence in opera — and later in ballet — was a spontaneous one which arose towards the end of the sixties in the mind of Lothar Barth, managing director of Stellenbosch Farmers' Winery. Strongly aware of the age-old connection between wine and the arts, he felt that it would be most fitting if a wine company were to pay tangible tribute to the achievement of performing artists of merit. At much the same time, a similar idea occurred to Andrew Marais, the group's public affairs manager, who tells how a superb performance in Cape Town's old Alhambra theatre by the soprano, Nellie du Toit, in Donizetti's *Lucia di Lammermoor*, moved him so deeply that he determined that such talent should not go unrewarded. It was fortuitous for him that in 1970 he was

LEFT
Ann Wixley, one of the youngest dancers ever to receive a Nederburg award, was honoured in 1990 for the dedication and enthusiasm with which she approached all her roles.
CENTRE
Two outstanding performances from tenor Deon van der Walt (Belmonte in Mozart's Il Seraglio and the Prince in Rossini's La Cenerentola) earned him one of the 1984 opera awards.
RIGHT
Soprano Carla Pohl's riveting performance as Aïda in the CAPAB production of Verdi's opera won her the coveted opera award in 1985.

employed by an enlightened company whose board of directors, particularly Lothar Barth, shared his appreciation of the finer things of life; and it did not require much persuasion to convince all concerned that there existed a unique opportunity to give recognition for excellence where it was due. And so it was that the now famous and prestigious annual Nederburg Prize for Opera was born.

At first the award was made only to members of the Cape Performing Arts Board since it was in the Cape that the idea was conceived and it is in the Cape that the vine is generally cultivated. Most eligible were the artists themselves, but it was agreed that recognition should also be given to anyone who made an outstanding contribution in any capacity to the particular art form in which she or he was involved. Not only South African citizens would be considered for the awards: they could also be presented to any overseas artist who had been living and working in this country for at least three years. The first award was made in 1971 — coincidentally the year in which the Nico Malan Opera House was opened — and the recipient was the well-known bass-baritone and CAPAB's resident producer, Angelo Gobbato. He was awarded the prize, at that

time worth R1 000, for his role as Papageno in Mozart's opera, *The Magic Flute*, which had been produced during the Nico Malan's inaugural season. Gobbato was to win the prize again ten years later and in 1987 was further honoured by being invited to be guest speaker at the award ceremony.

In 1972 the Nederburg Prize for Ballet was instituted at the Cape and the first to receive it was CAPAB's gifted and popular prima ballerina, Phyllis Spira, who was to win it again in 1979. Although it is usually a dancer who is selected, there have been occasions when the work and artistry of a non-performer have been recognized. For example, in 1974 Peter Cazalet won a Nederburg Prize for ballet for his costumes and spectacular stage designs, and credit was given to years of unseen snipping and stitching by wardrobe mistress Ruth van Aswegen by an award made in 1978.

In 1972 it was decided to allocate an annual prize for opera to the Performing Arts Council of the Transvaal (PACT). Lawrence Folley won it on this first occasion, as he did again in 1977 and 1983. It was decided not to award a Nederburg ballet prize in the Transvaal since, from 1972 onwards, PACT has benefited from the generous bequests made by Lilian and Ivan Solomon for

A concentration of award winners in Cape Town in 1989 prompted the awards' organizers to arrange a friendly get-together luncheon at Nederburg. Seen here, left to right, are Rouel Beukes, Sarita Stern, Gé Korsten, Nellie du Toit, Gerard Korsten, Aviva Pelham, Ben Illeman, Andrea Catzel and John Eager.

principal dancers in that province. However, in Nederburg's bicentenary year a ballet prize was awarded in the Transvaal.

The Performing Arts Council of the Orange Free State (PACOFS) and the Natal Performing Arts Council (NAPAC) have not been overlooked, for since 1973 prizes for opera have been presented in both these provinces. Bass Hans van Heerden was awarded the first Nederburg Prize in the Orange Free State, while Valerie Anderson was selected as winner in Natal. The first ballet award in Natal was made in 1985, the prize in that year going to Hugo le Roux, and annual awards continued to be made until 1989. Two awards have been made for the performing arts in South-West Africa, now Namibia and beyond the ambit of Nederburg. The first was won by Ernst van Biljon in 1986 and the second by the actor, Mees Xteen, in the following year. Winners in each category in each province are chosen by selection boards whose members are chosen for their experience and expertise.

Over the years since the first Nederburg Prize for Opera was awarded, three artists have been winners on four or more occasions. PACOFS' resident bass, Hans van Heerden, has won the opera prize four times in

PAGE 186: TOP
Captivating dancing from Nicolette Loxton as Aegina in Spartacus, for which she was awarded one of the 1987 ballet awards.
BOTTOM LEFT
1983 opera award winner Evelyn Dalberg.
BOTTOM RIGHT
Stellenbosch Farmers' Winery director Brian O'Grady congratulates Catinka van Vlaanderen and DeWet van Rooyen for their respective ballet and opera awards.
PAGE 187: TOP
Angelo Gobbato in his 1971 award-winning performance as Papageno in Mozart's Magic Flute.
BOTTOM LEFT
CAPAB tenor Sidwill Hartman, winner of a 1991 opera award.
BOTTOM RIGHT
Aviva Pelham, who received the 1980 CAPAB opera award.

his home province and once in Natal. Lawrence Folley has received one opera award in the Cape and three in the Transvaal. and another four-times winner is mezzo-soprano Evelyn Dalberg, who before she left South Africa to settle in Germany received two awards in the Cape and one each in the Orange Free State and the Transvaal. Several 'non-performers' have been singled out for awards: among them are Professor Leo Quayle, director of music and opera for PACT – he has won the Transvaal opera award three times – and Christine Crouse, CAPAB's resident director in 1990. She and her mother, soprano and three-times winner Nellie du Toit, were the first mother and daughter to be awarded Nederburg Prizes. A year earlier a father and son partnership was established when violinist-conductor Gérard Korsten won the CAPAB opera prize, his father, tenor Gé Korsten, having won the Natal opera award in 1975. By 1990, when CAPAB's Ann Wixley became the youngest dancer ever to win the ballet award, the prize money had risen from the original R1 000 to R7 000. Although the financial value of the award may have changed, the design of the original silver fluted

Johan Kotze, photographed here in the role of the Prince in Tchaikovsky's Sleeping Beauty, was the recipient of a ballet award in 1985.

trophy has remained precisely as it was when it was first presented. There are also those whose contribution to the performing arts in South Africa has been recognized by the award of special prizes.

The directors and staff of Stellenbosch Farmers' Winery continue to take a personal interest in the awards and each year are hosts at the presentation ceremony. On an occasion in the chandelier foyer of the Nico Malan Opera House in 1991, Nederburg itself, in an unprecedented gesture independent of prizes or judges, honoured Dr Dulcie Howes – gracious and graceful doyenne of her art and founder of CAPAB's predecessor, The University of Cape Town Ballet Company – for her life-long dedication and inspiration to ballet in South Africa.

Some of Nederburg's prize-winners – Deon van der Walt, Riki Venter, Carla Pohl, Marita Napier, Wicus Slabbert and Andrea Catzel among them – have left the country to make names for themselves in a wider world abroad. Invariably they return, if only for an occasional visit, to share their talents and experience with their original audiences in South Africa. ∎

NEDERBURG'S PRIZES FOR OPERA AND BALLET: THE WINNERS

CAPAB OPERA

1971 Angelo Gobbato
1972 Nellie du Toit
1973 Evelyn Dalberg
1974 Sarita Stern
1975 David Tidboald
1976 Christine Reynolds
1977 Manuel Escorcio
1978 Gregorio Fiasconaro
1979 Lawrence Folley
1980 Aviva Pelham
1981 Angelo Gobbato
1982 DeWet van Rooyen
1983 Evelyn Dalberg
1984 Deon van der Walt
1985 Carla Pohl
1986 Sally Presant
1987 DeWet van Rooyen
1988 Andrea Catzel
1989 Gérard Korsten
1990 Christine Crouse
1991 Sidwill Hartman

CAPAB BALLET

1972 Phyllis Spira
1973 David Poole
1974 Peter Cazalet
1975 Elizabeth Triegaardt
1976 John Simons
1977 Eduard Greyling
1978 Ruth van Aswegen
1979 Phyllis Spira
1980 Veronica Paeper
1981 Keith Mackintosh
1982 Catinka van Vlaanderen
1983 Eduard Greyling
1984 Carol Kinsey
1985 Johann Kotze
1986 Clare Shepherd-Wilson
1987 Nicolette Loxton
1988 Juanita Yazbek
1989 Johan Jooste
1990 Ann Wixley
1991 Terence Kern

PACT OPERA

1972 Lawrence Folley
1973 Leo Quayle
1974 Nellie du Toit
1975 Neels Hansen
1976 Evelyn Dalberg
1977 Lawrence Folley
1978 George Kok
1979 Anthony Farmer
1980 Douglas Brown
1981 Leo Quayle, shared with Neels Hansen
1982 Sue Braatvedt
1983 Lawrence Folley
1984 George Kok
1985 Marita Napier
1986 Riki Venter
1987 Rouel Beukes
1988 Neville Dove
1989 Wicus Slabbert
1990 Marita Napier
1991 Eugenie Chopin-Couzyn

PACT BALLET

1991 Laetitia Müller

NAPAC OPERA

1973 Valerie Anderson
1974 Bradley Harris
1975 Gé Korsten
1976 No award
1977 Mary Ashdown
1978 Rosalie Hunt
1979 Dawie Couzyn
1980 Robert Cross
1981 Barbara Knox
1982 Hans van Heerden
1983 Eugenie Chopin-Couzyn
1984 Lawrence Folley
1985 Oysten Liltved
1986 Riki Venter
1987 David Tidboald
1988 Angelica Novak
1989 Andrew Botha
1990 No award
1991 Leo Quayle

NAPAC BALLET

1985 Hugo le Roux
1986 Ashley Killar
1987 Robyn Segel
1988 Geoffrey Sutherland
1989 Mark Hawkins
1991 Judy Holme

PACOFS OPERA

1973 Hans van Heerden
1974 Nellie du Toit
1975 No award
1976 Evelyn Dalberg
1977 Dawie Couzyn
1978 Riki Venter
1979 Hans van Heerden
1980 Brian Evans
1981 Hans van Heerden
1982 Michael Renier
1983 Sheila Fox
1984 Eugenie Chopin-Couzyn
1985 Hans van Heerden
1986 Gerhard Geist
1987 Gwenyth Lloydë
1988 No award
1989 Andrea Catzel
1990 No award
1991 George Kok

CHAPTER THIRTEEN

NEDERBURG: THE HOUSE

Built in 1800 and graced by one of the Cape's most
beautiful gables, Nederburg homestead follows the 'H' ground-plan found
in many spacious country houses. In 1937, under the Graues,
it underwent extensive changes but many of the original features have
survived, including the stinkwood and yellowwood doors,
shutters and ceilings and a superb wall cupboard. Today the house
is used for entertaining Nederburg's many visitors.

*This handsome longcase clock whiles
away the hours in Nederburg's front hall —
once the Lyall's morning room, then
at the back of the house.*

Philippus Bernardus Wolvaart, Nederburg's first owner, was a simple man of scant education, yet the house that he built was one of the most elegant in the western Cape. The main gable, which bears not only the date 1800 but also the name of the farm, is described as transitional in design, for it combines the sweeping concave-convex lines of the earlier 18th-century 'holbol' style with a type of neo-classical triangular pediment that was just coming into fashion at the time when Nederburg was being built. Also typical of this period are the inner pilasters which frame the sides of the gable window and are linked to the outer

mouldings by means of short horizontal bands. But perhaps most interesting of all is the finial which surmounts the pediment, for it has graceful, inward-curving lines reminiscent of swans' necks.

And it is this 'swan's neck' pediment that calls to mind the famous sculptor, Anton Anreith, for in 1785 he placed a carving of this romantically beautiful bird, an emblem of Martin Luther, above the superb pulpit that he carved in Cape Town's Lutheran Church. Not long after he completed that masterpiece — in fact, just at the time Philippus Wolvaart was building his house at Klein Drakenstein — Anreith was commissioned to

The dining-room with table set for
luncheon. Originally, this was Nederburg's
main bedroom.
PAGES 192 AND 193
Nederburg: the original front elevation
with its 1930 extensions on either side.
There is a suggestion of the hand of master
craftsman, Anton Anreith, in the
elegant gable, which bears the date 1800
and the name of the farm.

execute the carvings on the organ in the old Dutch
Reformed Church in nearby Paarl. Could it have been
that the two men, both German-speaking, met at this
time and that Anreith's hand and genius left their mark
on Nederburg's beautiful gable? No records are known
to exist so one can do no more than speculate.

Local materials — sun-dried bricks bound with clay
mortar and painted with homemade whitewash, yellowwood beams, reeds of different thickness for ceilings
and thatch — were used for the building of Nederburg.
It must have seemed the very epitome of sophistication
when compared with its older neighbours for the floors,
instead of consisting of hard, well-trodden earth (preserved by a weekly rubbing with ox-blood or cow-dung)
were either laid with the very latest in yellowwood
boards or paved with squat, square Batavian tiles
brought to the Cape by sea as ballast. All the guests who
stepped over Nederburg's threshold in those early days
would have found their attention held by the marvellous wall-cupboard set in the wall opposite the front
door. A happy marriage of stinkwood and yellowwood,
it had — and still has — an ornate carved gable-top
which, again, leaves one wondering whether it was
Anreith, a master in the shaping of wood as well as of

plaster, who was responsible for its intricate flowers and stylized plume of feathers. Some authorities say that nowhere in Europe or in the Dutch colonial empire did the wall-cupboard reach such heights of perfection as it did at the Cape – and of the local examples, that at Nederburg is possibly the most beautiful.

No one can tell what furniture Philippus Bernardus Wolvaart owned or what his day-to-day style of living was like, for no inventories of his possessions have been traced. However, it is known that in the early days of colonization of the Cape, separate rooms, in general, were not kept for particular purposes: beds were to be found almost throughout the house and people simply slept anywhere, some in four-posters with elaborate hangings, others in simple *kadels*, or stretcher beds

TOP
Dining is a gracious experience in the handsomely proportioned and furnished dining room at Nederburg.
BOTTOM
A Mogul blue and white plate, displayed in Nederburg's wall-cupboard.

slung with *riempies* and covered with feather mattresses. Nor were any special arrangements made for the accommodation of the slaves – with a few notable exceptions such as Vergelegen and Groot Constantia, where they had quarters of their own. Probably those at Nederburg 'dossed down', usually on the floor, where it was convenient: the kitchen was comfortably warm in winter and the stoep under the stars pleasantly cool in summer, while the *brandsolder* or loft over the stables was a favourite spot in any season.

A feature of Nederburg in its early days was its carved wooden screen or *porte-de-visite* (sometimes pronounced '*porte difisi*') which divided the entrance hall, or *voorkamer*, from the main reception room. For dances, the slatted leaves of the screen could be folded

back on one another to lie almost flush with the side walls of the room, so making the *voorkamer* and *agter-kamer* into one long gallery. Alas for Nederburg, its original teak screen was removed some time during the 19th century and the only parts of it that survived were discovered years later converted into pantry shelves.

The first insight we are given into the furnishings of the homestead is provided by the inventory taken when Petrus Jacobus Hauptfleisch went insolvent in 1881. Details of the contents of the house, which are given in Chapter Three, indicate that Hauptfleisch — and in all probability Nederburg's three previous owners — were extremely simple people whose material possessions and creature comforts were minimal. Harry Currey, Nederburg's fifth owner, was an entirely different sort of

TOP
The voorkamer, with the portrait of Commissioner Sebastiaan Nederburgh to the left and, through the doorway, a glimpse of the music room.
BOTTOM
An English Doulton Burslem plate from the wall cupboard.

person. Whether at his home in Rondebosch or at Nederburg, he entertained frequently and formally and both houses were furnished accordingly. His sister-in-law, Dorothea Fairbridge, writing in *The State* in November 1911, recalls that when he bought Neder-burg in 1902 a wall had been built in the *voorkamer* to form a narrow passage, a state of affairs that Currey rapidly rectified, at the same time putting together what remained of the old screen and re-installing it. It is likely, however, that Harry Currey, the conventional Victorian gentleman, divided the two front bedrooms so that each had a dressingroom of its own and added a bathroom and separate loo inside the court formed by the north-side arms of the 'H' plan. Peter Pare, son of Harry Currey's successor, remembers that loo well.

With its back against the outside wall, the seat consisted of a teak 'throne' set above an ash bucket which was mysteriously emptied through a hatch at dead of night. Primitive though this arrangement might seem to modern minds, in the Curreys' day it was no doubt a tremendous advance over the time-honoured 'long-drop' hut camouflaged by convolvulus in an inconspicuous spot at the bottom of the garden.

This was how the Pares found the house when they moved into it in 1918 – and how they left it, according to a detailed and fascinating ground-plan drawn to scale and meticulously annotated by Catharine Lyall, wife of Nederburg's seventh owner. Every piece of furniture is shown on the diagram and neatly labelled: 'CBL's Wm. & Mary Writing Bureau' stood in the back hall or breakfast room and there was a 'pots & pan's shelf' (sic) in the kitchen. The various types of floor – 'old wood', 'old tiled' and 'modern' – are indicated, as well as the directions in which the doors opened. This plan indicates that Colonel Lyall restored the bedroom on the right of the front door by removing

PAGE 196: TOP LEFT
*The Batavian floor tiles in
Nederburg's front hall.*
TOP RIGHT
*Nederburg's wall cupboard was moved by
the Graues from its original position in the
agterkamer to the present front hall.*
BOTTOM
For 200 years the wall cupboard has displayed the treasures of Nederburg's owners.
PAGE 197: TOP LEFT AND RIGHT
*Decorative swags and urns embellish
this handsome French armoire in
Nederburg's voorkamer.*
CENTRE
*One of Nederburg's plaster urns, seen here
through the voorkamer window.*

the wall separating it from the dressingroom and added a 'modern' floor – probably consisting of Oregon pine boards. Outside stairs led up to the loft from the north-side court – an interesting part of the house since it contained the 'present milk room, future wood hole' as well as a pump, which, with the water barrel in the kitchen, indicates that tapped water had not yet been laid on.

In the diaries that he painstakingly kept, Colonel Lyall mentions every guest – and they were legion – who called on him at Nederburg. 'Lord de Villiers came to tea,' he wrote on Sunday 10 January 1926 and, six weeks later, 'Young Lieut. Currie (sic), son of late owner of Nederburg, arrived with surprise party at tea time.' One hopes the Lyalls had a store of *soetkoekies* stashed away somewhere or the surprise arrival of the uninvited young naval officers stationed at Simon's Town might have turned out to be a shock. At all events, they remained close friends, for five years later Colonel Lyall's diary records that Phil Currey paid another visit to Nederburg, this time bringing with him his young

PAGE 198: TOP
The Bagnall family who lived at Nederburg during the 1960s. Left to right, public relations officer 'Bags' Bagnall, his daughter, Gorry Bowes-Taylor, Mrs Fay Greene, and her daughter, Bags's wife, Dorothy.

BOTTOM LEFT
Lit by the afternoon sun, the armoire in the voorkamer is seen in all its splendour.

BOTTOM RIGHT
Tea — or wine, depending on the time of day — is served to visitors in the comfortable agterkamer.

PAGE 199: TOP
The front hall at Nederburg, formerly the morning room.

BOTTOM
This handsome Dutch kist, with its bun feet and decorative brass, stands proudly in Nederburg's front hall.

bride, Rona, and that they spent an idyllic weekend camping in Nederburg's woods.

Years later — on 27 August 1951 — Philip Currey, survivor of two world wars and captain of H.M.S. *Bermuda*, then flagship at the Cape station, visited Nederburg yet again. Once more Rona was with him; this time their hosts were the Graues and they were accompanied by two friends, the well-known wine merchant, Harry Tayler, and his wife, Marge. Fortunately for posterity it was Rona who kept a diary on this occasion. 'Nederburg,' she wrote when she returned to Simon's Town that evening, '. . . is the farm that was bought for Phil when he was born (1902) and sold when he went into the Navy. Now some Germans called Graue own it. Phil says it was like coming back to look at a favourite

old bicycle and finding it turned into a Rolls Royce. I remember, from the time we were out here in 1929-31, the small main room with the heavy wooden screen . . . across it, a fine old specimen in this lovely old Dutch house, so cool in summer. On the right and left of this main room were doors leading to bedrooms. But now the screen has gone, making the room larger and lighter, and they have also put in larger windows and made the two bedrooms on the right of the front door [the bedroom and the dressing room] into one lovely drawing room and the bedroom on the left into a dining room. The whole character of the place is changed and yet each version of the house is beautiful in its way. At first the Graues appeared severe but soon relaxed into the charming, cultured people they are. We had drinks

before lunch, Marge and I preferring soft drinks. Normally neither of us drinks wine with our lunch but as we were on a wine farm we decided to waive this habit and make a day of it. The table was beautiful and set with exquisite lace, silver and glass and there followed a most delicious meal. The only odd thing about it was that we ate fish before the soup. We tasted two wines, one dry and one less dry but not too sweet. Then more glasses were brought out and we tasted a wine I thought horrid but Harry, the wine merchant, was beside me and told me what was wrong with it: it was immature. Then the Nederburg Cuvée, their "champagne" or sparkling white wine, was brought out. This, though not as dry as the French, was delicious. When we protested at drinking so much the Graues said: "Not to drink — just to taste."

'It was all so much interesting fun. Their son (and only child), Arnold, aged 27, was pourer-out in chief at lunch . . .'

Later, he showed the Curreys and their friends the

neighbouring farm that the Graues had recently acquired. In her diary Rona Currey wrote that it had on it 'the most delicious little house in the Dutch style. This place, called Highlands [later the name was changed to Hochheim], Arnold has chosen as his own . . . He has not yet moved in and the place is still being painted and done up. The views from there are quite, quite lovely, wherever you look . . . I cannot imagine a more inspiring place in which to begin one's married life, when you cannot have too much of the beloved's company and everything is fun! Left alone in that house, with its views of the Drakenstein, the vineyards sloping away below it, I could sing all day . . . Arnold is inordinately proud of his new flush sanitation! Also his bath with shower . . .'

That was 1951. Arnold never married and before the decade was out both he and his father were dead, Ilse Graue had moved away, Hochheim had been sold and Nederburg had become the property of Monis. For some time it was occupied by a retired army officer,

Brigadier Cilliers, who acted as public relations officer and bought a considerable amount of furniture for the homestead. He died in 1966 and his place was taken by the well-known radio personality and wine expert, Mr A. 'Bags' Bagnall, who had just retired as public relations officer for a large advertising company in Cape Town. One of his instructions was to develop the house 'as a gracious, open-hearted centre of old-world hospitality'; another was to furnish the ground-floor rooms (the Bagnalls' accommodation was in the adjoining wing or 'flat') 'in keeping with Nederburg's history as one of the finest Cape-Dutch homes of two centuries ago'. With these orders in mind, Bags immediately made it his business to discover all he could about the early history of Nederburg and to hunt for authentic items of furniture to add to those already in the house. It was neither practical nor possible to furnish the house as it had been at the end of the 18th century and although Bags did pick up suitable Cape pieces when he could find them, he also explored other sources for items that were suitable and beautiful.

Fortunately, Cape furniture blends happily with English and French antiques, as it does with both Persian and English carpets, and Bags Bagnall kept a meticulous inventory in June 1966 of the furniture that he bought. For the 'cobbled entrance hall' he acquired an antique long case clock (it cost R136), a stinkwood kist and two medieval Dutch chairs (obtained from Brigadier Cilliers' estate for R8 each), while 11 pieces of antique porcelain — English, German and French costing, together, just less than R50 — were acquired for display in the fine old wall-cupboard. A modern blackwood dining-room suite (a table, ten chairs and a sideboard) was bought from a well-known furniture manufacturer in Knysna (price: R570) and a Persian carpet (size not specified) from a Cape Town dealer for R214. Bags and Dorothy Bagnall made Nederburg worthy of its heritage, but they also ensured that it would be comfortable as a home by furnishing it with bedside lamps, Wilton carpets, an antique stinkwood

With an 18th-century huntsman and hound above the clock face and his quarry in the spandrels, the timepiece in the front hall is probably even older than Nederburg.

table (round, with ball and claw feet), two Cape ladder-back chairs with *riempie* seats (R14 for the pair), an Italian marble-top table-cum-showcase (bought from Robert Moni for R200) . . . The inventory, occupying two closely typed foolscap pages, reveals what seem, to anyone caught in the maelstrom of inflation whirling through the nineties, the absurdly low prices paid for furniture and furnishings less than 30 years ago.

For the three years that Bags and Dorothy Bagnall were host and hostess, Nederburg scarcely knew an idle moment, for it was company policy to restore the house as one of the showplaces of the Cape and open it up to

visitors. The Bagnalls, with mother-in-law and small daughter, moved in only a month after Stellenbosch Farmers' Winery had taken over from Monis in 1966 and, although Nederburg was still very much a family home, they found themselves involved in a tremendous amount of official entertaining. Those were the days before South Africa had become the outcast of the world and parties of sightseers arrived at Nederburg from all corners of the earth. The scrapbooks of Press cuttings that Bags Bagnall kept so assiduously reveal that Nederburg's guests included international rugby teams, such as the British Lions; naval officers and marines from

Paved 200 years ago with fireproof sun-dried bricks, the thatched solder still proves a convenient place for storing odd bits and pieces of furniture.

foreign ships calling at Simon's Town, then still a Royal Naval station; the Günter Kallman Choir (during the week of Robert Kennedy's assassination in June 1968); groups of businessmen, such as a party of Japanese sugar importers; and cultural societies, including the Van der Stel Foundation. It became fashionable for companies and institutions in Cape Town to entertain delegates to conferences by putting them on board a special train (with a cordon bleu meal provided) bound for Huguenot station, where waiting cars whisked them off to Nederburg for wine-tasting. Often, for instance when groups of sportsmen arrived, a meal had to be provided,

and of course in summer nothing was more popular than a *braaivleis*. An enormous bonfire would be lit at a safe distance from the thatched house and rows of chickens would be set to roast upon its embers. When large parties visited a friendly traffic policeman from Paarl, an expert at the job, would roar up on his motorbike to supervise the *braai*. For smaller groups, the Graues' faithful gardener, Bayman Jacobs, would be called in, for over the many years he was at Nederburg he had learnt to be a Jack-of-all-trades. Fires indoors as well as fires in the open were among his specialities: he used to lay them early in the morning in the

ponderous German fireplaces the Graues had installed and on the dot of four in the afternoon would come in to light them. Four o'clock was the magic hour, not a moment before or after, because it was at four o'clock that he had always lit the fire for Mrs Graue.

The Bagnalls inherited Bayman as a gardener and, with him, the superb garden that Mrs Graue had created. There were roses everywhere: they grew in blocks of every imaginable colour and swept right round the garden in front of the house. Dorothy Bagnall remembers those roses as the loveliest she has ever seen and she remembers, too, that it was Bayman who cared for them after Ilse Graue had moved away.

The Bagnalls left Nederburg in 1969 shortly after

TOP
During its two centuries, Nederburg has provided hospitality to thousands of guests. Here the British Lions, on tour in the 1960s, relax on Nederburg's front lawn.
BOTTOM
Lothar Barth, managing director of Stellenbosch Farmers' Winery from 1970 to 1980 and non-executive chairman from 1980 to 1986.

the south-western Cape had been shaken by an unforgettable earthquake on the night of 29 September. Many of the old Cape houses were damaged on that occasion — some had to be almost rebuilt — but Nederburg, firm on its foundations, survived.

It was at the end of the sixties that the directors of Stellenbosch Farmers' Winery initiated a new policy towards Nederburg homestead. Today it is common practice for wine farms to encourage visitors, but at that time Nederburg was one of the few — and it had been one of the first — to do so. In 1969, under the leadership of Lothar Barth, the directors modified their attitude towards Nederburg, for they began to perceive it not just as a farmhouse where tourists and other interested

204

TOP
Public relations officer, 'Bags' Bagnall, his wife, Dorothy (front left) and his mother-in-law, entertain a Japanese trade delegation.

BOTTOM
Bruno Mori, a director of Nederburg from 1959 to 1966 and a former chairman of the Cape Distilling Merchants' Association.

people could be hospitably wined and dined, but as compatible with their concept that wine and wine farming are closely associated with culture and all that civilized living means. Until then, Nederburg had been a family home, but one with its doors open to visitors for the purpose of enjoying relaxed entertainment; now the directors wanted its status to be elevated and enhanced. With its vineyards and cellars, it was to become the epitome of the gracious life and all that a wine estate stood for. To Nederburg, the house, special guests would from now on be invited for entertainment at the most elegant and sophisticated level. Nederburg's wines, at that stage, had won more awards than those produced by any other wine estate: in the words of Lothar Barth, they had become the flagship of the S.F.W. group and its directors linked the high quality of this achievement with the concept of cultivated hospitality enjoyed in an elegantly furnished homestead. What better, then, than to bring people of importance to a house of stature and grace set in surroundings as spectacularly beautiful as those of Nederburg? What more satisfying, than to entertain them with the best food and the finest wines in its beautifully furnished rooms? This is the use to which Nederburg was put in 1970 and the role which it still plays today. Again to quote the words of Lothar Barth, Nederburg has become a jewel; it is a far cry from the simple dwelling in which the elder Willem Petrus Retief 'laboured with

14 persons in his house under a severe sickness' way back in the days of Lord Charles Somerset.

In keeping with this concept was the decision made in the early seventies to pay visible tribute to the Graues, father and son, by placing a fitting memorial to them in the entrance to the cellars. Karl Wilhelm, a Stellenbosch sculptor of German origin, and his son, Karl-Heinz, then 21 years old, were commissioned to undertake this task which entailed, in the first place, creating wooden plaques embossed with portraits in copper of Johann Georg and Arnold Graue. Using photographs as models, Karl Wilhelm worked on the likenesses until Ilse Graue was perfectly satisfied with them — even to the details of her husband's spectacles. Since the installation of the plaques, every visitor taken on a

TOP
The culinary team in Nederburg's kitchen, under chef Rozetta Adams, left, prepares a luncheon for V.I.P. guests.
BOTTOM
A reminder of the Cape's Dutch days, this oval meat platter is now displayed in Nederburg's wall cupboard.
PAGE 207: TOP
A tour group is entertained in Nederburg's wine tasting room.
BOTTOM
Only seen by the observant, this unusual shutter-fastener at Nederburg is in the shape of a man's head.

cellar tour has been moved by their dignity and significance for they call to mind the two men who first placed Nederburg's wines on the world map. It was the expansion that followed the Graues' initiative that necessitated the building of the cellars, lofty as a cathedral and spacious enough to shelter the great vats — some oak and others steel — where those wines reach their maturity.

When the plaques were completed, Karl Wilhelm and his son began the second phase of their commission: to enhance the already beautiful old oak casks with symbolic and appropriate figures and significant local scenes. Working on site for three months, father and son created a collection of figures, some sprightly, others serious — from pert *putti* to solemn 18th-century

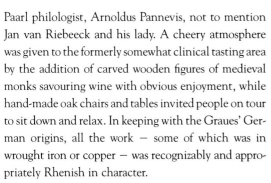

Paarl philologist, Arnoldus Pannevis, not to mention Jan van Riebeeck and his lady. A cheery atmosphere was given to the formerly somewhat clinical tasting area by the addition of carved wooden figures of medieval monks savouring wine with obvious enjoyment, while hand-made oak chairs and tables invited people on tour to sit down and relax. In keeping with the Graues' German origins, all the work — some of which was in wrought iron or copper — was recognizably and appropriately Rhenish in character.

The new concept of Nederburg as a visitors' centre meant that a hostess had to be found to receive and entertain the guests, but it was not until December 1973 — after one or two incumbents had held the post briefly — that Ansie Kemp arrived. She had given

up teaching in a well-known Johannesburg school to take on the post of public relations officer at Nederburg, but she very soon found that, being alone in the house and living on the spot, she had to do a great deal more than she had expected. Fundamentally, her task was to meet and greet the visitors, take them on cellar tours, tell them about Nederburg and about the wine industry, entertain them to wine-tasting and then say good-bye. For someone who, at that stage, knew little about wine-making, this was a tall order, but Ansie threw herself on the mercy of Günter Brözel and production manager, Gottfried Jost, who had joined Nederburg's staff in 1964, and together they taught her all she needed to know. Before long she was able to impart her new-found knowledge in the cellar

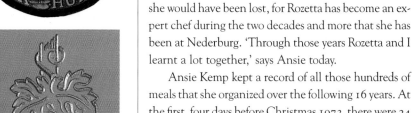

with the same skill with which she had formerly enlightened the classroom.

Coping with the entertainment in the homestead was rather more difficult. When Ansie arrived, the directors had asked her whether she would be prepared to organize and act as hostess at luncheons now and again. 'Not more than once or twice a month,' they told her; but soon the luncheons — and later the dinners — became once or twice a week and then even more frequent than that. It was fortunate for Ansie Kemp that her years of teaching experience had taught her how to structure her day to the last second for she had to do all the shopping in Paarl, give instructions and supervise in the kitchen, and meet the guests and take them on a cellar tour and wine-tasting, which had to conclude at the precise moment when lunch was ready to be served. She admits that without her assistant, Rozetta Adams,

she would have been lost, for Rozetta has become an expert chef during the two decades and more that she has been at Nederburg. 'Through those years Rozetta and I learnt a lot together,' says Ansie today.

Ansie Kemp kept a record of all those hundreds of meals that she organized over the following 16 years. At the first, four days before Christmas 1973, there were 24 guests, all opera singers, and she served crayfish as a starter followed by the traditional Cape dish, *hoenderpasteie*, accompanied by salad and followed by watermelon balls, cheese and biscuits. In mid-January 1974 Ansie was serving *langoustines*, ham, tongue and chicken to 50 hefty lifesavers from Australia and New Zealand, Britain and America, and before the month was out had provided three more meals — all different — for 20 more people. Ansie Kemp entertained a titled English couple one day and a prince of Iran (in the days of

WEIN IST
ARBEIT,
WAHRHEIT,
WEISHEIT.

PAGE 208: TOP LEFT
This vat commemorates the landing of
Jan van Riebeeck and his wife, Maria de la
Quellerie, at the Cape on 6 April 1652.
TOP RIGHT
Surrounded by trailing vines, Bacchanalian
putti greet the on-looker from this wine vat.
CENTRE
This carved medallion was a gift from the
New Zealand company, Fletcher Humphreys.
BOTTOM
One of the etched glass panels in the door
to the wine cellar.
PAGE 209: TOP LEFT AND RIGHT
Nederburg's carved vats are always a point of
interest to visitors.
BOTTOM
Nederburg's well-known heraldic logo.

the Shah) the next; she offered fillet of beef to cele-brated soprano Mimi Coertse and *escalopes de veau* to Minister of Economic Affairs, Owen Horwood, while the prime minister of the Ciskei and three of his ministers were entertained to kingklip with tar-tare sauce. In her first year at Nederburg, Ansie Kemp, trained teacher but untrained cook, provided 54 different meals to over 500 people and never al-lowed a guest to be given a dish he (or she) had been served before.

In July 1974 she undertook an additional culinary responsibility as well as a social one when the first of Nederburg's winter chamber concerts was presented in the music room. Once more her ingenuity was put to the test in providing a selection of different menus to be enjoyed by both audience and performers throughout each season. Smorgasbord was popular fare on these occasions; so was a selection of hors-d'oeuvres and gen-erous snacks; or one could be offered a cheese board, pâtés and pastas of various kinds, and paella. Again, Ansie refused to repeat a menu and went to her usual lengths in acting hostess to her guests, who numbered up to 80 on occasions. Every now and then Ansie added a comment of her own to the menus she methodically recorded: 'sauce too thin' or '*nie baie lekker nie*' and now and then a mouth-watering '*heerlik!*'

About the guests themselves she recorded little be-sides their names – but those alone are fascinating. The late Percy Qoboza, one-time detained editor of the banned newspaper, *The World*, was among the guests in 1976; so was Professor Chris Barnard, the heart sur-geon. A random glance at the guest list reveals that Anneline Kriel and Margaret Gardiner were among a number of beauty queens entertained by Ansie Kemp.

Other guests included Ian Smith, then prime minister of Rhodesia; cricketer Basil d'Oliviera; Lucas Mangope, chief minister of Bophuthatswana; and world-renowned photographer, Lord Lichfield. Groups of parliamentarians, butchers, cricketers, rugby-players, gynaecologists, wine-tasters, bottle-store owners, retired airways pilots, have been entertained at Nederburg, while opera singers and ballet dancers are among the 'regulars'. And, during the years when South Africa's image abroad was at its lowest and sanctions were at their most stringent, Ansie Kemp's guest list shows that Nederburg was host to guests from Germany, England, Holland, France, Portugal, Italy, Switzerland, Japan, Paraguay, Uruguay, Australia and New Zealand. Among the special occasions that Ansie recorded was Bayman Jacobs' farewell party after some 60 years on the staff and the splendid commemorative dinner held on 6 February 1986 in honour of the 30th anniversary of Günter Brözel's arrival at Nederburg.

When Ansie Kemp took on the post of public relations officer, entertainment facilities at Nederburg were

LEFT AND RIGHT
These amusing carvings adorn one of the walls in Nederburg's wine cellar.
CENTRE
Carved from the trunk of one of Nederburg's old oaks, this sculpture depicts labourers at work in the vineyard.

not as sophisticated as they are today. For instance, wine-tasting in the old days always took place in the music room — Mrs Graue's drawing room — and it was only in 1977 that a special area was set aside for this purpose. Until then the ground floor of the 'flat' — the wing added by the Graues — had consisted of two apartments: one had provided accommodation for the Graues' guests and the other was occupied by their German housekeeper. Now, walls were broken down and this entire area was converted into one very large room where wine-tasting involving large groups of visitors could take place comfortably. Smaller groups, which Ansie encouraged, were still entertained in the house itself. It was at this time, too, that the parquet floor in the *voorkamer* was replaced by red tiles in keeping with those from Batavia that had been in the hall (now at the front of the house, but originally at the back) since Nederburg's earliest days. A new fireplace with chimney piece made by the well-known wood-carver, Dietrich Kruger-Haye, was also installed in the *voorkamer* and, at the suggestion of restoration architect,

Dirk Visser, the plaster ceiling with which Mrs Graue had concealed the original yellowwood beams of the music room was removed — to very good effect.

Ansie Kemp was becoming so busy that it was obvious that she needed an assistant to help with the cellar tours and so free her to supervise the entertaining. In 1980 a new member of Nederburg's staff, destined for long association, arrived as her assistant. This was Serena, now married to one of Nederburg's former winemakers, Hein Hesebeck. Rozetta remains in charge of the much-modernized kitchen.

Ansie Kemp made Nederburg her home for 16 years. She lived in the upper floor of the flat and in her 'spare' time she took charge of the garden. It had changed considerably since the days when it was a bower of roses, though a few of the hardier varieties still grew and blossomed. Ansie moved some of them to the back of the house and, with the addition of hydrangeas and other shade-loving plants, transformed the large circular bed, planted with oaks and surrounded by the drive, into what Günter Brözel called 'Ansie's fairyland'.

Details taken from the fascinating wood carvings in Nederburg's cellar.

In the Graues' day the ancient oaks below the front *stoep* had been replaced by plane trees, but some of the old-established trees in Nederburg's garden remain to this day. Every November the jacarandas planted by Colonel Lyall scatter their lavender-blue flowers on the lawn below the house, while visiting children always delight in scrambling up the massive and contorted limbs of the marvellous old camphor tree opposite the wine cellars. Believed by forestry experts to be well over a century old, it was probably introduced to Nederburg as a sapling by Petrus Jacobus Hauptfleisch. Some of Colonel Lyall's cork oaks still grow behind the vastly enlarged cellars and offices but, despite investigation by experts, they have never provided Nederburg's bottles with a single cork.

In 1990 Nieske Hiemstra-Weitz became Nederburg's new hostess and one of considerable elegance and charm. Formerly private secretary to Lothar Barth, she had been on the staff at Nederburg since 1986, so she was well acquainted with the obligations and demands of the work she was undertaking. Nieske more

than maintained the high standard of entertainment set by Ansie Kemp, so it was a considerable responsibility that Serena Hesebeck inherited when she took over as hostess on Nieske's retirement. With the support of expert caterer Elsa van Dyk, Serena was hostess and liaison co-ordinator at Nederburg until the beginning of 1992.

A close association exists between all members of Nederburg's staff, whether at the homestead, in the reception building – originally the manager's house – in the offices built in the 1970s or in the cellars themselves. Managing director, Ernst le Roux, and his team – including his secretary, Shirley Fenton, who has been at Nederburg since 1965 – are to be found in the administrative offices, as is group farm manager, Hannes van Rensburg. He has the weighty task of keeping all the wheels of Nederburg's farming operation turning and of supervising the day-to-day organization of the vineyards. Master of the cellar is Newald Marais, with

PAGE 212: TOP
The music room, enlarged in the 1930s to accommodate Ilse Graue's Bechstein piano and used today for chamber concerts.
BOTTOM
When concerts are not in progress, music can be provided by this antique polyphone.
PAGE 213: TOP LEFT
One of Nederburg's shutter hinges.
TOP CENTRE
Gleaming for 200 years, brass escutcheons adorn Nederburg's stinkwood and yellowwood doors.
TOP RIGHT
Colonel Lyall's diary records the day on which he added this brass dolphin to Nederburg's front door.
BOTTOM LEFT, CENTRE AND RIGHT
These decorative tiles, which surround the music room fireplace, were imported by the Graues.

an increasing number of trophies and awards to his credit. The other managers are Gottfried Jost, in charge of production; chief engineer, Johan Steyn; marketing manager, Schalk Burger; commercial manager, Pieter Joubert; and human resources manager, Johann Briedenhann. Public relations manager, Pieter Marais, has his offices at the reception building and caterer, Elsa van Dyk, moves between Nederburg and Plaisir de Merle, where she lives and undertakes a considerable amount of V.I.P. entertaining for Nederburg as well as for Stellenbosch Farmers' Winery. Indispensable to the perpetuation and enhancement of Nederburg's image are its five tour guides. Fluent in a variety of languages and familiar with every stage in wine-making, they have the task of informing, enlightening and entertaining all the hundreds of visitors who pass through Nederburg's cellars each year.

These are the people who take the responsibility for

running Nederburg. There are also those who labour in the vineyards and the cellars, who keep the vehicles in order and service the vital machinery. Others maintain the garden, while some sweep and dust, prepare food and wash dishes. Without them Nederburg could not continue to exist and it is upon their loyalty — sometimes through succeeding generations, as with the Jacobs family and the Fortuins — that Nederburg relies.

How would Nederburg's former owners react were they to return to it today? No doubt Philippus Bernardus Wolvaart would scarcely recognize it, so changed is it from 'zekeren plaats genaamd Nederburg' that he hewed from the stony earth. The Retiefs, once they had got over an amazing sense of wonder, would look for the graveyard where all their dear dead lay buried — only to find that it had disappeared years ago, perhaps under the vineyards flanking the Palmiet River or even beneath the floor of the huge new cellars. Petrus Jacobus

PAGE 214: TOP
Framed by an archway of leaves, the original jonkershuis, now the reception centre, still has an air of antiquity.
CENTRE LEFT
Poplars have replaced the oaks that once shaded Nederburg's homestead.
CENTRE RIGHT
The classic beauty of the twin urns, guardians of Nederburg's entrance steps.
BOTTOM LEFT
In the 'mellow fruitfulness' of autumn, a gardener tidies Nederburg's lawn.
BOTTOM RIGHT
Though trees have come and gone at Nederburg, there are still oaks to witness the quiet procession of the seasons.
PAGE 215
In the soft light of autumn, leaves are gathered in before the onset of the winter rains.

Hauptfleisch would undoubtedly gaze with admiration at the burgeoning vineyards and shake his head sadly at memories of the dreaded *Phylloxera* and of the devastation that it wrought a century ago. Harry Currey would certainly taste Nederburg's wines, this time with unfeigned pleasure, admitting with admiration that they are very different from the 'horrible vinegar' that he used to make. Maurice Pare might look in vain for the fruit trees that he planted, finding only vineyards in their place; while the vastness of the cellars would inspire a feeling of reverence — and envy — in Colonel Lyall who did, so desperately, long to make really good wine at Nederburg. And what of the Graues, Johann Georg, Ilse and Arnold? Theirs would be an overwhelming sense of pride (but a pride tinged with sorrow) at the knowledge that without their vision and skill, their inspiration and example, Nederburg, as it is today, could never have been. ∎

GLOSSARY

agterskot	final payment	solder	loft
agterkamer	back room	stalknecht	stablehand or foreman
alle sodanige goederen en		stoep	veranda
effecten	all goods and effects	Strooidakkerk	thatch-roofed church
bo-en-onder (door)	'above and below', stable door	Uitlanders	foreigners (in the Transvaal prior
braai, braaivleis	traditional barbecue		to the South African War)
brandsolder	loft with a layer of bricks laid over	venduemeester	auctioneer
	the ceiling to catch burning thatch	voorkamer	front room
	in the event of fire	voorskot	advance payment
Diamandt eende Peerl berg	Diamond and Pearl Mountain	weiland	grazing land
dominee	minister of religion	zeeker plaats ofte hofsteede	certain farm and building named
dop system	system in which wine forms	genaamd Nederburg	Nederburg
	part-payment		
drift	ford		
fynbos	general term for numerous species		
	of narrow-leaved indigenous shrubs		
	common to winter rainfall areas		
griep	influenza		
hoenderpastei	chicken pie		
Hottentot *See* Khoikhoi			
huisgezinnen	household		
opgaaf	income and property taxes		
jonkershuis	bachelor quarters		
jukskei	a game originally played with		
	yoke-pins		
kadels	stretcher beds with thongs		
kaross	animal skin used as clothing or		
	covering		
Khoikhoi	'Men of men'; indigenous people		
	formerly known as 'Hottentots'		
	(now a pejorative word).		
kingklip	a highly-esteemed edible fish		
koeksisters	twisted doughnuts deep-fried in		
	syrup		
konfyt	jam or preserves		
laatlammetjie	a child born long after the others		
	in a family, an 'afterthought'		
lamoen en nardges	oranges and nartjies		
muurkas	wall cupboard		
nachtmaal	('evening meal') Holy Communion		
oblietjies	thin wafer biscuits		
ofgaafrol	tax list		
opstal	farm complex		
porte de visite	carved screen		
reekening	calculation or account		
riempies	leather thongs		
rusbank	a wooden, open-armed settee		
sjambok	a stout whip with a long hide		
	thong		
soet	sweet		
soetkoekies	sweet spice biscuits		

SOURCES

PRIMARY AND UNPUBLISHED SOURCES

PRIVATE PAPERS, CORRESPONDENCE AND DIARIES

Currey Papers, Cape Town
Currey, Rona: Papers, Isle of Man
Graue Papers, Paarl
Lyall Papers, Truro, Cornwall
Nederburg Papers, Scrapbooks and Ledgers, Paarl
Nederburg Auction Press Cuttings
Merriman Papers, South African Library, Cape Town
Pare Papers, Somerset West

UNPUBLISHED MEMOIRS

Brooke, A.: *I can see it all now* . . .
Currey, R.F.: *From Victoria to Fouché*
Currey, H.L.: *Memoirs*

MASTER'S OFFICE, CAPE TOWN

Death notices: Maurice Pare; Johann Georg, Ilse and
Arnold Graue

DEEDS REGISTRY, CAPE TOWN

Farm Registers
Old Cape Freeholds
Old Stellenbosch Freeholds
Stellenbosch Quitrents
Transfer Deeds

CAPE ARCHIVES

Reference letters are given for a selection of the documentary
sources that were used:

AGR   Secretary for Agriculture 1881-1912
CCP   Cape Colony Publications
CO   Colonial Office Papers
G2   Dutch Reformed Church Records, Stellenbosch
G3   Dutch Reformed Church Records, Paarl
GH   Government House Papers
J   Returns for Taxation Purposes (*Opgaafrolle*)
M   Maps
MOIB Minutes of Meetings of Creditors
MOIC Liquidation and Distribution Accounts
MOOC Wills, Inventories and Death Notices
PIO   Immigration Office Records
QRR   Quitrent Registers 1792-1919
SO   Slave Office Papers
VO   Joint Commissionaries of Vendue
WT   Wine Taster's Records

PUBLISHED SOURCES

BOOKS

African Court Calendar and Directory (Cape Town, 1816)
BARROW, J.: *An Account of Travels into the Interior of Southern
    Africa* (Reprint, New York, 1968)
BORCHERDS, P.B.: *Autobiographical Memoirs* (Cape Town, 1903)
BOTHA, C.: *The French Refugees at the Cape* (Cape Town, 1970)
BOTHA, C.: *Social Life in the Cape Colony* . . . (Cape Town, 1976)

BOUCHER, M.: *French Speakers at the Cape* (Pretoria, 1981)
BROWN, W.H.: *A Century of London Co-operation* (London, 1928)
BURCHELL, W.: *Travels in the Interior of Southern Africa*, 2 vols
    (London, 1953)
CAMPBELL, J.: *Travels in South Africa* (Cape Town 1974)
Cape Almanac, 1824-1880 (Cape Town)
CORDER, C.: *Coat of Many Colours* (Cape Town, 1977)
CURREY, J.B.: *John Blades Currey 1850-1900* (Johannesburg, 1986)
DE BOSDARI, C.: *Cape Dutch Houses and Farms* (Cape Town, 1953)
DE BOSDARI, C.: *Wines of the Cape* (Cape Town, 1966)
DE VILLIERS, C.C. AND PAMA, C.: *Geslagregisters van die Ou Kaapse
    Families*, 2 vols (Cape Town, 1981)
Dictionary of National Biography, Vol. 34 (London, 1893)
Dictionary of South African Biography, Vols 1-5 (Pretoria,
    1968-1987)
DURAND, SIR M.: *The Life of the Right Hon. Sir Alfred Comyn
    Lyall* . . . (Edinburgh and London, 1913)
EDWARDS, I.: *Towards Emancipation* (California, 1942)
FAIRBRIDGE, D.: *Historic Farms of South Africa* (London, 1931)
FAIRBRIDGE, D.: *Historic Houses of South Africa* (London and
    Cape Town, 1922)
FORBES, V.: *Pioneer Travellers of South Africa* (Cape Town, 1965)
FLEMING, P.: *News from Tartary* (London, 1936)
FRANSEN, H. AND COOK, M.A.: *The Old Buildings of the Cape*
    (Cape Town, 1980)
GARDNER, B.: *Allenby* (London, 1965)
GARDYNE, C.G.: *The Life of a Regiment*, 2 vols (Edinburgh, 1903)
GIRD, H.: *A Memorandum on Cape Wines* (Cape Town, 1846)
HATTERSLEY, A.: *An Illustrated Social History of South Africa*
    (Cape Town, 1969)
HOGE, J.: *Personalia of the Germans at the Cape 1652-1806*
    (Cape Town, 1946)
HUGHES, D., HANDS, P. AND KENCH, J.: *The Complete Book of
    South African Wine* (Cape Town, 1989)
JOELSON, A.: *Memoirs of Kohler of the K.W.V.* (Cape Town, 1946)
JOHNSON, H.: *The World Atlas of Wine* (London, 1977)
KOLBE, P.: *Present State of the Cape of Good Hope* (Facsimile
    edition, New York, 1968)
LEIPOLDT, L.: *300 Years of Cape Wine* (Cape Town, 1952)
LEWSEN, P.: *John X. Merriman* (Johannesburg, 1982)
LICHINE, A.: *Alex Lichine's New Encyclopaedia of Wines and Spirits*
    (London, 1974)
LICHTENSTEIN, M.H.K.: *Travels in South Africa* (Cape Town, 1930)
MACMUNN, G.: *The History of the Sikh Pioneers* (London, n.d.,
    c. 1932)
MARAIS, J.S.: *The Cape Coloured People, 1652-1937* (London,
    1939)
MENTZEL, O.: *Description of the Cape, Parts 1 and 2*, (Cape Town,
    1921 and 1925)
OBERHOLSTER, A.G. IN ASSOCIATION WITH VAN BREDA, P.:
    Paarl Valley, 1687-1987 (Pretoria, 1987)

OPPERMAN, D.J. (ed.): *Spirit of the Vine* (Cape Town, 1968)

OVINGTON, J.: *A Voyage to Suratt* (London, 1696)

PEARSE, G.E.: *Eighteenth Century Architecture in South Africa* (Cape Town, 1968)

PEARSE, G.E.: *The Cape of Good Hope* (Pretoria, 1956)

PERCIVAL. R.: *An Account of the Cape of Good Hope* (London, 1809)

ROTBERG, R.: *The Founder* (Johannesburg, 1988)

South African Who's Who (Johannesburg, 1953)

SPARRMAN, A.: *A Voyage to the Cape of Good Hope* (London, 1785)

Standard Encyclopaedia of Southern Africa, 12 vols (Cape Town, 1976)

STAVORINUS, J.: *Voyages to the East Indies* (London, 1798)

Thackers Indian Directory, 1899-1921 (Calcutta, 1926)

THEAL, G.MCC.: *History of South Africa before 1795* (London, 1922)

THEAL, G.MCC.: *History of South Africa 1795-1872* (London, 1919-1927)

THEAL, G.MCC.: *History of South Africa South of the Zambezi* (London, 1922)

THOMPSON, G.: *Travels and Adventures in Southern Africa*, 2 vols (Cape Town, 1970)

VAN RIEBEECK, J.: *Journal*, 3 vols (Cape Town, 1954)

VAN ZYL, D.J.: *Kaapse Wyn en Brandewyn* (Cape Town, 1975)

Who Was Who 1941-1950 (London, 1952)

Wine Book of South Africa (Cape Town, 1936)

NEWSPAPERS AND JOURNALS

Agricultural Journal

The Argus

Die Burger

Cape Argus

Cape Times

Cape Town Gazette and African Advertiser

Farmers Weekly

Financial Mail

Government Gazette

Hotelier & Caterer

Paarl Post

South African Commercial Advertiser

South African Hotel Review

South African Liquor Trade News

Wine & Spirit

Wynboer

De Zuid Afrikaan

ACKNOWLEDGEMENTS: ILLUSTRATIONS AND DOCUMENTS

PAGE

TITLE Alain Proust.

6 Haverfield, J.T., Africana Museum, Johannesburg.

7 Cape Archives, Cape Town. AG 7402.

8-9 Lyall family.

10 Bowler, T.W., Africana Museum, Johannesburg.

12 Top: Mallet, A.M., Africana Museum, Johannesburg.

13 Reid, A., Africana Museum, Johannesburg.

14 Top: Bogaert, A., *Historische Reizen door d'oostersche Deelen van Asia . . .*, Africana Museum, Johannesburg.
Bottom: Cape Archives, Cape Town. L 1038.

15 Top: William Fehr Collection, The Castle, Cape Town.
Centre: William Fehr Collection, The Castle, Cape Town.
Bottom: Kolb, P., *Caput Bonae Spei hodiernum . . .*, Africana Museum, Johannesburg.

16 Top: Cape Archives, Cape Town. AG 12906.
Bottom: Cape Archives, Cape Town. M 148.

17 Van Schley, J., *Vies des Gouverneurs Generaux . . .*, Africana Museum, Johannesburg.

18 Top: Cape Archives, Cape Town. AG 6795.
Bottom: Volcker Miros.

19 Top: Van Stade, E., The Mendelssohn Collection, Library of Parliament, Cape Town.
Bottom left: Van Stade, E., The Mendelssohn Collection, Library of Parliament, Cape Town.
Bottom right: Kolb, P., S.A. Library, Cape Town.

20 Cape Archives, Cape Town. M 227.

21 Top: Schumacher, J., engraving by I.H. Schneider (1778), reproduced by C. Struik (Pty) Ltd (1973), Cape Town.
Bottom left: Cape Archives, Cape Town. AG 7359.
Bottom centre: Cape Archives, Cape Town. AG 5818.
Bottom right: Nederburg.

22 Top: Schumacher, J., Cape Archives, Cape Town. E 2668.
Bottom: Burchell, W.J., *Travels in the Interior of Southern Africa*, S.A. Library, Cape Town.

23 Top: Gubbins, J.G., Africana Museum, Johannesburg

24 D'Oyly, Sir Charles, Library of Parliament, Cape Town.

25 Cape Archives, Cape Town. M 112.

26 Top: Poortermans, J.C., Library of Parliament, Cape Town.
Bottom: HAUM Publishers (Pty) Ltd, (Engelbrecht, S.P., *Die Kaapse Predikante van die 17de en 18de Eeu*, Cape Town, 1952).

27 Top: Frederici, J.C., Mendelssohn Collection, Library of Parliament, Cape Town.
Bottom: Danloux, H.P., Africana Museum, Johannesburg.

28 Top: Cape Archives, Cape Town. M 929
Bottom: Cape Archives, Cape Town. M 360.

29 Top: Daniell, S., Africana Museum, Johannesburg.
Bottom: Cape Archives, Cape Town. AG 7827.

30 Top: Cape Archives, Cape Town. AG 7078
Centre: Cape Archives, Cape Town. M325.
Bottom: Barrow, Sir John, *Travels in Southern Africa . . .*, vol. 2, S.A. Library, Cape Town.

31 Centre: Eddis, E.U., Africana Museum, Johannesburg.

32 Cape Archives, Cape Town. Vendue Rolle, 1/STB 19/47 (P.B. Wolvaard, April 1810).

33 Left and right: Cape Archives, Cape Town. Liquidation and distribution account, MOOC 13/1/94, 15 Feb. 1841).

34 Top: Campbell, John, 'Mr Retieff's Dragensten', grey wash, Africana Museum, Johannesburg.
Bottom: Steeb, I.F., portrait of J.J. Haupt, watercolour, Africana Museum, Johannesburg.

35 Top: Burchell, W.J., *Travels in the Interior of Southern Africa*, S.A. Library, Cape Town.
Bottom left: Steeb, I.F., portrait of Ester Loret, watercolour, Africana Museum, Johannesburg.
Bottom right: Cape Archives, Cape Town. E 435.

36 Top: Bell, C., Mendelssohn Collection, Library of Parliament, Cape Town.
Bottom: Cape Archives, Cape Town. CCP 8/1/7.

37 Top: Knyvett F., Library of Parliament, Cape Town.
Bottom: Cape Archives, Cape Town. M363.

38 Top: Anderson, W.J., Library of Parliament, Cape Town.
Below: Africana Museum, Johannesburg.

39 Trench, P.C., watercolour, Cape Archives, Cape Town.

40 Cape Archives, Cape Town. M 178.

41 Top: Surveyor General's office, Nederburg papers, sheet BH-6D. BI-5C, Stel.Q.8.44.
Bottom: S.A. Library, Cape Town.

42 Top: Cape Archives, Cape Town. Slave Register 1816-1834, SO 6/101, p. 102.
Bottom: Cape Archives, Cape Town. E 332.02.

43 Top: Cape Archives, Cape Town. No. E 2365
Bottom: Cape Archives, Cape Town. M 383.

44 Top: Angas, G.F., photograph of painting, Cape Archives, Cape Town. E 4661.
Bottom: I'ons, F.T., Africana Museum, Johannesburg.

45 Comfield, J.F., photograph, Mendelssohn Collection, Library of Parliament, Cape Town.

46 Top: Cape Archives, Cape Town. M 899.
Bottom: Cape Archives, Cape Town. E 4095.

47 Top left: Cape Archives, Cape Town. CO 756, p. 2.
Top centre: S.A. Library, Cape Town.
Top right: Die Genootskap van Regte Afrikaners publication.
Bottom: Krynauw, D., 'Voorhuis, Eenzaamheid', Africana Museum, Johannesburg.

48 S.A. Agric. Pamphlets, S.A. Library, Cape Town.

49 Top: Gribble, J., Gribble's Photo House, Paarl. AG 208 HP.
Bottom: Cape Archives, Cape Town. AG 7512.

50 Top: Cape Archives, Cape Town. AGR 61.
Bottom: Cape Archives, Cape Town. AG 9617.

51 Top: Cape Archives, Cape Town. M 925.
Bottom: Cape Archives, Cape Town. AG 6343.

52 Top left: Cape Archives, Cape Town. E 7581.

PAGE NUMBERS IN ITALICS REFER TO ILLUSTRATIONS

SPONSORS' EDITION

This edition, limited to 26 copies, has been reserved for Nederburg.

COLLECTORS' EDITION

Steve Bales

Hans Beetge – Mopane Safaris

Eberhard Bertelsmann

W.F.L. Blanden

Sarah, Caroline & Simon Borchert

The Brenthurst Library

Jim Gerard Paul Broekhuysen

Phillida Brooke Simons

S.F. Cairns

P.D. Corder

Andrew Currey

Dr J. & Mrs K. Dhansay

Diners Club International

Kevin J.Dunkley

Dr H.B. Dyer

John & June Fannin

Dr Leslie F.G. Frankel

Sidney L. Frankel

Pauline Friedman

Hope Gain

Lydia Gorvy

M.F. Keeley

G.G. Leslie

Kelly & Carol Manson

Nederburg Wines

Rupert & Garda Pardoe

S.H. Prior

S.C. Rees

Carl Schlettwein

Robert J.W. Spanjaard

Stellenbosch Farmers' Winery

Pieter Struik

Struik Winchester

Ian R.F. Trollip

H.J. van Wyk

Penelope Williamson

STANDARD EDITION

V.G. Achadinha

AEB Africa (Pty) Ltd

Africana Book Collectors

Brian Archibald

Baldwins Steel

Thomas Barlow

Peter Bayly

Lady Beadle

Herbert & Jacqueline Becker

Hans Beetge – Mopane Safaris

Hanns-Gerd Bergs

Berry Bush De Villiers Di Bella & Bellamy
(Pty) Ltd.

Craig Bracken

John P. Brimble

W.J. Christians of Hillcrest

Ted & Estelle Clayson

Peter & Sally Cobbold

Johan Coetsee – Sasolburg

Corrie Coetzee

Susanne Collins

Dr E.N. Costa

Andrew Currey

Rona Currey

Barbara de Villiers

B.E. de Vos

Don Africana Library

Enid P. du Plessis

Gillian & Tessa du Plessis

J.C.M.D. du Plessis

Wilhelm P. Egeler

Ronald Robert Emmett

Anton A. Endres

Carla & Felix Ernst

J.M. Faure

Ferdinand Postma-Biblioteek,
Potchefstroomse Universiteit vir CHO

Russouw Ferreira

E. Folli

Z. du T. Fonternel

Kenneth Forrester

M.J. Forster

Johann Fourie

Ulrich Gericke

Johannes Cornelis Matheus Gerrits

Rupert Gettliffe

Dr Aubrey M. Goldman

Neale Gordon

Dave & Margie Hidden

M.A. Hinton

Eugen A. Huber

John & Margaret Hughes

G.N. Hunt

Indian Ocean Export Company (Pty)
Limited

J.S. Gericke Library

Clive & Aliki Kelly

Bruce Knoefel

Landzicht Kelder

Johan Latsky

Betty Louw

Christopher James Lyall

Malcolm Maclennan of Toronto

Stan & Karen Matthews

Dr Peter McGregor

Lin Mehmel

Ruth & Walter Middelmann

David B. Mitchell

Wynand Nel

J.M. Neser

Gisela & Michael Pardoe

Hugh G. Peatling

Anne, Belinda, Carolyn &
Anthony Peepall

Jeffry Perlman

George & Penny Poole

George Raftopoulos

Thomas W. Richardson

David Robertson

Daniel Rooks

Malcolm Ross

Con & Carol Roux

Ulrich Ruch

Carl Schlettwein

Douglas M. Simons

Genard Russel William Sizer

M. Francois Smuts

Clare & Patricia Storrar

Summerhill Stud C.C.

Graham Thiele

Christopher Thompson

Pieter Toerien

Antony Tooley

H. van Kerken

M. & M.A. van Rijswijck

Michael van der Spuy

Dr Ashton Vice

Mr & Mrs Hack Wilson